15 Days ___________________
Drawing and Painting Course

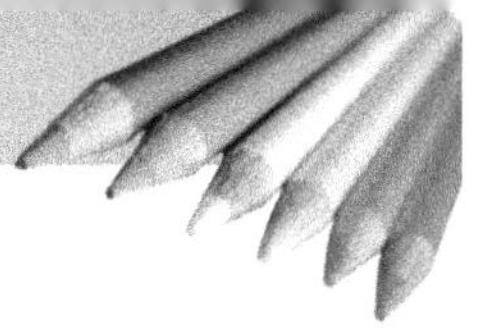

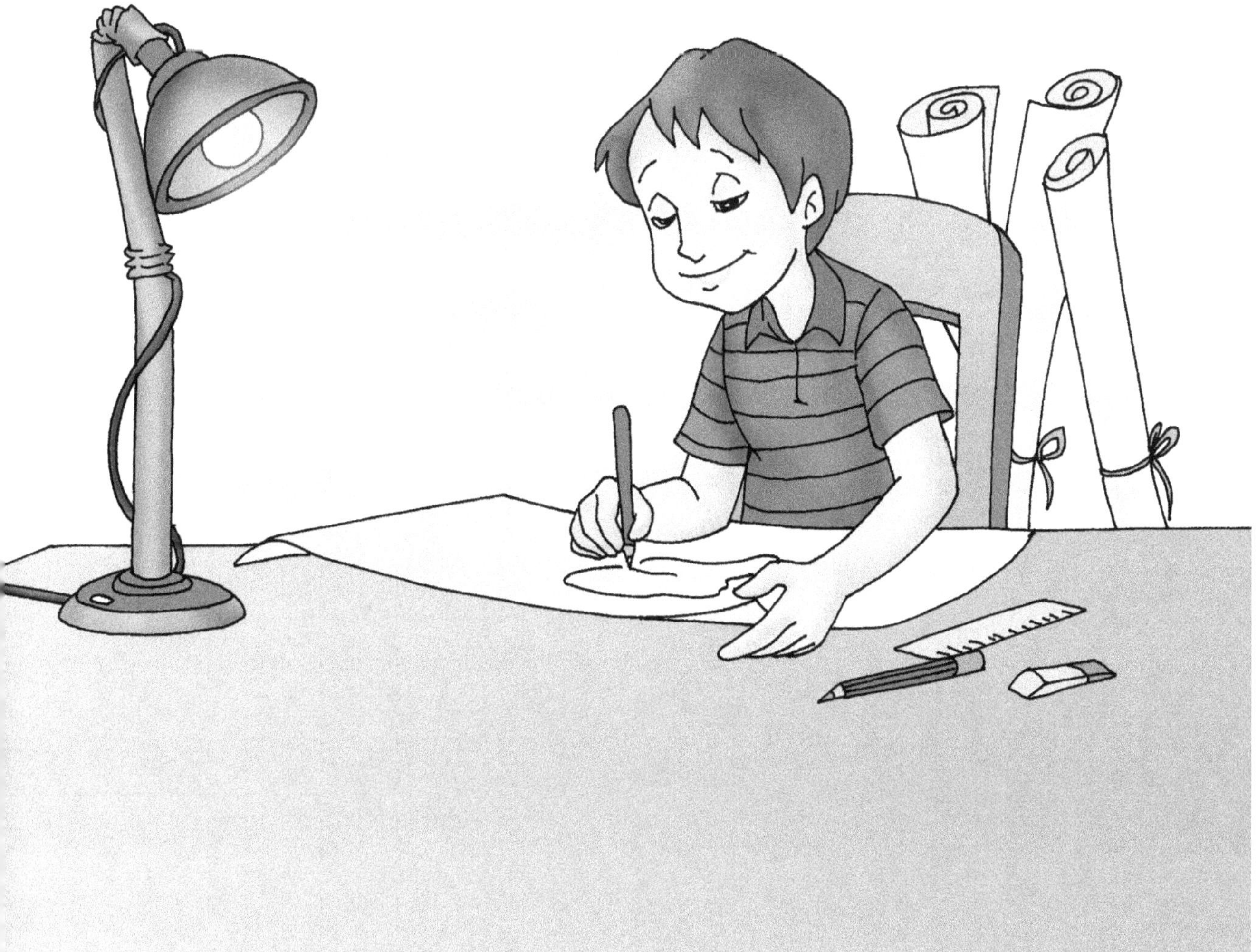

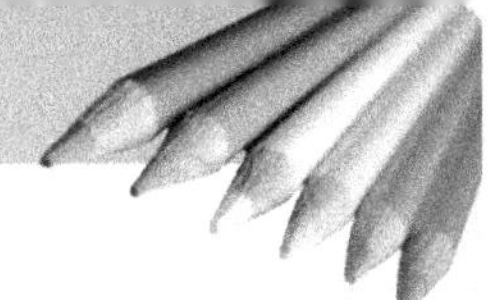

______15 Days______
Drawing and Painting Course

(Prepared by an experienced Artist, a simple and effective course to teach

Author
A.H. HASHMI

Redesigned by :
SUMIT SAKHUJA, SONAL

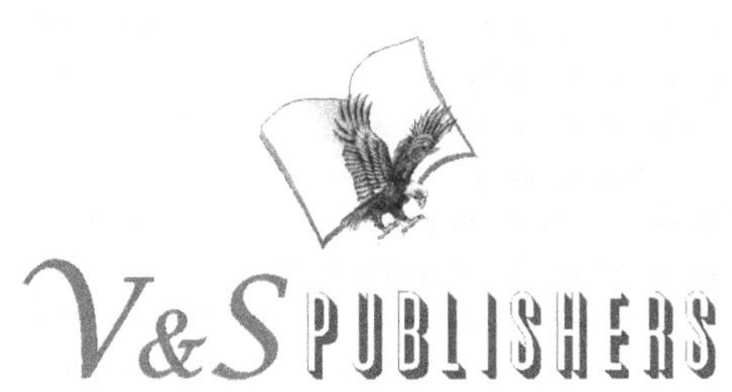

Published by:

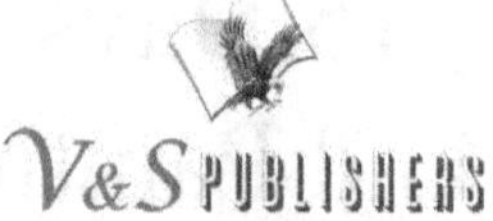

F-2/16, Ansari Road, Daryaganj, New Delhi-110002
011-23240026, 011-23240027 • *Fax:* 011-23240028
Email: info@vspublishers.com • *Website:* www.vspublishers.com

Regional Offi ce : Hyderabad
5-1-707/1, Brij Bhawan (Beside Central Bank of India Lane)
Bank Street, Koti, Hyderabad - 500 095
040-24737290
E-mail: vspublishershyd@gmail.com

Branch Offi ce : Mumbai
Godown # 34 at The Model Co-Operative Housing, Society Ltd.,
"Sahakar Niwas", Ground Floor, Next to Sobo Central, Mumbai - 400 034
022-23510736
E-mail vspublishersmum@gmail.com

ISBN 978-81-920796-6-0
Edition 2015

Printed at : Deep Colour Scan, Shahdara, Delhi-110095

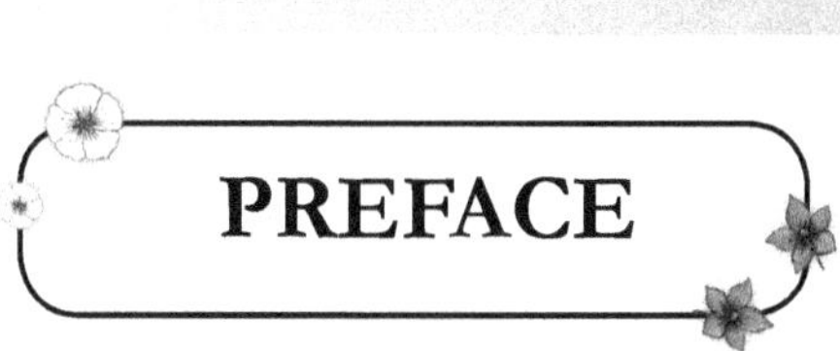

PREFACE

The modern youth has developed a craze for drawing and painting. This is quite understandable in view of the human nature which has been an ardent seeker of beauty, beauty in its subtle and varied manifestations. This perennial search for the sublime has prompted man to draw and paint the diverse forms of fl ora and fauna, of gods and men, of rivers and mountains—in a nut-shell the entire universe. The ever-lasting monuments of the creative genius of man can be found in the celestial paintings still preserved in the age-old caves and temples.

The bookshops are fl ooded with a plethora of books claiming to teach drawing and painting. However, it is well nigh impossible to locate a single title which would teach all the aspects of drawing and painting in a systematic and phased manner—from the handling of a pencil to the practising of modern art. The present book specifi cally serves this purpose.

The book is divided in fi fteen chapters, and as the title suggests, it is planned as a fi fteen days course wherein all the relevant aspects of drawing and painting have been explained in a simple and lucid language with hundreds of illustrations and diagrams. The students while pursuing the course will gradually learn the importance of lines—thin line, thick line, straight line, dotted line, curved line, zig-zag line, horizontal line, cross line, slanting line etc. They will appreciate the role of shape, light, texture, balance, harmony, contrast, rhythm, tone, emphasis, span, colours, etc. They will develop a perspective and a point of view and will be able to distinguish between light and highlight, between shade and shadow.

The book, it is hoped, will be found useful by all those persons, men and women, young and old, professionals and amateurs, who have some taste, some love for art and artistic creations.

We are sure that most of our readers, if they carefully follow the guidelines given in this book, can blossom into mature artists. They may even aspire to adopt commercial art as their career, a sure means to earn their livelihood. They can as well decorate their dwellings with their own art work.

The author of the book is himself an experienced artist of considerable standing and as such we feel confi dent that millions of our readers will welcome this publication as a practical and pragmatic exposition to the much sought after world of drawing and painting.

—Publishers

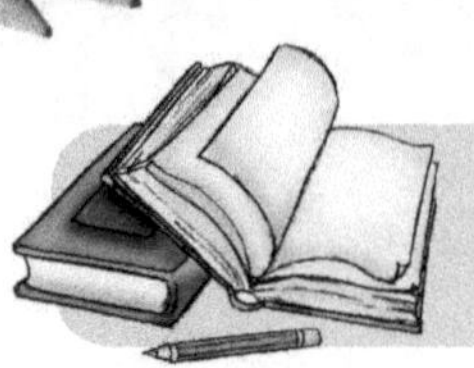

CONTENTS

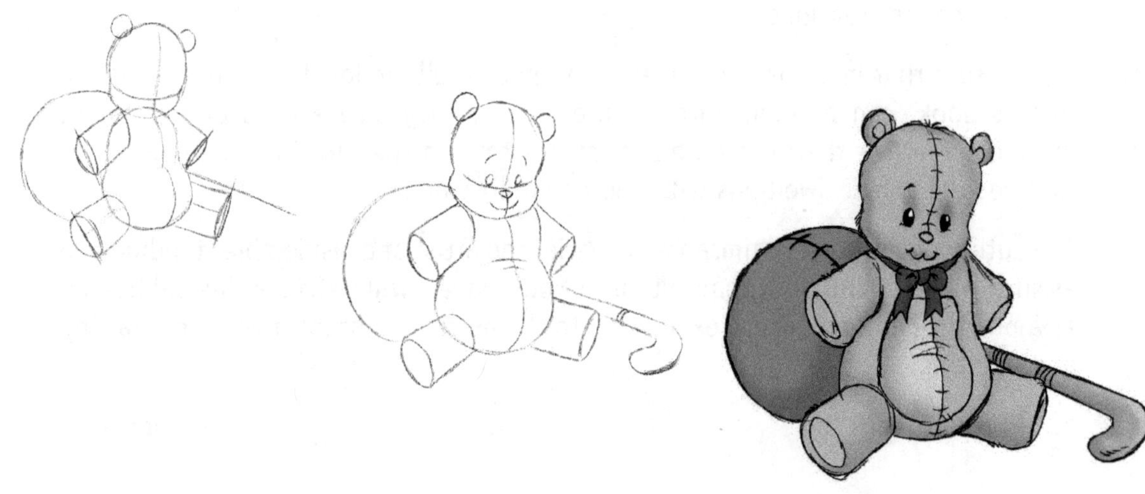

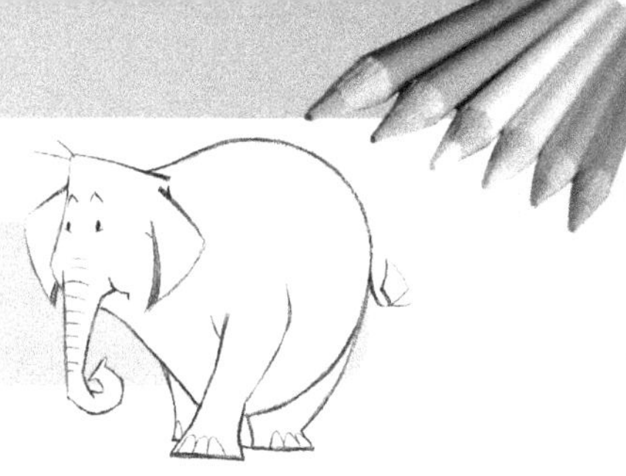

7th Day	:	Drawing of Birds.
8th Day	:	Drawing of Animals
9th Day	:	Sizes and Proportions of Different Parts of Body.
10th Day	:	Drawing of Eyes, Nose, Lips, Ears, Face.
11th Day	:	Profi le of Head or Face.
12th Day	:	Front Position of Hsead.
13th Day	:	Drawing of Hands and Postures, Structure of Feet and Postures, Drawing of Other Parts of Body.
14th Day	:	Different Methods of Making Illustration.
15th Day	:	Water Colour Painting, Method of Filling Colours, Oil Painting, Acrylic Painting, Batik.

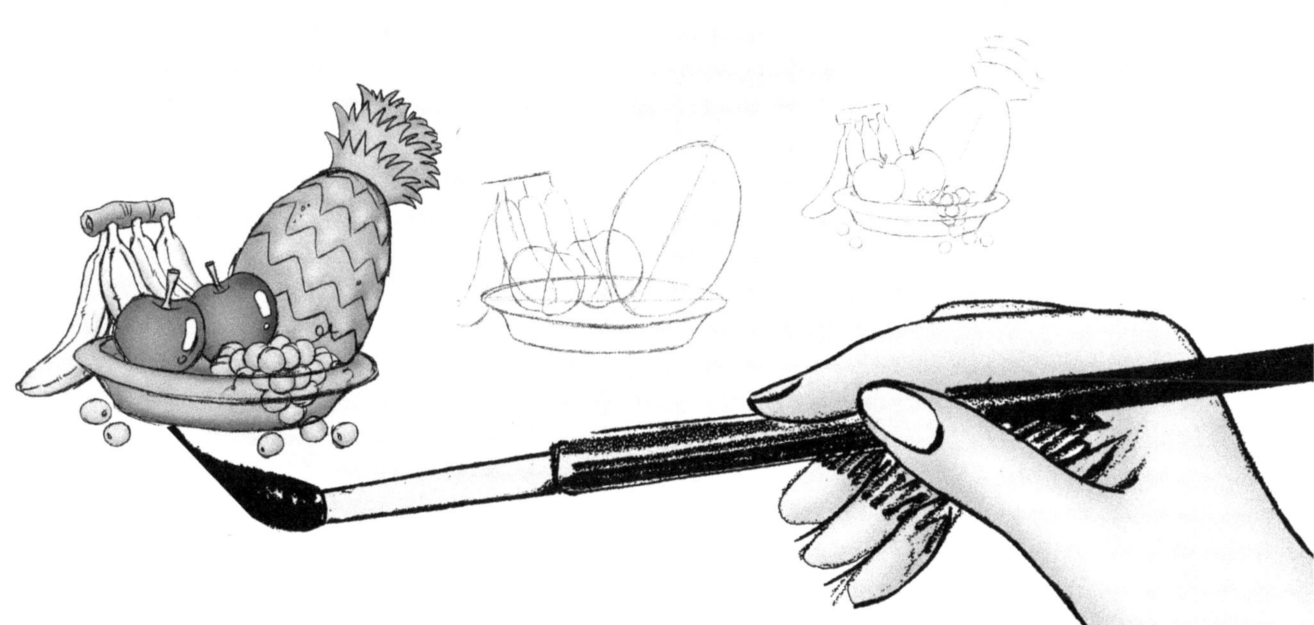

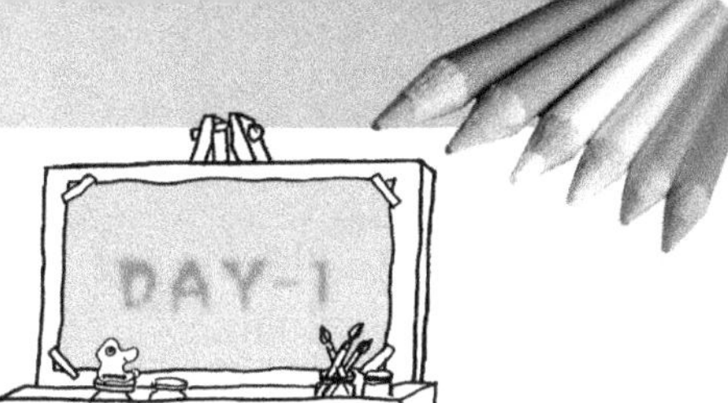

Dear readers, man has been attracted towards art since the beginning of civilization. Today, though man is very busy in his day-to-day life, still he has some spare time to appreciate art. No doubt, art is a very useful and attractive subject. The attraction for beautiful and colourful things in life is but the gift of art.

Our 15-day course is in your hands. We appreciate your interest in drawing and painting. Our course's aim is to help you learn art to perfection and become a good artist. So, we invite you to join us. We will solve your problems, if any. But remember, art is a subject which requires special attention and regular practice. Therefore, you promise us that for 15 days you will stay with us, sincerely follow the instructions given in each lesson and do the exercises regularly. And, we will try our best to make you feel confi dent while making drawings, and sharpen your analytical power. We believe that you will become successful by sincerely following the lessons of this book.

If you are ready to enter the world of art, then believe us, making you a successful artist is our foremost aim. And, there is no better reward for our efforts than your becoming a good artist.

Before you formally learn the techniques of drawing and painting, you must be familiar with the things which you will require as an artist. For ordinary drawing, you may need only pencil, paper and colours. But for making your art work beautiful and appealing, you must have the following essential materials which you can buy from the local art store —

Pencil, rubber, foot ruler, T-square, set-square, curves, instrument box, crowquill, speedball nibs, brushes, colours, water-proof ink, colour palette, a mug, drawing sheet (glazed or rough), tracing paper, drawing board, board pins, rubber solution, cloth, etc.

Now let us understand the uses of the above mentioned things.

Pencil

Pencil is very essential for drawing. It can be both hard and soft. Depending upon their hardness, pencils are given the following different numbers—

HB—This is a medium pencil. It is used very much in drawing because it is neither too black (soft), nor too hard, and does not break easily. Lines drawn by this number of pencil can be easily erased.

B—This pencil is slightly soft and lines drawn by it are a little darker.

2B—This pencil is soft and a little darker. It is used in drawing dark and clear lines.

3B—This is very soft and also very dark. This should be used with light hand, or else its lead breaks off.

4B—This is quite black and is used in drawings to show the light and shade areas.

5B—This pencil is very black and is used to show light and dark areas.

6B—This pencil is very soft and black. It is thicker than others. It is used to show the darker areas.

Along with the above mentioned pencils, carbon pencils are also used in drawing. These are more black. Their speciality is that their darkness goes well with pastel and water colours. These pencils are of the following types-

HB—Ordinary soft and black. It is used in drawing lines.

B—Used in drawing and showing a little darkness.

BB—This is a bit more black. It is also used in shading.

BBB—This is very dark and thick. It is useful in dark shading.

You will use these pencils according to your need, but you must also know how to sharpen a pencil's tip. Pencil should by cut with a sharp knife or a pencil cutter in such a way that its tip becomes conical. Its lead should be straight, long and pointed, but not so long as to break with slightest pressure.

Rubber

Howsoever perfect an artist you may be, you will still have to use rubber to erase wrong and useless lines. Rubber should be of superior quality. It should be soft, not very oily as to leave any stains behind. Before using a rubber, it should be cleaned properly with a clean and rough cloth. After rubbing a line, the rubber should be cleaned again as the blackness of the lead sticks onto the rubber. For drawing, an ordinary Indian rubber is suffi cient. But other varieties like plastic rubber, or art erasers, are very useful. Remember one thing that you must not use rubber frequently. A good artist makes very little use of the rubber.

T and set square

T square is made up of wood and set squares are of transparent plastic. These are used to make parallel lines. They are not used in freehand drawing but are very essential for commercial art.

Instrument box

It has all the instruments needed by an artist. The compass is one of these instruments. The compass is of two types—one of pencil and the other of ink.

Necessary Instruments

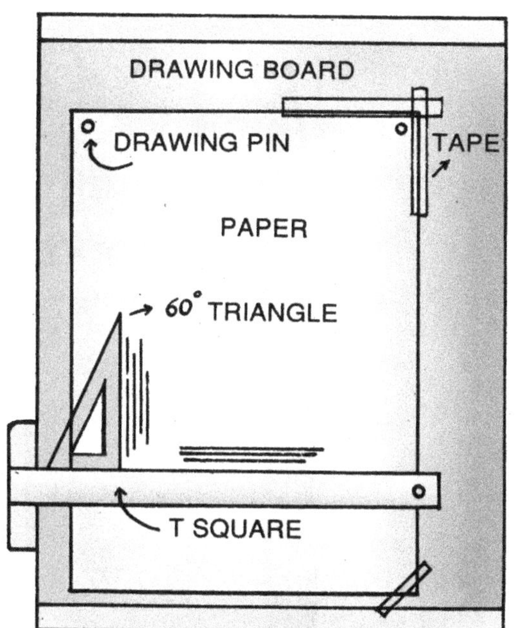

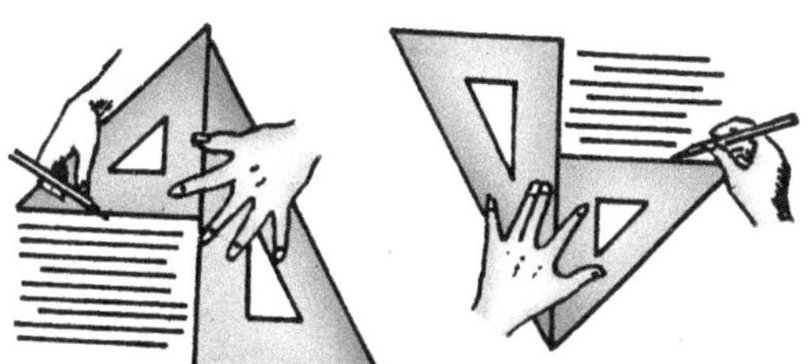

Use of set square

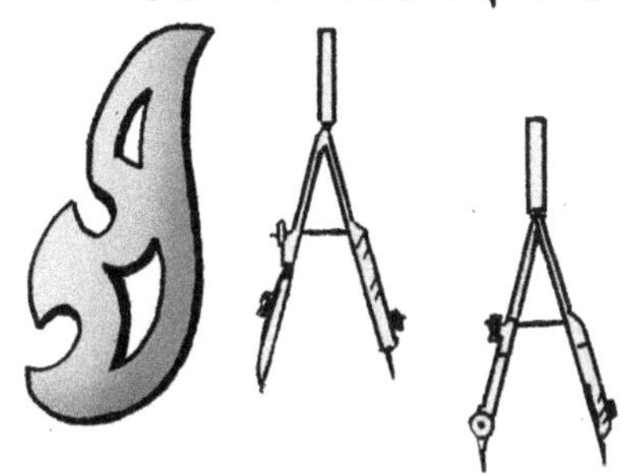

Curve Compass

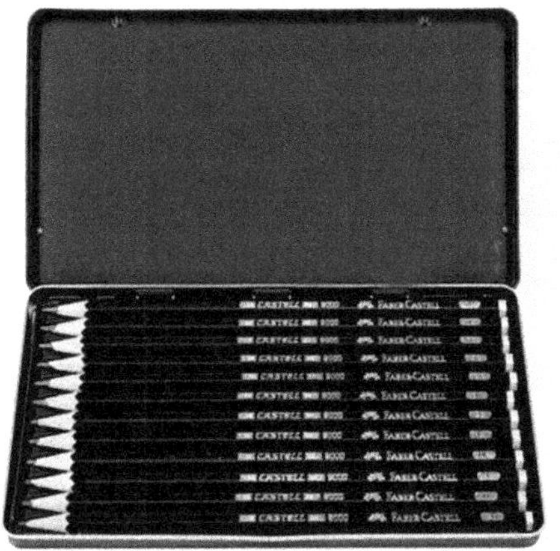

Dry colours

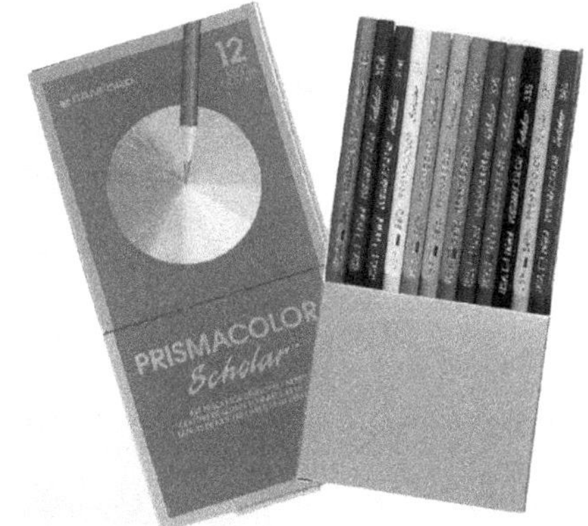

Pencil

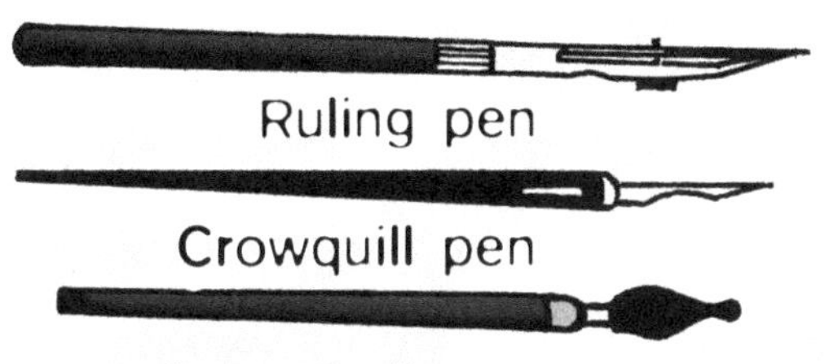

Ruling pen

Crowquill pen

Speedball pen

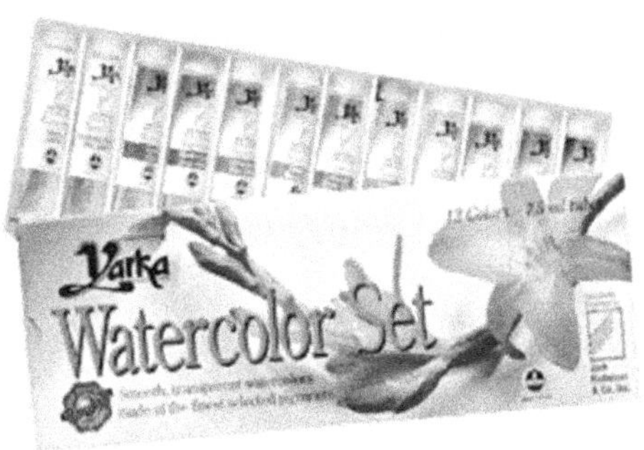

Oil colours

Wet-Medium Tools

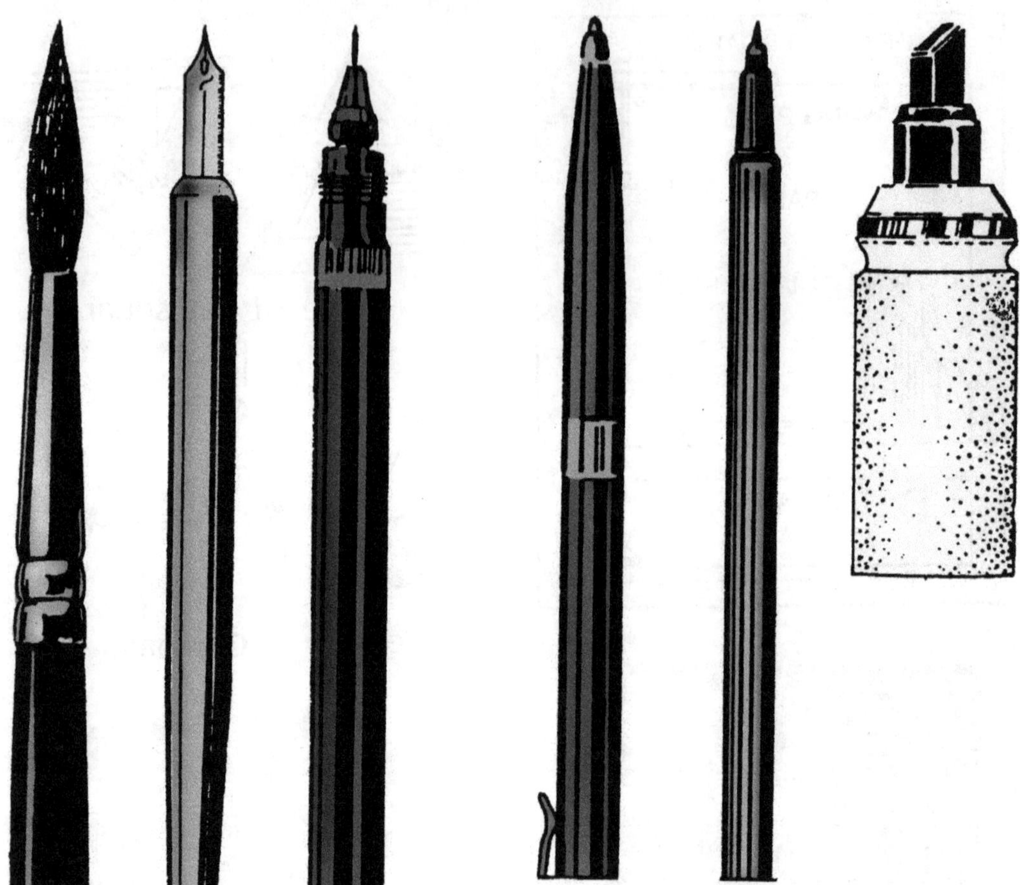

The most popular wet-mrdium tools are:

1. Brush
2. Writing pen
3. Technical pen
4. Ball-point pen
5. Felt-tipped pen
6. Broad-tipped felt pen

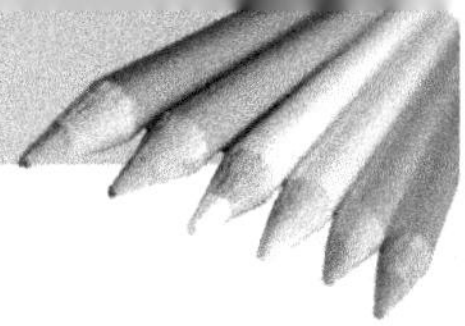

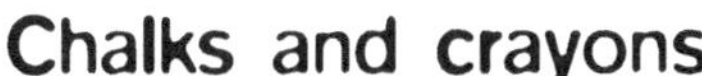

Chalks and crayons

Working with charcoal sticks, crayons and chalks, offers you the opportunity to build up areas of tone as well as vary the line thickness qualities. The major advantage of these tools is the wide variety of tones and marks available, some created by blurring with your fi nger, or highlighting with an eraser

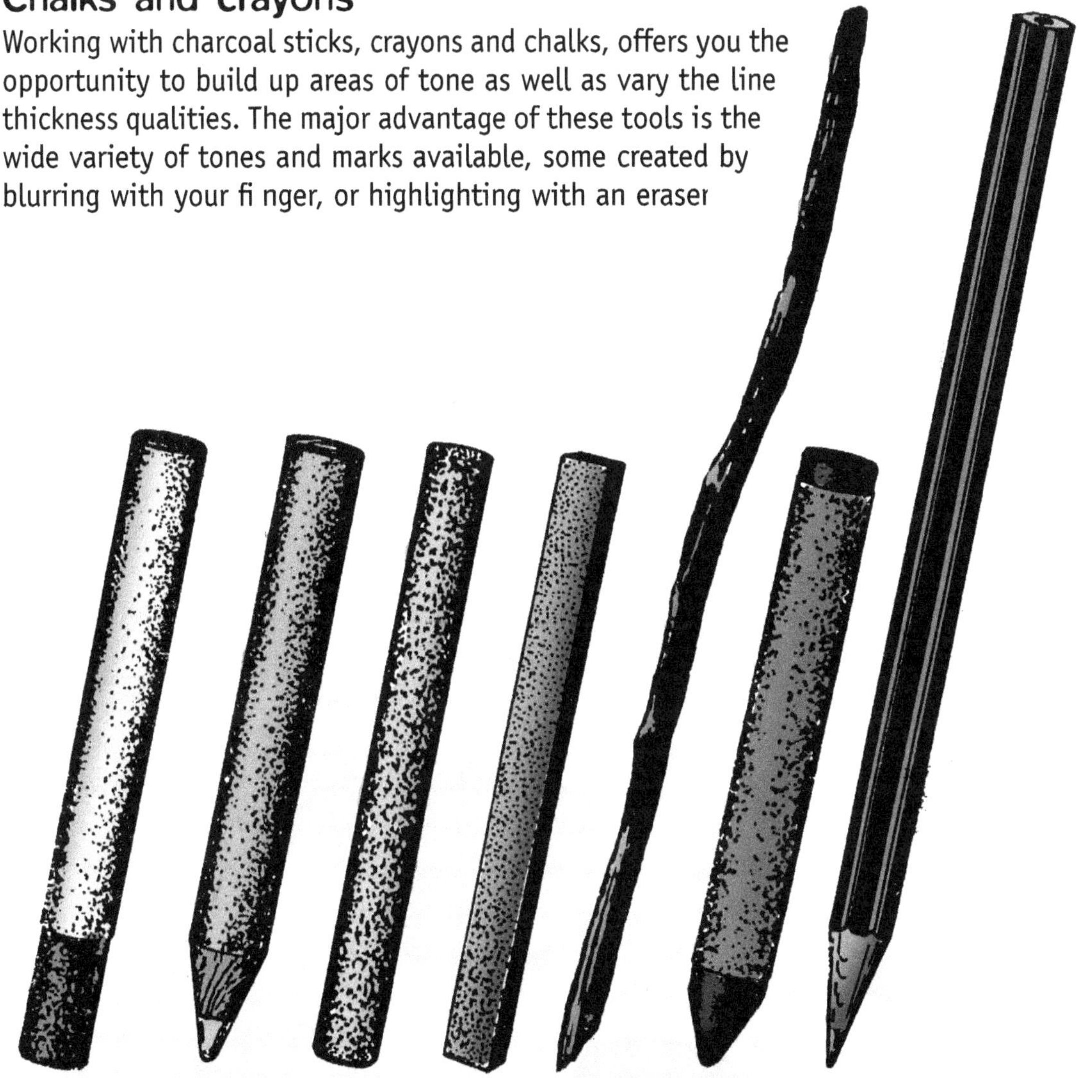

Types of Tool

1. Pastel sticks with protective paper cover.
2. Pastel pencils
3. Chalks
4. Graphite stick
5. Charcoal
6. Wax crayons
7. Coloured pencils

Use of crayon and brush

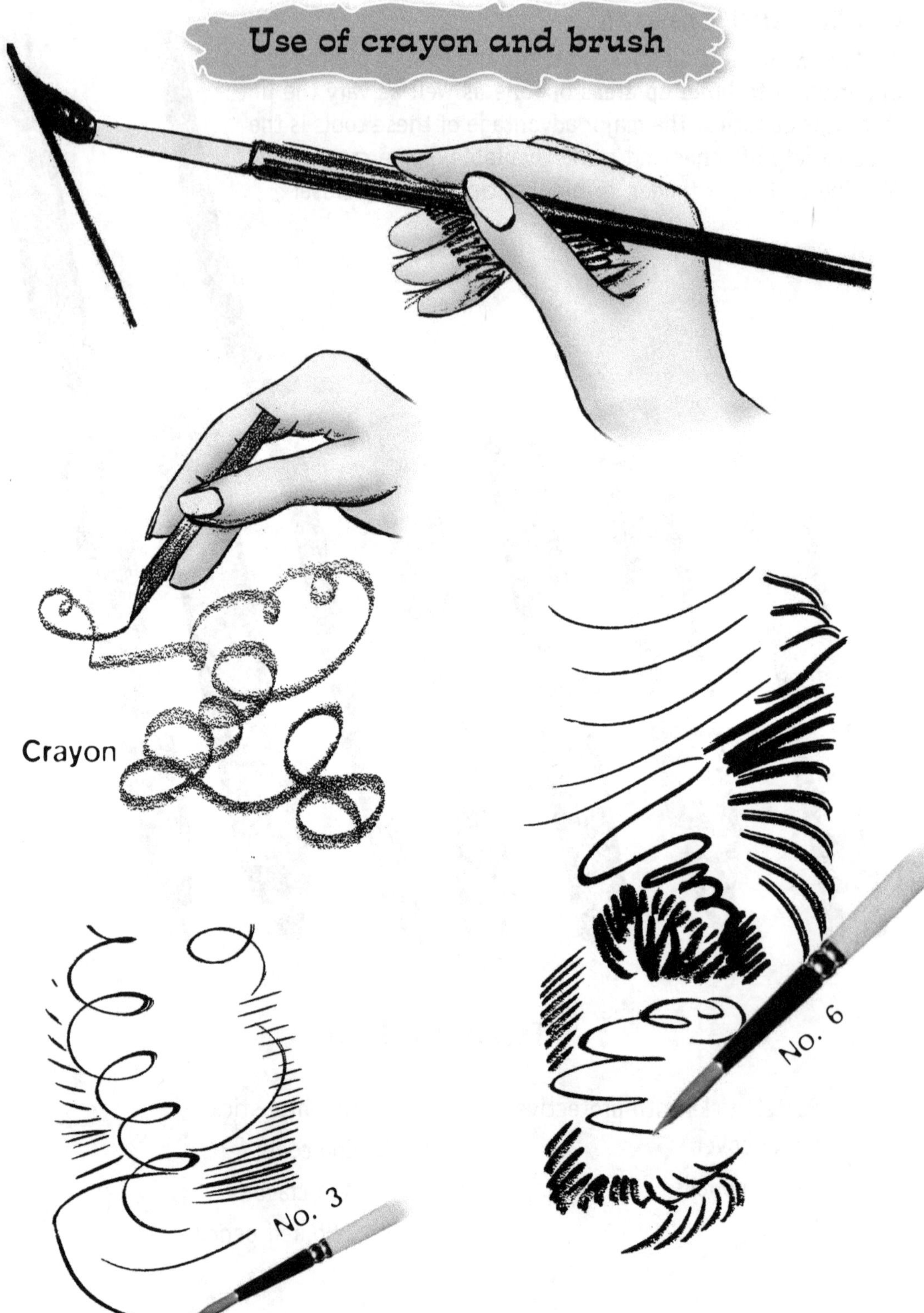

Pens

Different pens are used in a drawing for different requirements. A crowquill pen is more useful to you. In commercial drawing various sizes of speedball pen, ruling pen and sketch pen, ball-point pen, felt-tipped pen and technical pen are used.

Easel

If you want to stand and work, then you can make use of easel. You can take this out of your home also. And according to your need, you can also move it upwards and downwards.

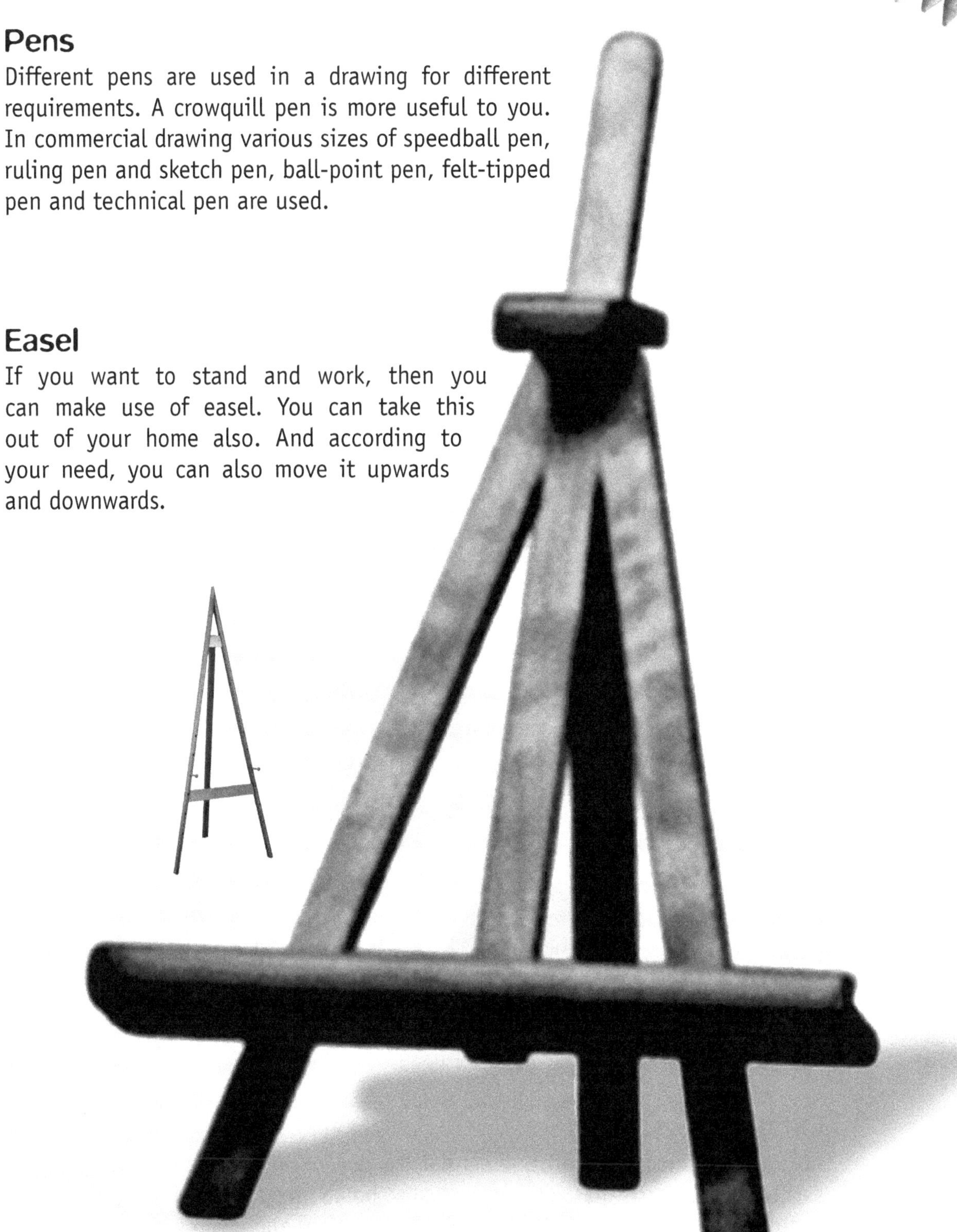

Brushes

Like pencil, brush is also an essential instrument for an artist. They can be of various types—thick, thin, round or fl at. The hair of animals are used in it. The hair can be both soft and hard. The brushes are used according to the needs of drawing. Brushes meant for water colour should be long and soft. Sable hair brushes give good results. Usually, brushes of 0, 1, 2, 3, 4, 5 and 6 numbers are used. You must always buy good quality brushes. Cheap brushes may affect the quality of your drawing.

Colours and ink

Nobody can deny the importance of colours in the fi eld of art. The colours make a drawing beautiful and attractive. In fact, the colours impart a glimpse of reality to a picture.

Colour is used according to the nature of creation and paper. In painting, usually three kinds of colour are used—dry colours, water colours and oil colours. Dry colours are pastels, pastel crayons, colour pencils and colour sketch pens. In water colour, there are tubes, tablets, transparent photo colours and poster colours. Oil colours are usually available in tubes and these are used by mixing turpentine or linseed oil in it. Water-proof ink is used as black ink.

Paper

Various kinds of paper are used for making drawings. For sketching with pencil any kind of white paper can be used, but it is better to use a drawing paper. You can buy the paper as per your requirement. The paper can be smooth, rough and extra rough, illustration board or mount board. For tracing, you must go for good quality tracing paper.

Drawing board

Drawing board is an essential item for an artist. This is made of wood and is available at any art store in standard sizes. For drawing and painting, Donkey or Easel is also used.

You can buy any of these as per your need.

Other things

An artist requires some other essential items such as porcelain, glass or other small bowls, palette, glass or mug for water, board pins for attaching paper to the board, rubber solution and fevicol for sticking paper and clean white cloth, etc.

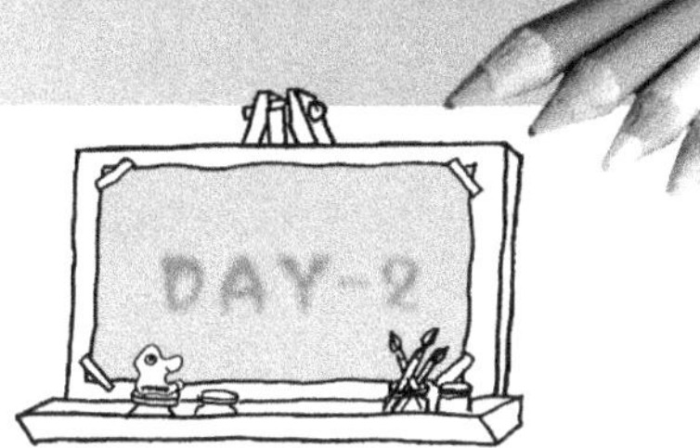

Dear readers, yesterday we introduced you to the things which you will have to use while making drawings. And, you must have bought them. Just now, you need a pencil, paper, rubber, drawing board and board pins.

Before you start work, check that all the above things are in order. Keep these ready by your side. And, sit at a place where you can work quietly without any hindrance or disturbance.

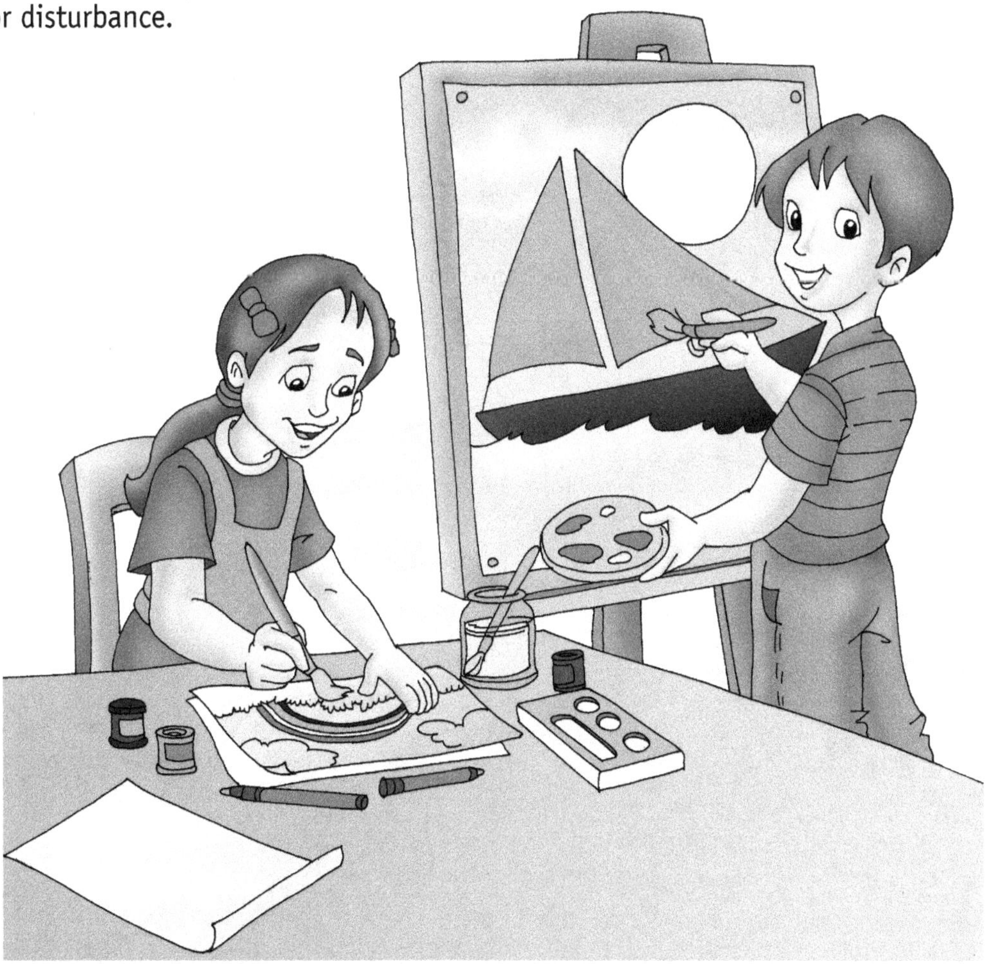

Would you like to sit and work, or keep standing?

Yesterday we had told you that you can stand and work on an easel. If you are working at home then keep your drawing board on the table. Make the drawing board a bit slanted by placing some books under it at the far end. Now sit on a

Lines

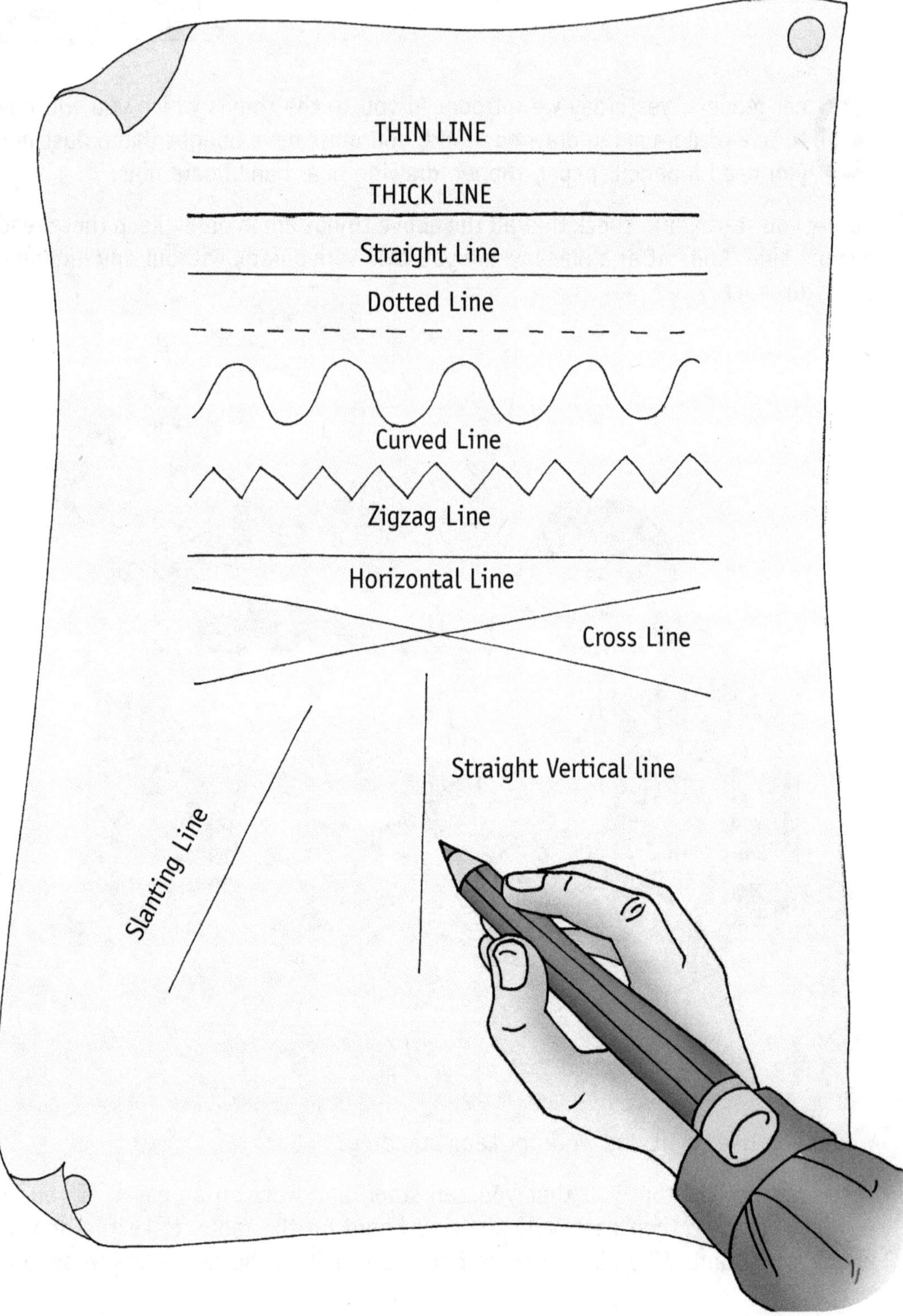

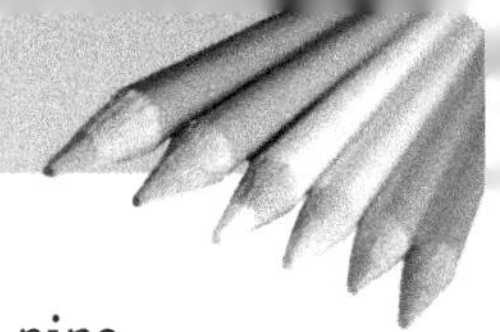

chair and place your paper at the centre of the drawing board, put drawing pins on the four corners of the paper so that it does not move.

To learn drawing, first of all, you must know how to use your pencil. Hold your pencil almost 1½ inches away from its tip. Do not press the pencil. This will enable you to draw soft lines. The lines should be drawn from top to bottom or from left to right.

Draw some lines on the paper for practice. The mystery of art is hidden in these lines only. You will be surprised to know that the invention of writing was based on these very lines. Without these lines man would not have been able to write or make a drawing.

Before you make a drawing, you must know the basic elements and principles of a picture. For the creation of good pictures the basic elements are line, shape, space, light and colour. The principles are balance, rhythm, contrast and emphasis.

Line

Line is the beginning of painting. You know that a line is drawn by joining any two points. It shows its effect in the design. It can be continuous or broken, thick or thin, clear and hard or smudged and soft, dark and heavy or very faint and delicate. It all depends on how you draw a line. Line in painting often suggests movement.

Every line of any type has some meaning. A line can be straight or dotted, horizontal or vertical, curved or slanting, zigzag or crossed, or parallel to some other line.

Shape

The form enclosed within drawn lines makes the shape of a picture. It has height and width.

Light

As an element of painting, light reveals shape. The light and dark areas contribute in balancing the picture surface. In the treatment of light and shade we come across tonal values. Tones are the gradations between black and white. With it we get depth in a picture. In colours, tones have special importance. The low and high tones of colours strengthen the effect of light and shade.

Texture

It reveals the nature of surface plane. The surface can be soft or rough. It can be experienced by touching things like the tree trunk, a carpet, a cloth, a table, etc. A flat surface of picture is made lively by texture. The texture in a picture is created by using some instruments, cross-hatching, by colour, texture board or paper.

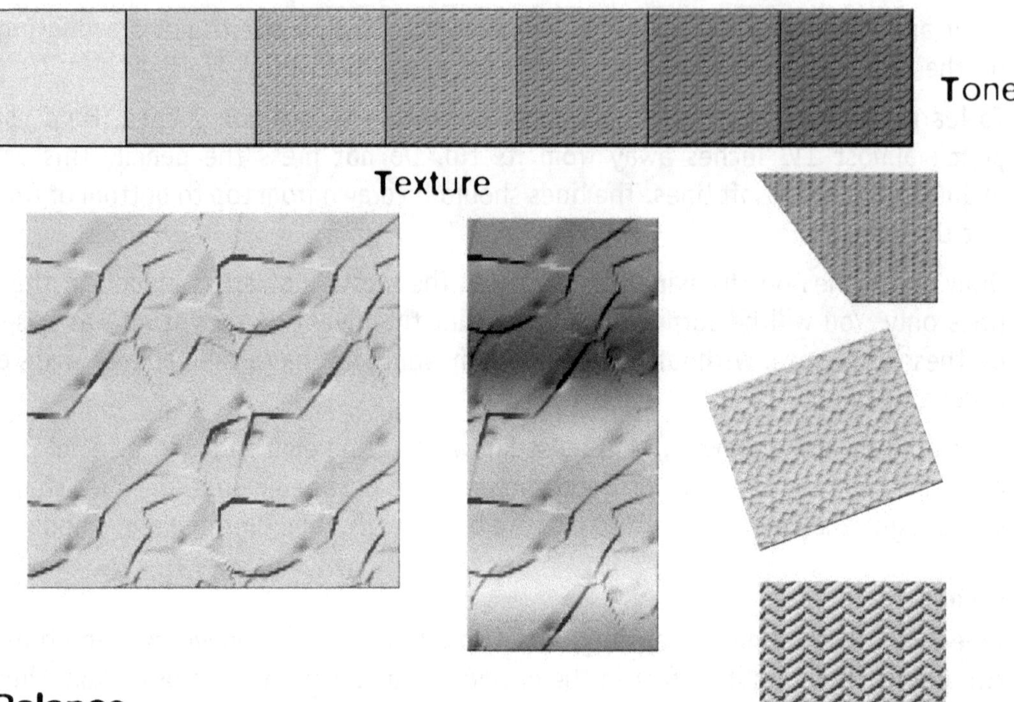

Balance

Balance is very essential for a picture. A picture is balanced when the two halves of the picture have equal forms or colours. For example, object drawn on the left hand side should be balanced by another form on the right hand side. Balance of colours and forms is a test of an artist's effi ciency.

Harmony

Some forms of a picture are similar in appearance. Or, you can say they are of the same family. For example, square, rectangle, or a parallelogram. Similarly, we have colours of the same family, like red, orange and yellow. These types of forms and colours are said to be in harmony. While making a picture, special attention should be paid to harmony of forms and colours.

Contrast

Contrast can be achieved by placing together colours and objects with opposite qualities. It is important in any kind of design as it makes the fl at surface lively. For example, red used with green, orange with blue, black with white, thin with fat, tall with short, etc., present a good contrast.

Rhythm

Forms repeated within the picture give rise to an effect called rhythm. Rhythm in a picture suggests movement and life, the feeling of energy and force. It is of special importance in decorative designs.

Balance

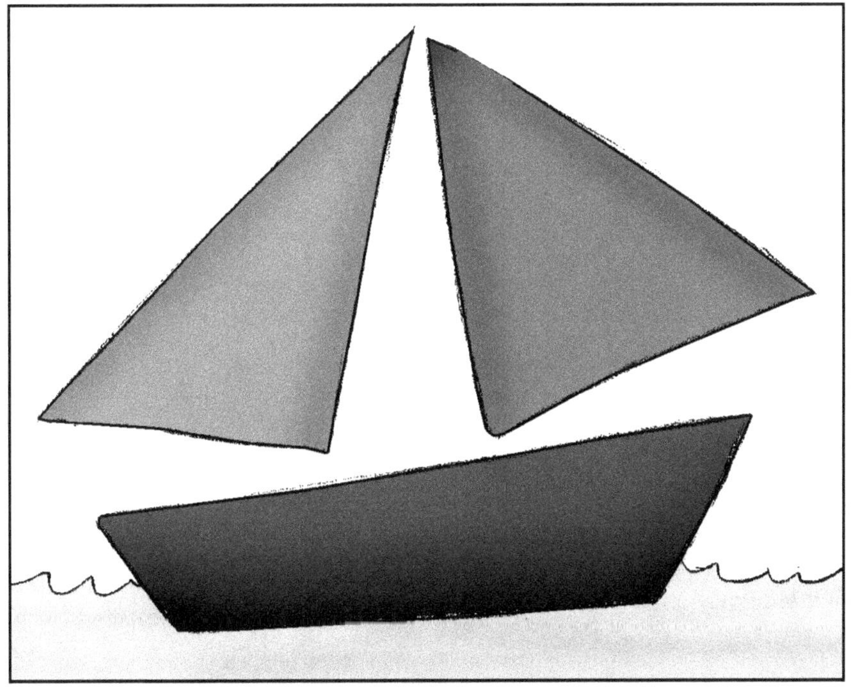

Harmony

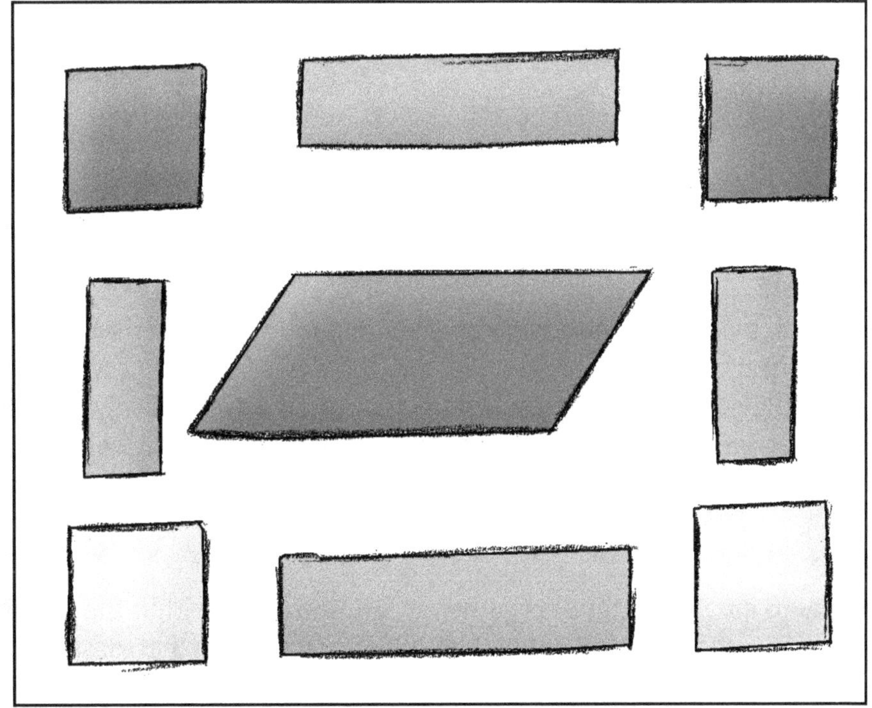

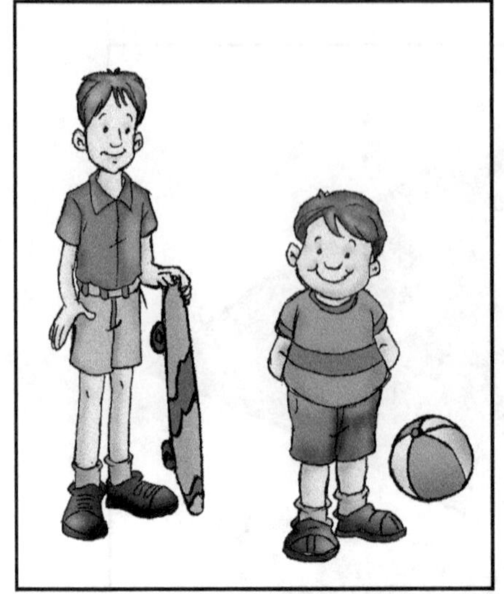

Contrast

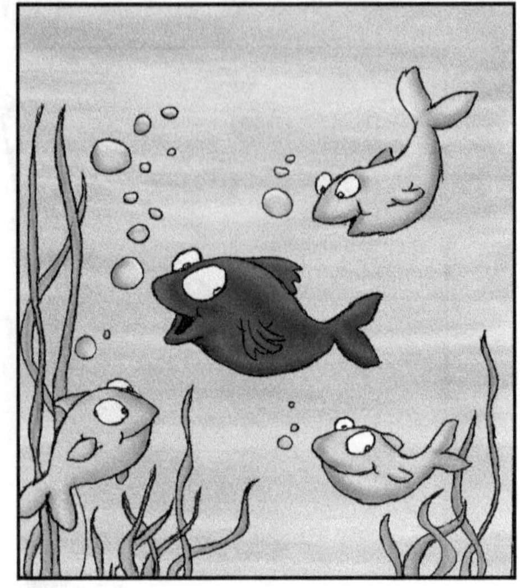

Emphasis

Rhythm

Emphasis

In a picture, a particular part is given more importance than others. This effect is called emphasis. Actually, in every drawing there is a focal point which highlights the main theme of the drawing. And, for a picture to be lively, the emphasis of the focal point is necessary. This can be created through contrast in forms and colours.

Space

All the forms employed, taken together, create the space within the picture frame. This created space can be either two-dimensional i.e. a flat design, or three-dimensional i.e. illusionistic.

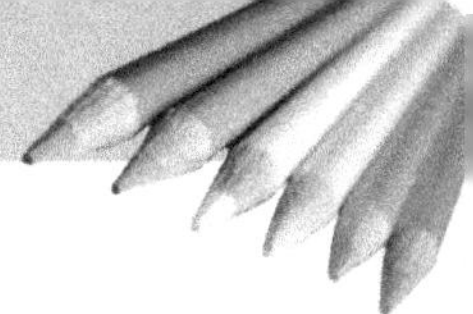

Colours

Colours have an important role in a drawing. They make a picture attractive and lively. Various emotions and feelings can be expressed by colours. For example, red corresponds with anger, danger, fi re, youth, strength, etc.; yellow symbolises wealth, sun, joy, etc.; blue represents longing, and so on.

Red, yellow and blue are considered as **primary colours**. These colours cannot be made by inter-mixing other colours. Red when mixed with yellow gives orange, blue with yellow gives green, and red with blue gives violet. Orange, green and violet are **secondary colours**. A similar inter-mixing of secondary colours will give **sub-secondary colours**. Black and white are **neutral colours**.

When **white** is added to a pure colour, **a lighter tint of that colour** is obtained. When **black** is added **a darker shade is created**. Opposite colours on the colour wheel are complementary colours. **The warm colours** are red, orange, yellow and brown. They give the effect of thrusting forward. The cool colours are green, blue and grey. They give the effect of withdrawal. When only warm or only cool colours are used in a picture, they create harmony. They are called harmonious colours.

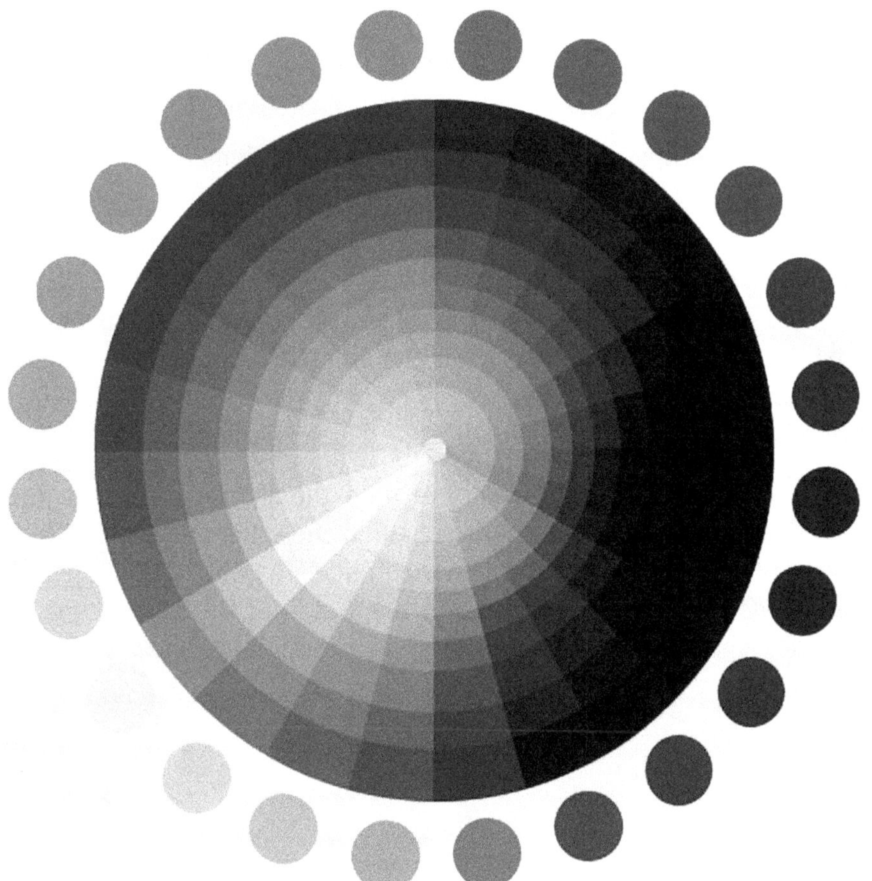

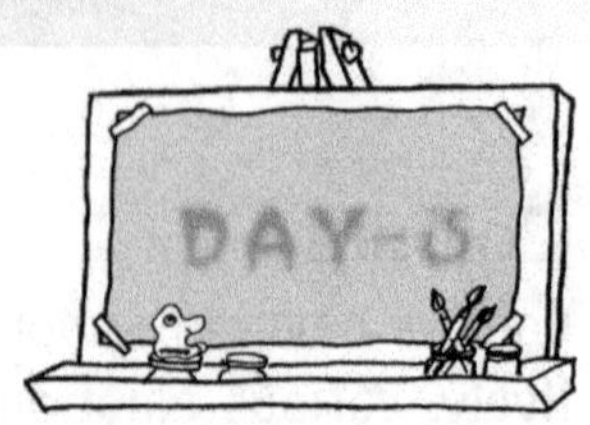

Yesterday, you had learnt about the elements of basic design, which are line, shape, composition, light and shade, harmony, balance, contrast, rhythm, emphasis and colours. We are sure that after gaining this knowledge you must feeling more confi dent now. Though every day you will learn new things, yet you will feel that you know it all. Today, we start with still life or object drawing.

Still Life or Object Drawing

In still life drawing, we draw the forms just as we see them. In this type of drawing, compass, protractor, scale or other instruments are not used. To become successful in still life drawing, it is necessary to practice free hand drawings of objects used in daily life.

To make a drawing beautiful and exact you must have an acute observation power. Before you make a drawing, observe minutely the model before you. Try to draw its forms, its beauty, colour scheme and impressions just as they appear on the model.

Object drawing is based on straight and curve lines. Remember, while doing the drawing, the rules of perspective must be followed.

Perspective

Any object seen from near seems to be big, while the same object seen from a distance looks smaller. In other words as the object gets away in distance it starts looking smaller. And, when the object is coming closer, it starts looking bigger. This is a natural phenomenon and you must have experienced it.

In vast fi elds while seeing far away, we fi nd the sky meeting the ground. This place is called the horizon. If a line is drawn on the same plane as the eyes and is parallel to the ground, it is called the horizon line. The horizon line gets higher or lower according to the plane of sight. In the sketch of the railway line and trees on both sides, the place of horizon and point of vision are shown.

Perspective can be divided into three types—

1. Linear perspective
2. Circular perspective
3. Colour perspective.

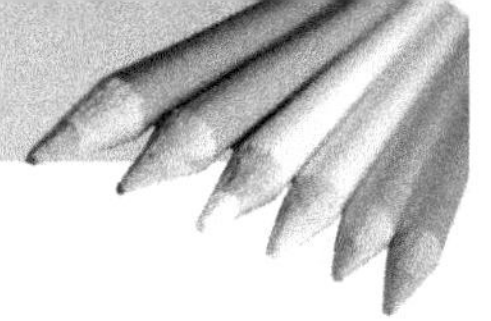

Linear perspective

Any object as it goes farther in distance becomes smaller in height and width. For example, see the picture given below. The height of the tree trunk that is nearest to you, is seen the biggest, while the second that is farther is seen smaller and the third one that is still farther is seen more smaller. All the lines when increased in distance, seem to meet at the horizon.

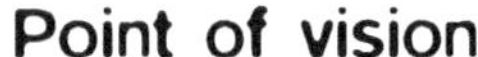

Point of vision

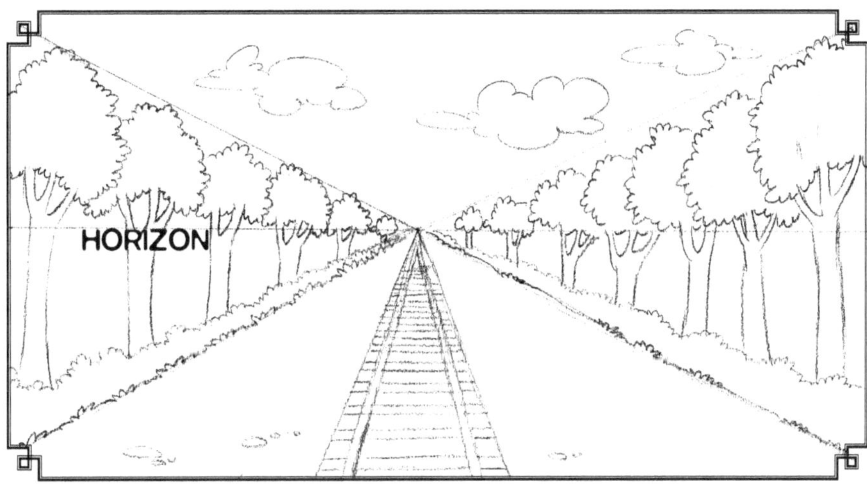

Circular perspective

In this perspective, all the circular lines tend to become more circular when raised above the eyesight. Similar effect occurs again when the circular lines are seen below the eyesight. On both sides of the eyesight level, if the object is placed at an equal distance, the ovals on both the sides look similar. And these ovals while

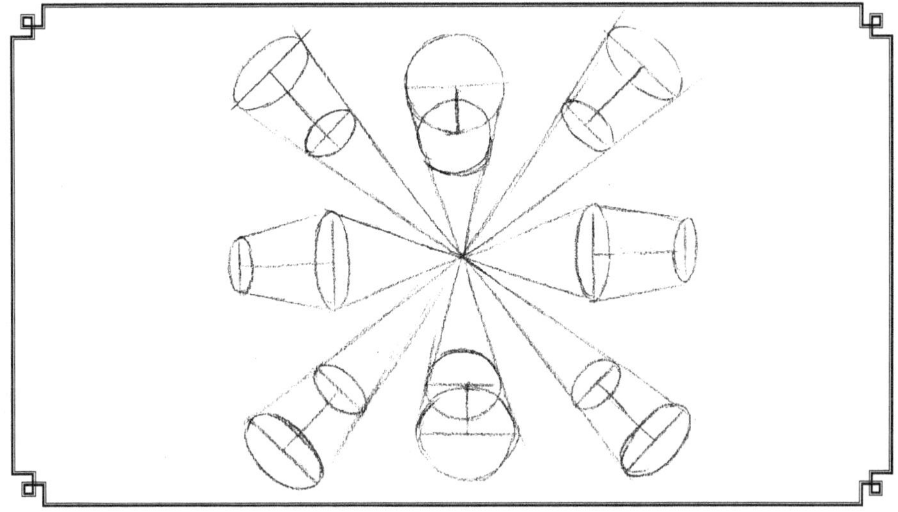

Various states of the glass

moving away from eyesight become smaller. See the different states of glass in the picture.

Colour perspective

A still life does not look beautiful and realistic till the colours are filled in it. Colours show the completeness and solidity of the objects. The effects of light and shadow have to be created carefully while putting the colours.

Points of view

1. Objects seen flat on and from afar have vertical sides and horizontal features. Both the vertical and horizontal elements are parallel to similar parts on the subject. **2.** Objects seen at an oblique angle; you see more than one side, and if viewed from afar they have vertical sides but converging horizontals. **3.** As you approach the subject the vertical parts appear to converge. This rule is true when working up at a subject (3), or down (4).

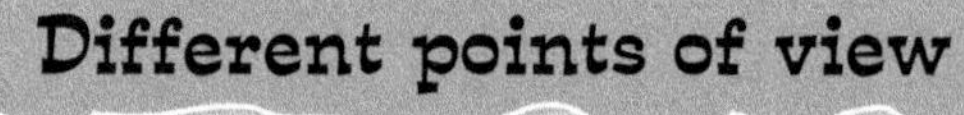

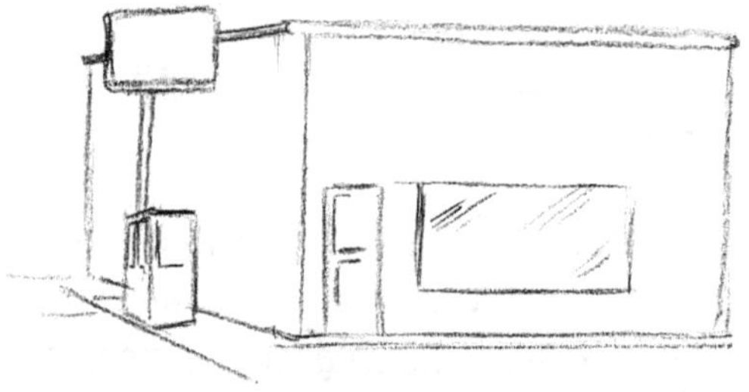

View - 1

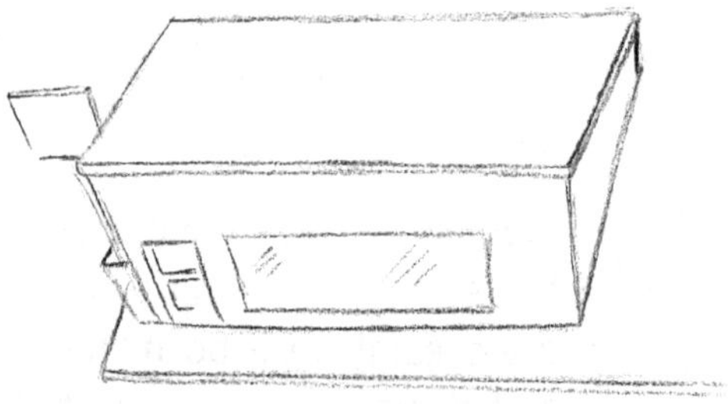

View - 2

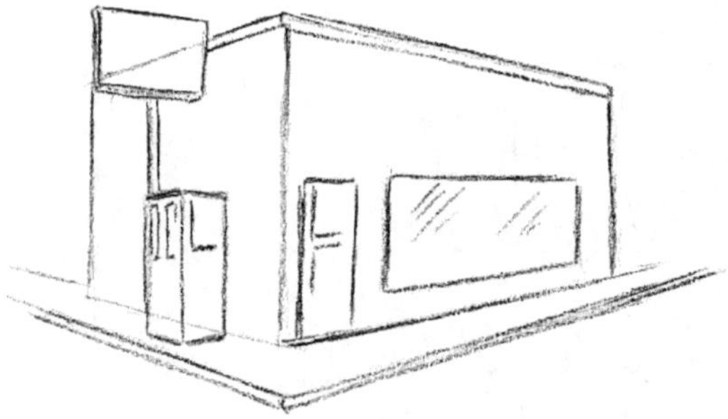

View - 3

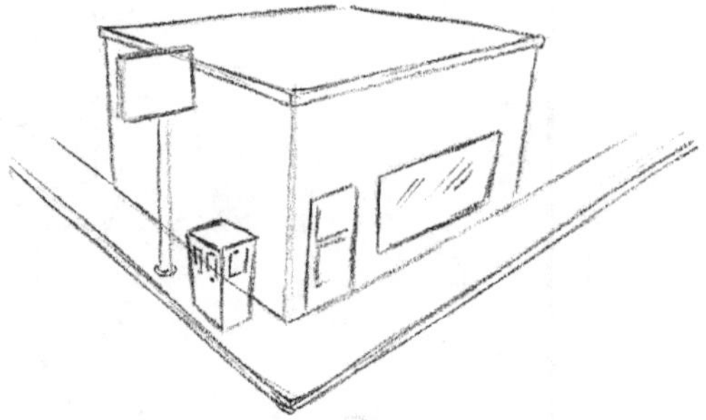

View - 4

The measurement of objects

Small objects can be drawn without measuring them. But when many objects have to be drawn in a picture, the right proportions of their relative sizes should be known, to make an effective picture.

To measure the size and proportion of an object, fi rst of all you must sit straight on your chair. Now hold a pencil in such a way that the little fi nger is below and the other three fi ngers are above the pencil, while the thumb is placed in such a way that it can be moved upwards and downwards according to the size of the object. Measurement should be taken by closing the right eye and keeping the right hand forward exactly in line with the right shoulder. While measuring all the lines, the pencil should always be held either vertical or horizontal to the ground.

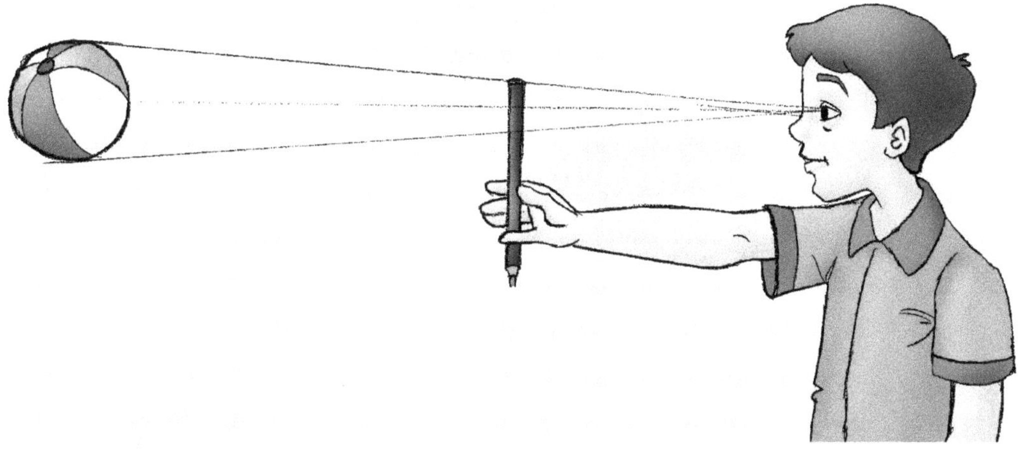

Different states of the shape of squarish object

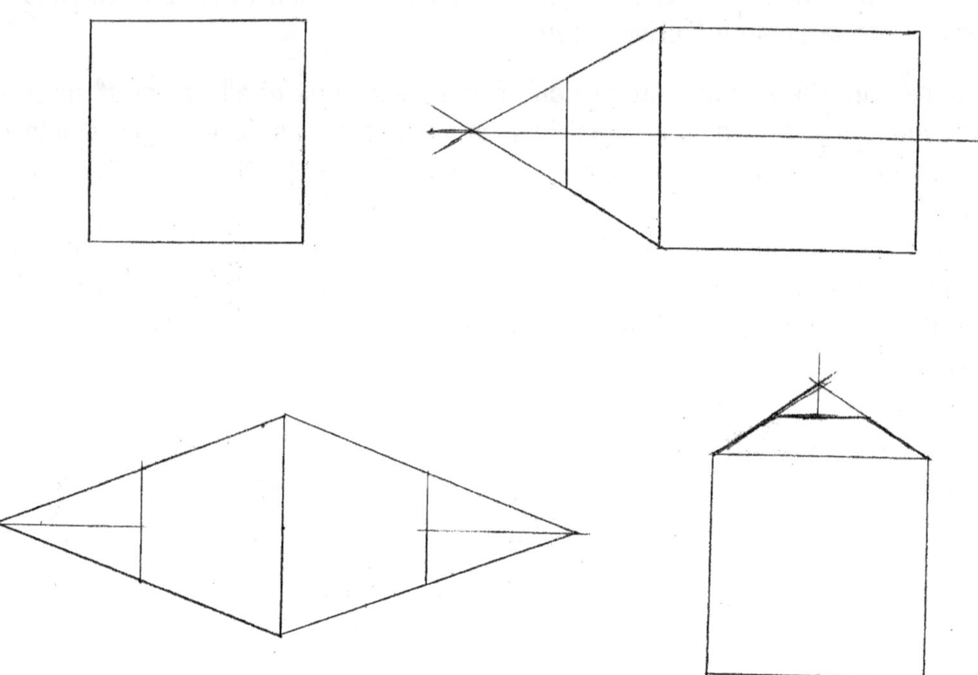

Horizon line

Plane of ground

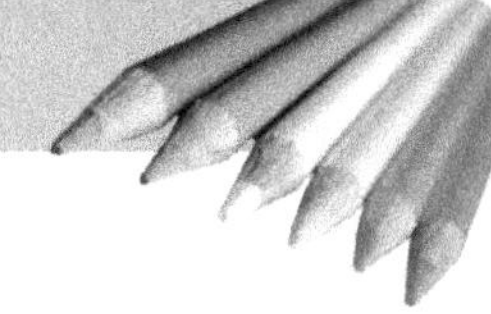

What do your draw?

Selecting what to draw is often the hardest part of the task; for example, where to look, which section to choose and which feature to examine, beginners often feel inhibited by the complexity of the real world. One simple method of selection is to direct your attention to one aspect of the subject. Draw the skyline to the exclusion of the middle distance and foreground.

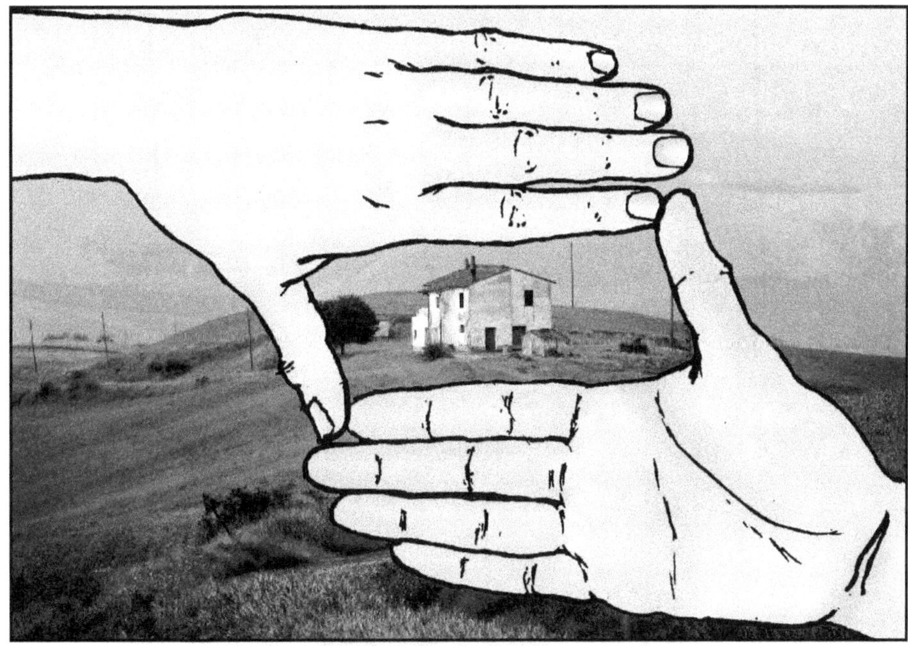

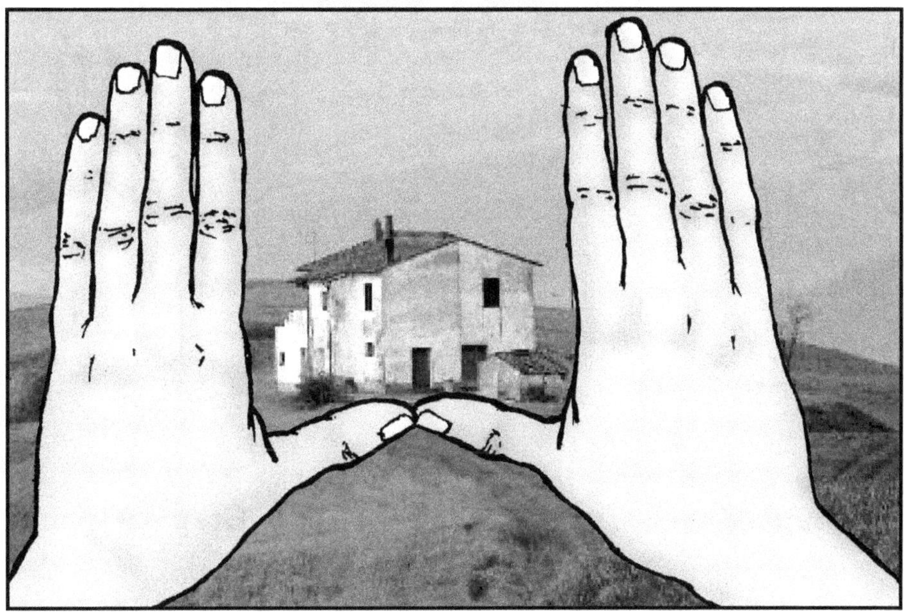

Drawing of still objects

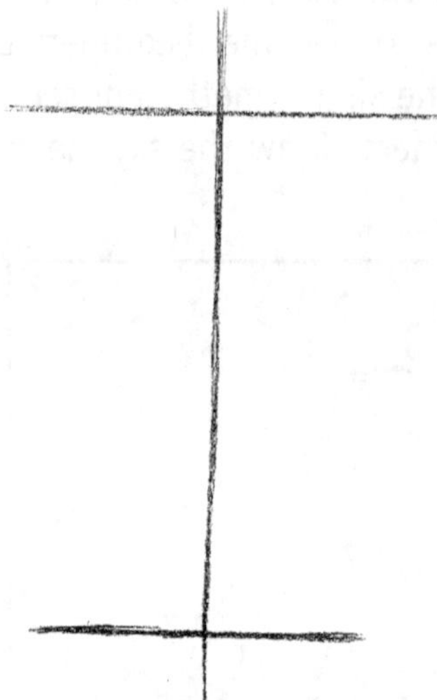

Step - 1

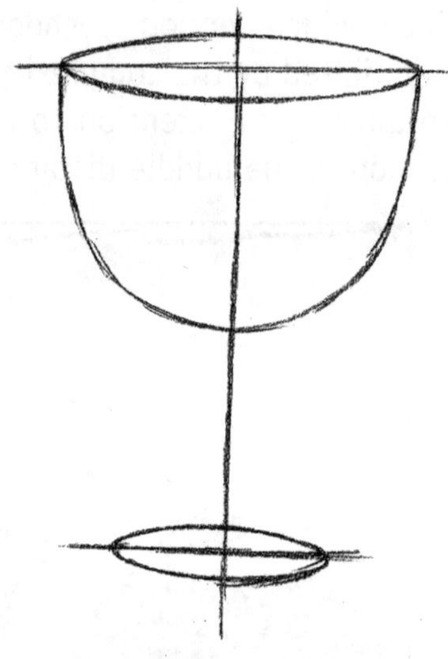

Step - 2

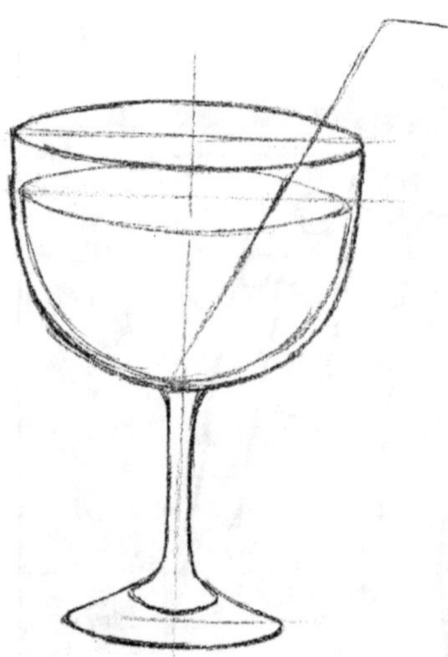

Step - 3

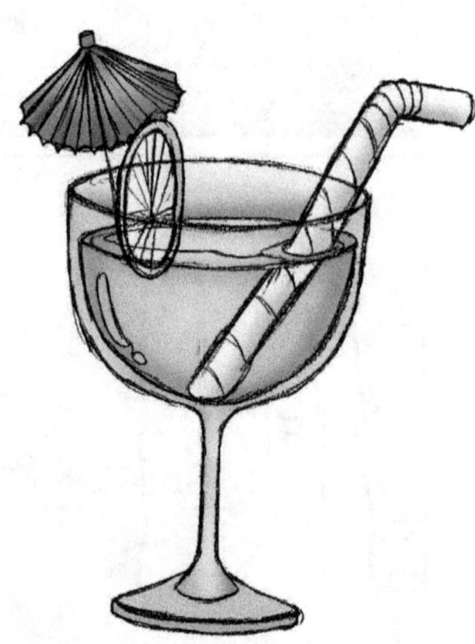

Step - 4

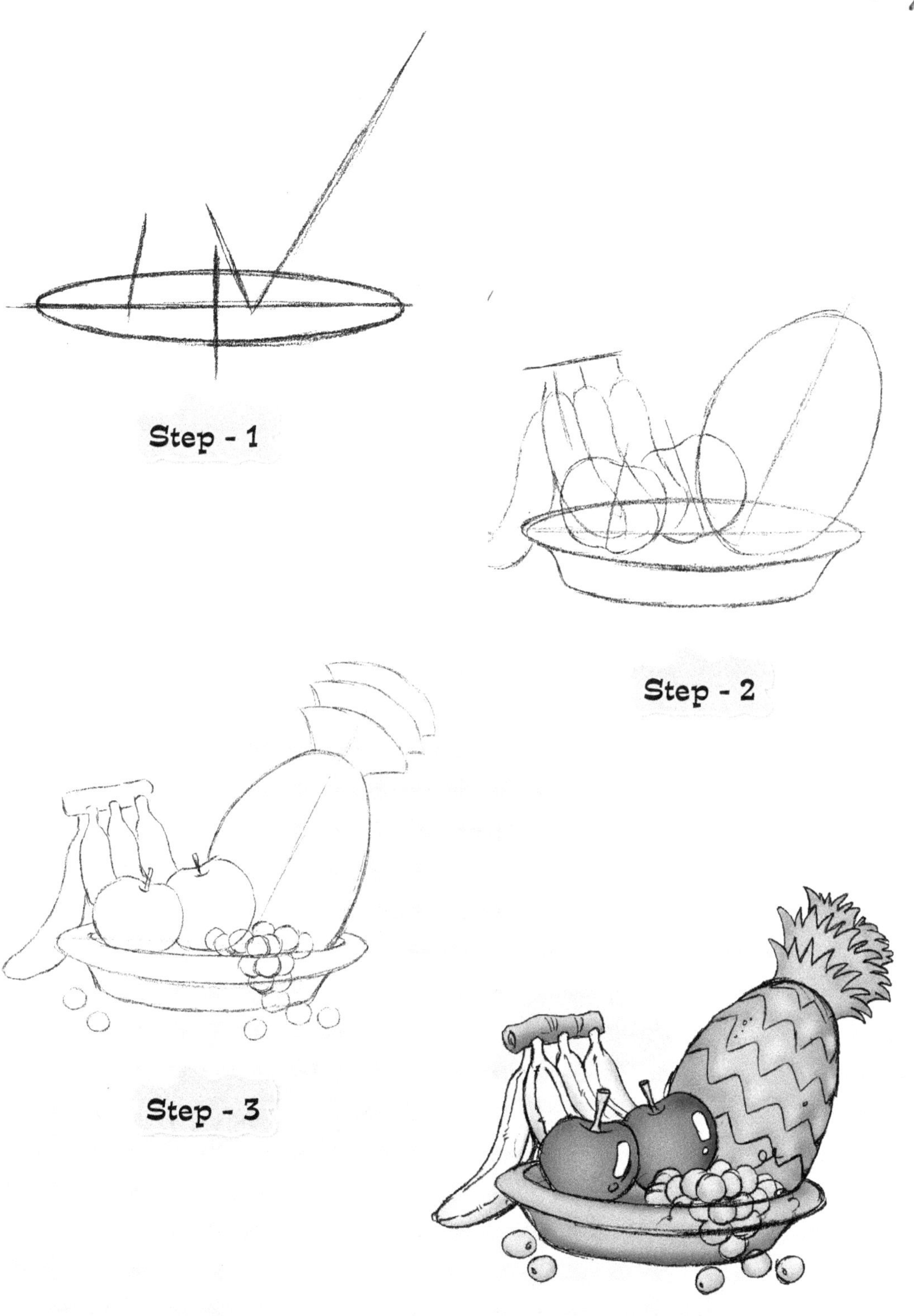

Step - 4

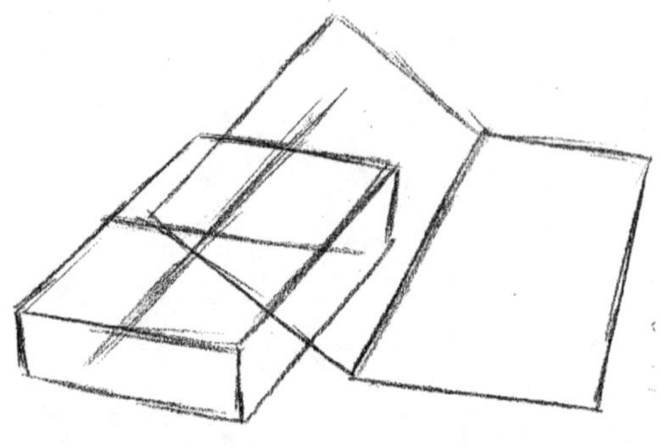

Step - 1

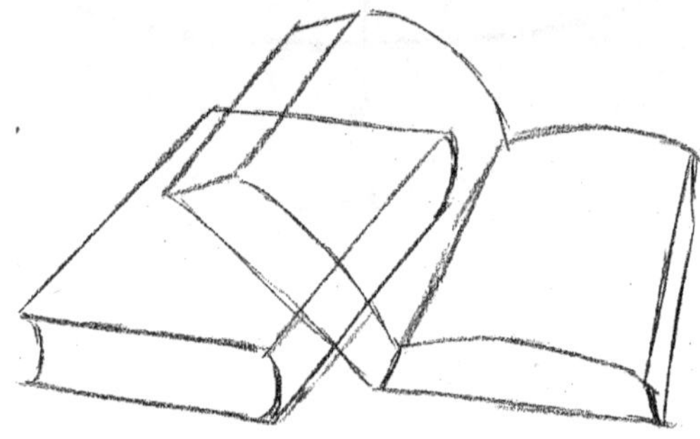

Step - 2

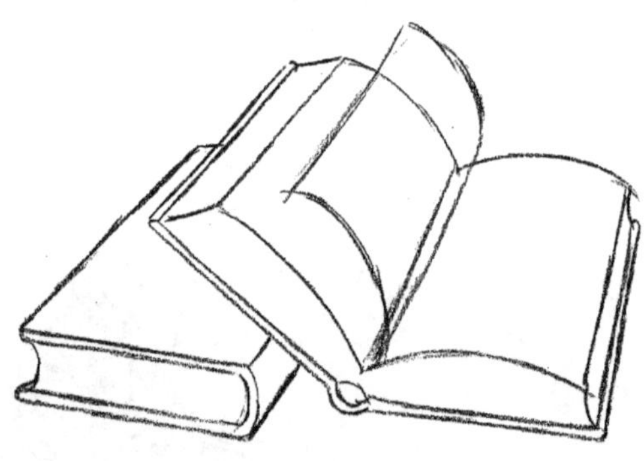

Step - 3

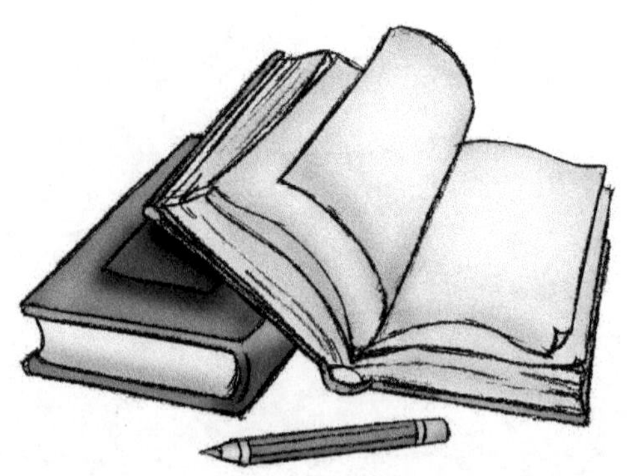

Step - 4

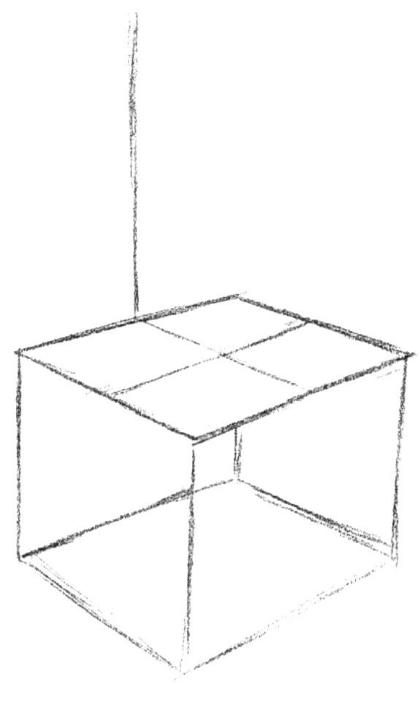

Step - 1

Step - 2

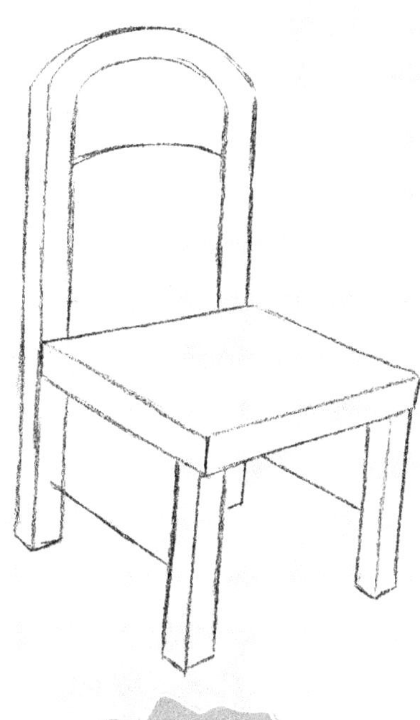

Step - 3

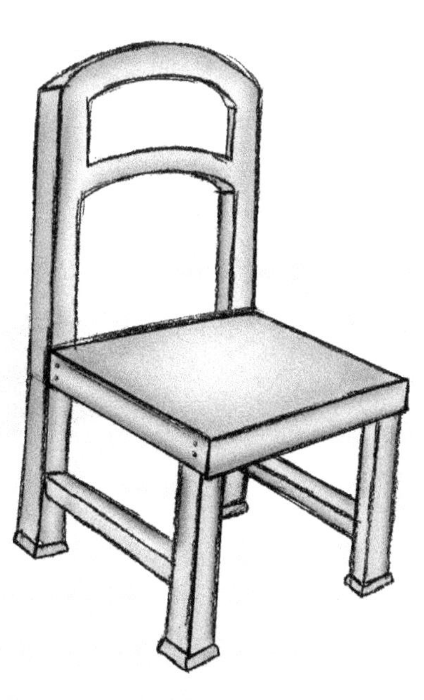

Step - 4

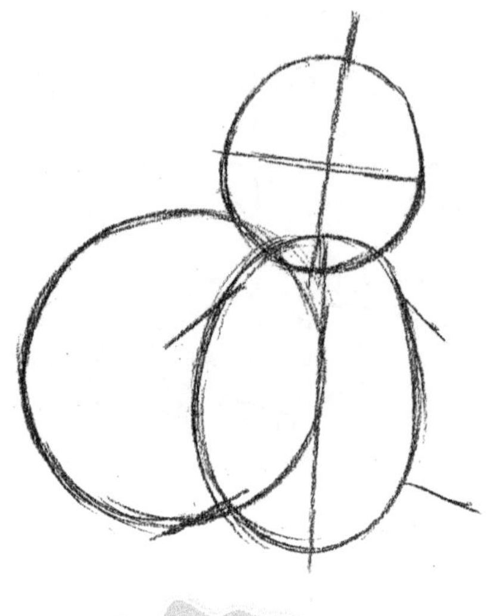

Step - 1

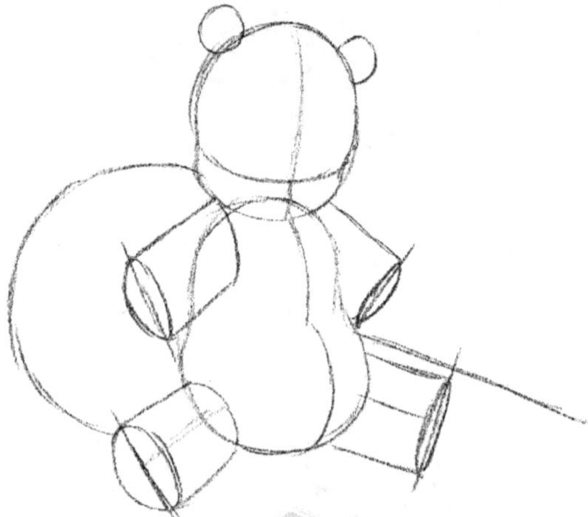

Step - 2

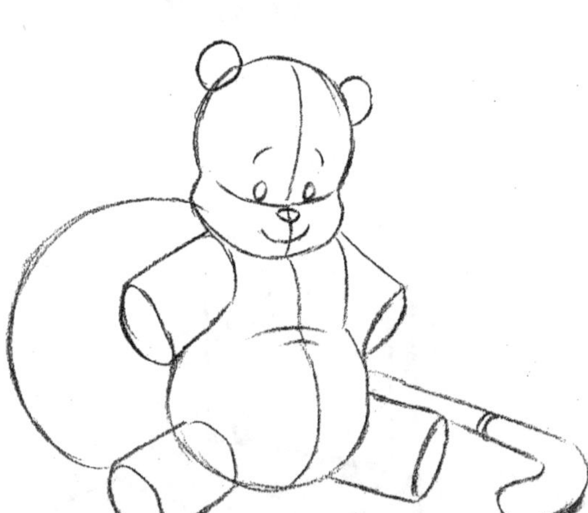

Step - 3

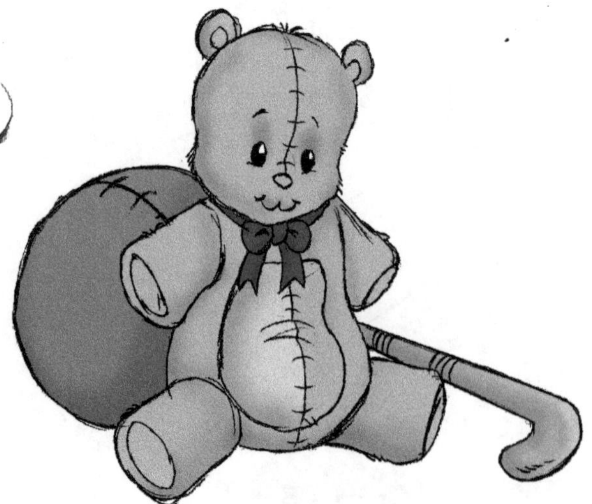

Step - 4

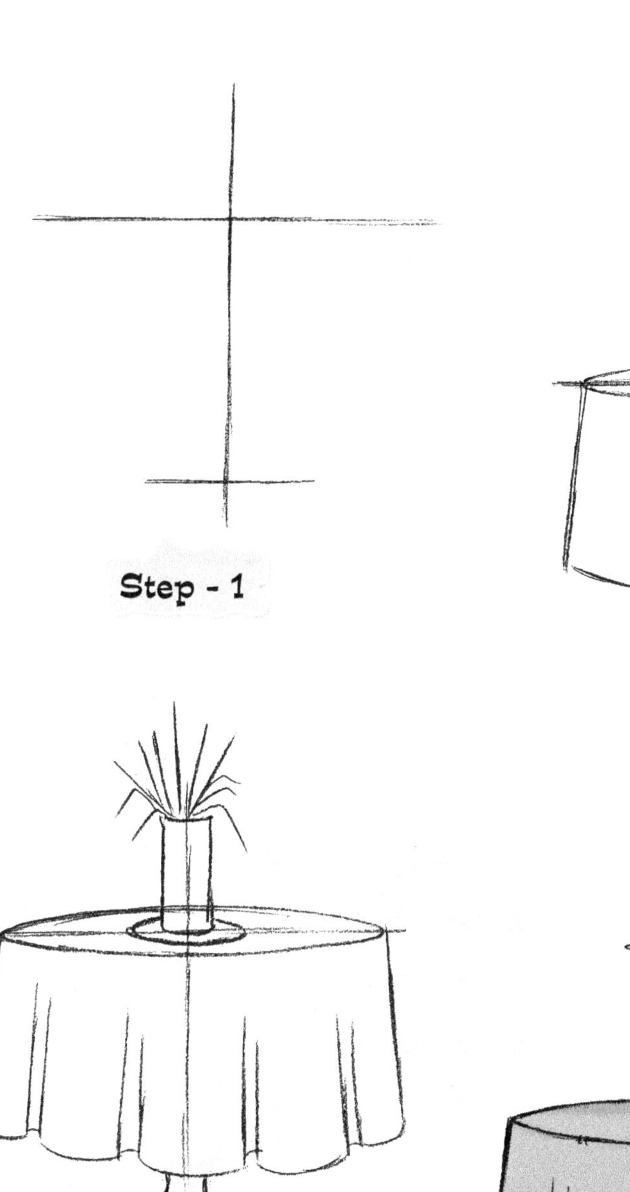

Step - 1

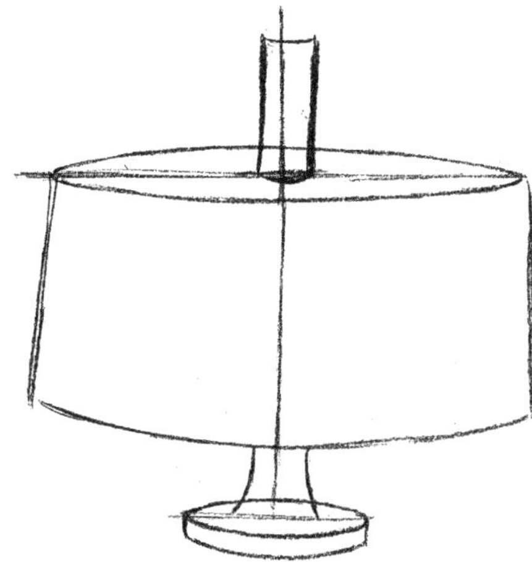

Step - 2

Step - 3

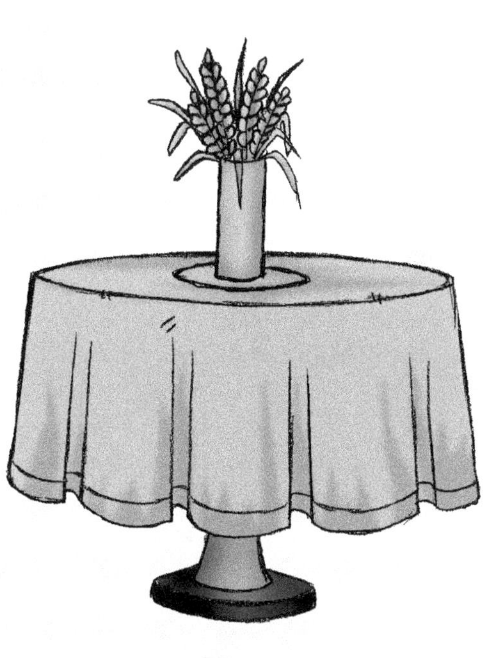

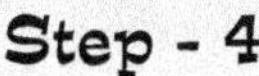

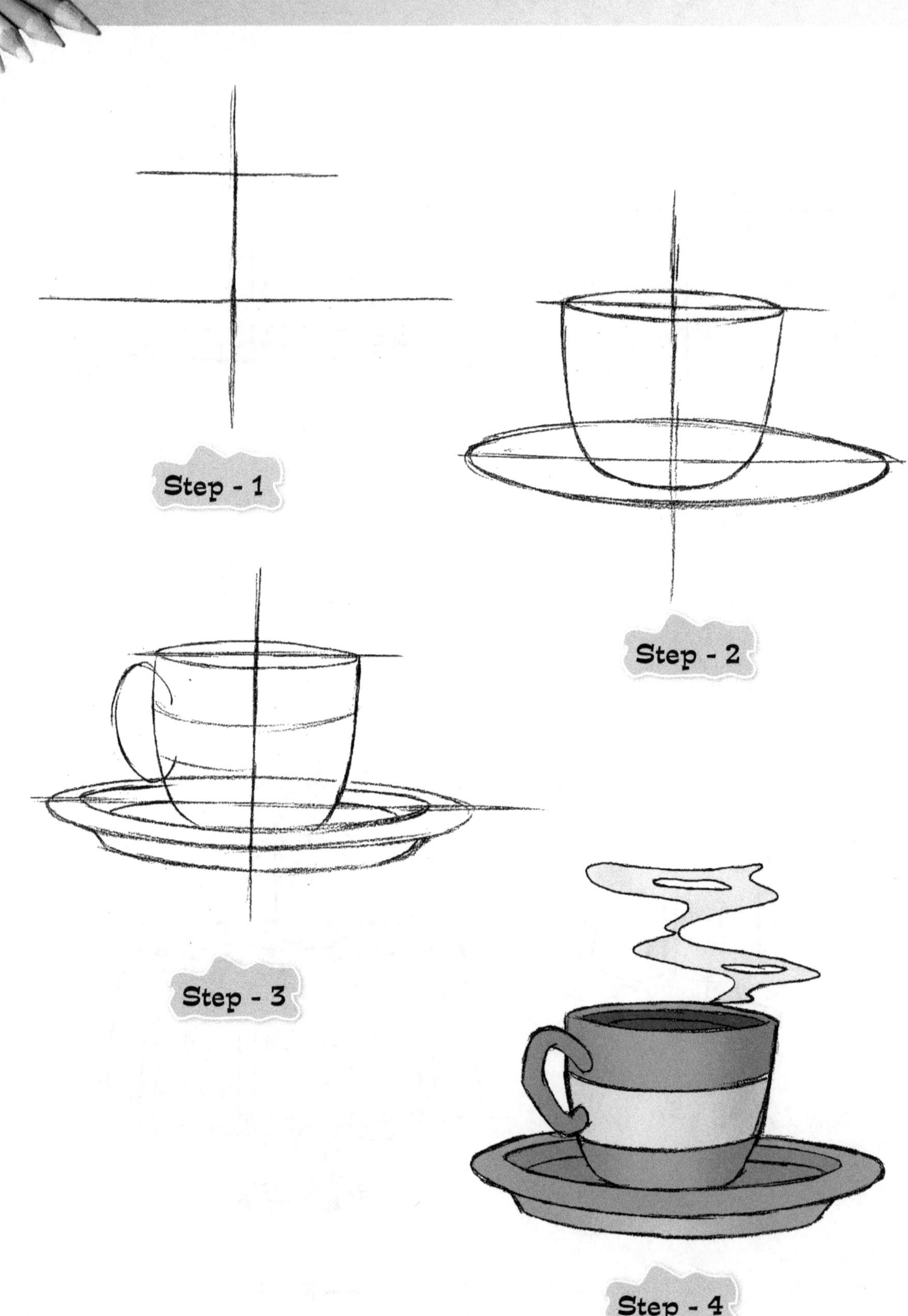
Step - 1
Step - 2
Step - 3
Step - 4

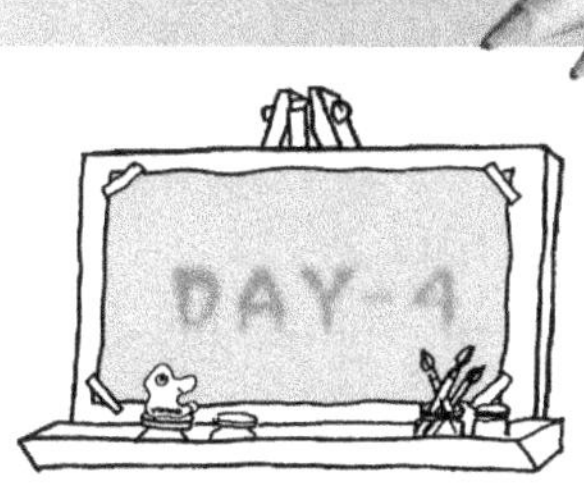

So, we had been telling you about object drawing. You must have practiced object drawing by following the rules that you had learnt yesterday. Probably, you might have committed some mistakes in the beginning, or you might not fi nd your work satisfactory. But, don't lose heart. Keep on trying. After some practice, your sketching will certainly improve. We are sure that you are now more enthusiastic and eager to learn new techniques of drawing.

Till now you have only drawn the outlines of objects with pencil. The objects do not become clear by this kind of drawing. After making the forms, in order to make them more clear, realistic, solid and lively, it is necessary to create the effect of light, shade and shadow on these forms.

The room you are working in must be having a door or a window, which should be opened completely from one side, so that there is one source of light. And, before opening a window or a door, keep a cubical or spherical object on your table. Now see the object carefully. The side on which the light is falling is completely lighted, while on the second side, there is slight darkness and the side just opposite to light seems most dark.

In object drawing, in order to show the right effect of light and shadow, you must carefully observe the direction of light falling on the object. Even while drawing a group of objects, the light must seem to come from one side only.

Light

The light that falls on the object refl ects and shows us the object. The part of the object that is facing the light is called lighted.

Highlight

It is the lighted area of the object on which maximum light is directly falling. In other words, it is that part on which the light rays are falling straight. This heavy light comes directly from the source of light. The effect of highlight increases the realism of the object.

Shade

It is that part of the object on which the light does not fall directly. In other words, that part on which there is not enough light is called shade.

Shadow

When light falls on an object from an opposite direction, the object leaves a shadow on the ground. This shadow is darkest on its edges and becomes lighter away from it. The shadow becomes big or small according to the angle at which the light is falling. The shadow takes the shape of the object.

Reflected light

When the light of a shining object falls on an object next to it, or when the light of the nearby object falls on the shining object, it is called refl ected light.

Reflected shade

When the effect of a light or dark object falls on a nearby object, it is called refl ected shade.

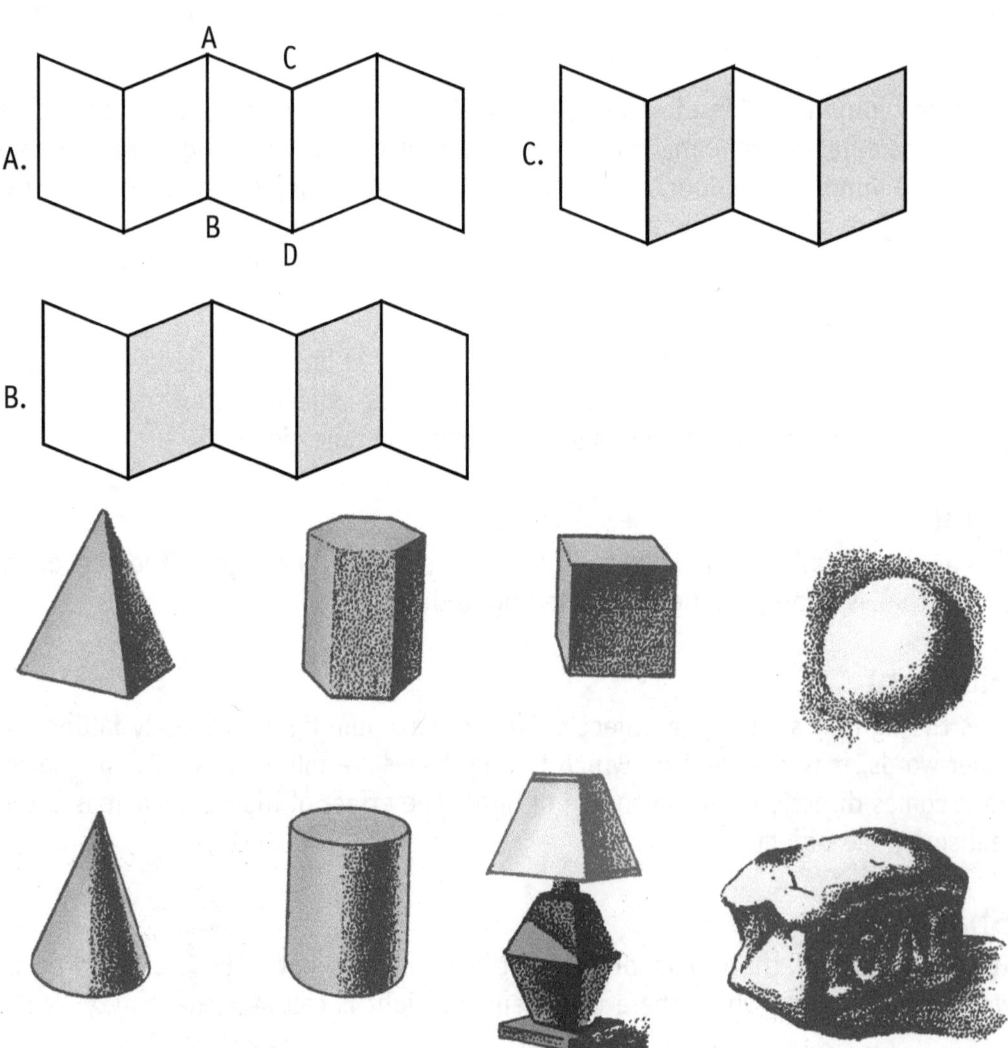

Different Techniques of Showing Light, Shade and Shadow

In the beginning you must use a pencil to show various shades. You can use pencils like HB, 2B, 4B, 6B. For the practice of colourful drawings, initially it is better to use pastels or crayons. When you are satisfi ed with your work, then you can try other techniques also. Among these, water colour, pen, brush and ink are important techniques.

Light and shade in lines

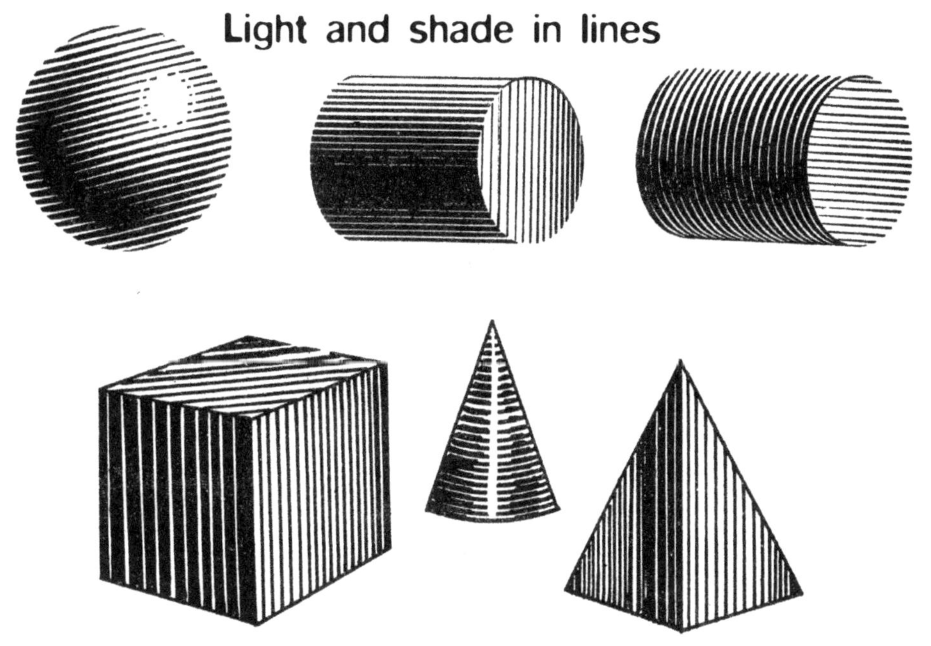

Light and shade with pencil

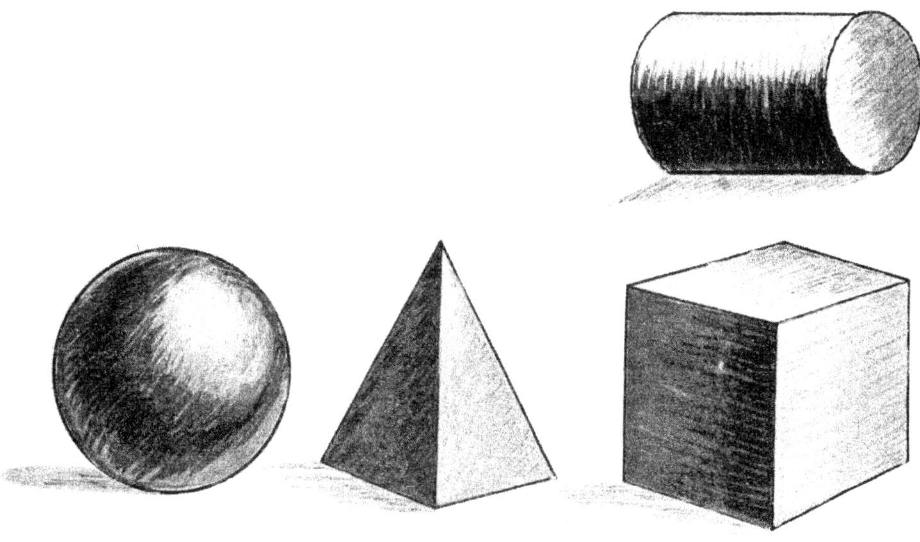

Light and shade with pencil

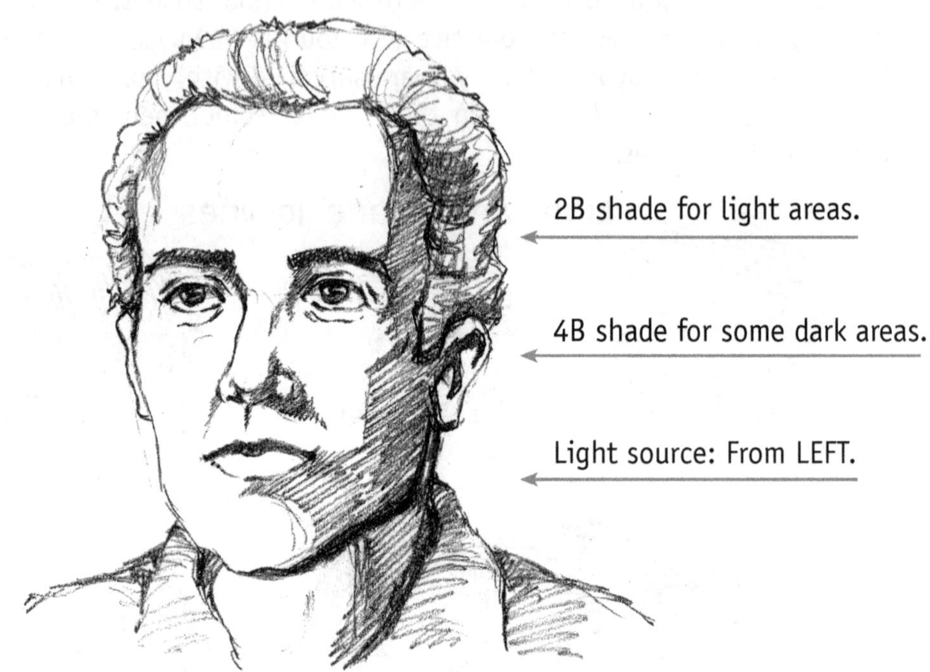

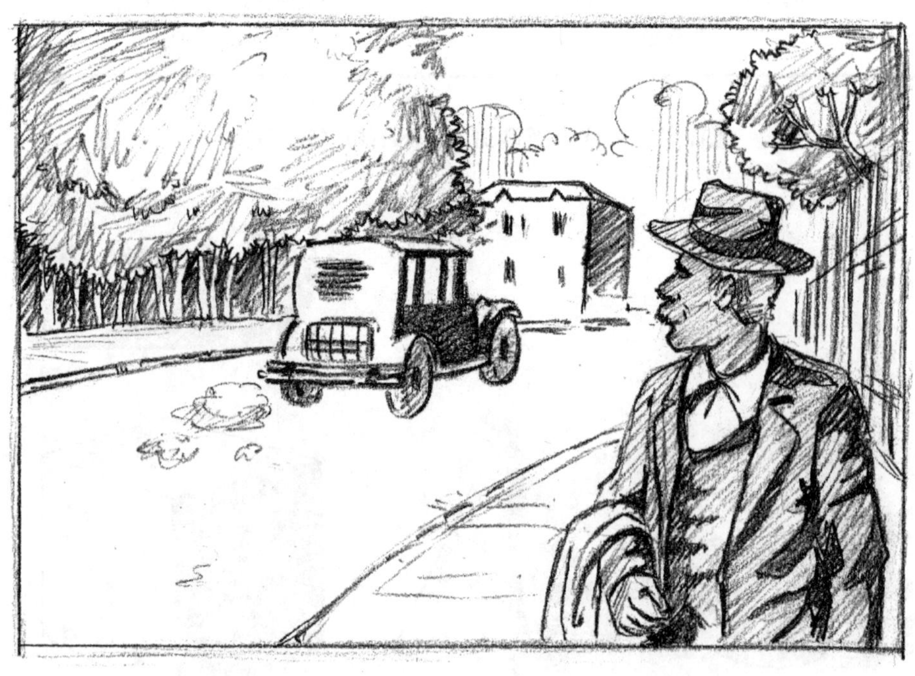

Light and shade with pen and ink

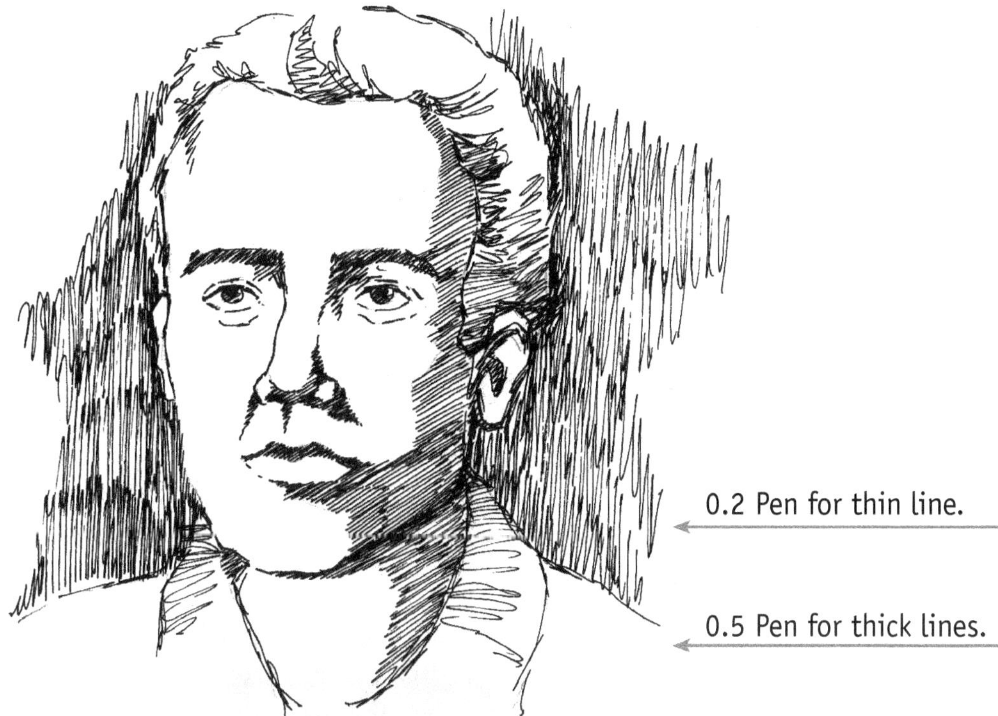

0.2 Pen for thin line.

0.5 Pen for thick lines.

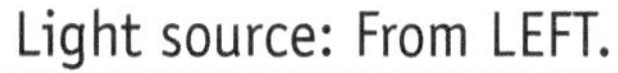

Light source: From LEFT.

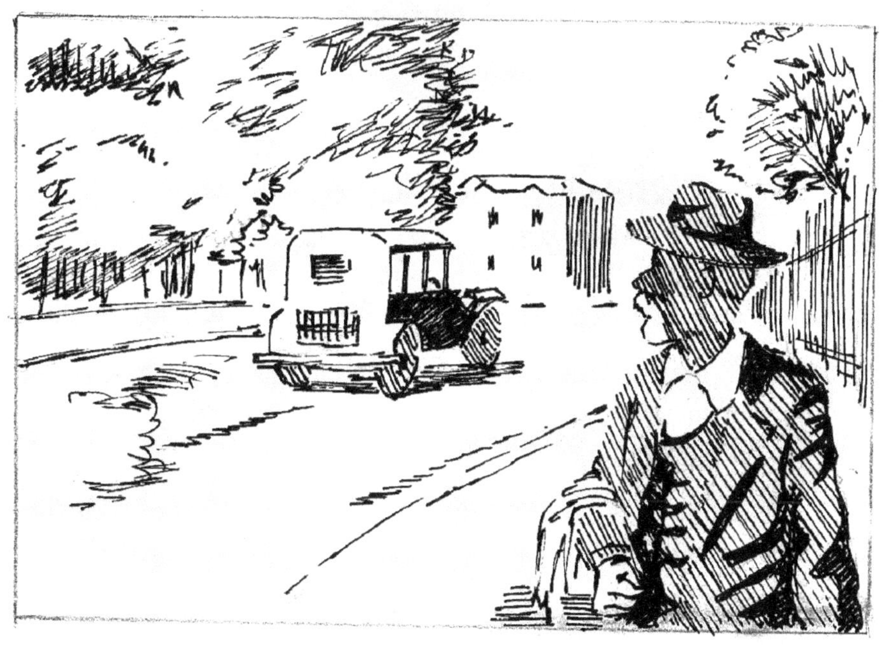

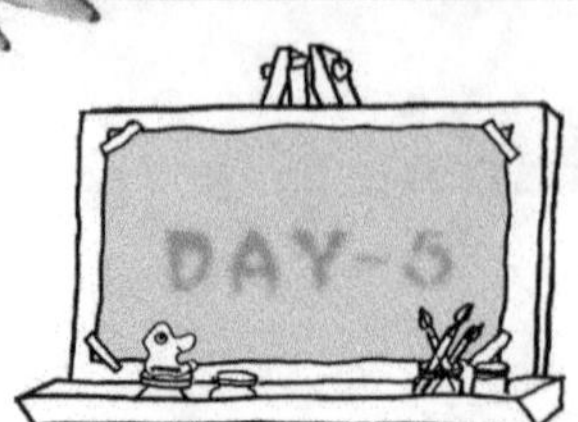

You have already learnt object drawing. You also know how to create the effects of light, shade and shadow in drawings. Let us proceed further. Today we will tell you about the leaves, fl owers, trees and plants. This kind of sketching is not much diffi cult. Before sketching, you must carefully examine the object. See what kind of shape it has, and also note down the proportionate measurements of its height and width.

Drawing of Leaves

There are various kinds of leaves. They differ in size—big or small, and have different shapes—round, oval, etc. Some leaves have rough edges, while those of others are plain. Before sketching a leaf, you should observe it closely. First, make an outline of the leaf according to its edges, and then give it the appearance of real leaf.

In drawing a leaf be careful of its edges and veins, as failure to recognize them will result in bad drawing. After drawing the edges, fi rst make the thick vein in the middle, then draw the thin veins all over the leaf.

Apart from this, carefully draw that portion of stem from where the leaf comes out of the branch, keeping in mind the ratio of their measurements. Otherwise, the rose leaf will look like a neem leaf. When the drawing is complete erase the rough pencil outlines.

Drawing of Flowers

Just like leaves, there are various kinds of fl owers. Before drawing them, observe their structure carefully. The fl owers can be round, oval or triangular. First, make a rough outline of the fl ower according to its shape, and then fi ll the petals in it.

In the drawing of fl owers, special attention should be paid to their petals. Some fl owers have many petals while others have very few. When the drawing is complete, rub out the rough outlines of pencil.

You have practiced the drawing of a fl ower, now make a drawing of fl owers along with their buds, leaves and branches. Create the effect of light and shade with the help of pencil.

Drawing of Trees and Plants

Before making the drawing of any plant or tree, observe it carefully. This kind of drawing can be made easy with the help of the basic shapes of circle, square, triangle and cone. First of all, make the tree trunk. They are of various types. Some trunks are straight and smooth, like the palm; some are thick and rough, like peepal and banyan. Similarly, some trunks are fat and rough, like mango and neem. The trunk of date palm is rough and tall while that of babool is smooth and black.

After sketching the trunk, make its branches and leaves. While doing the drawing, special attention should be paid to the joints of branches and the natural bend of the branches. They sprout from the trunk in a natural way, and the trunk is a bit thicker at the place from where the branches come out. In the same way, the leaves come out of the branches. In order to impart a real look to a tree's drawing, the branches should be drawn carefully.

Go to any garden. Observe closely various fl owers, leaves, plants and trees. For practice, make as many drawings as possible of various plants and trees.

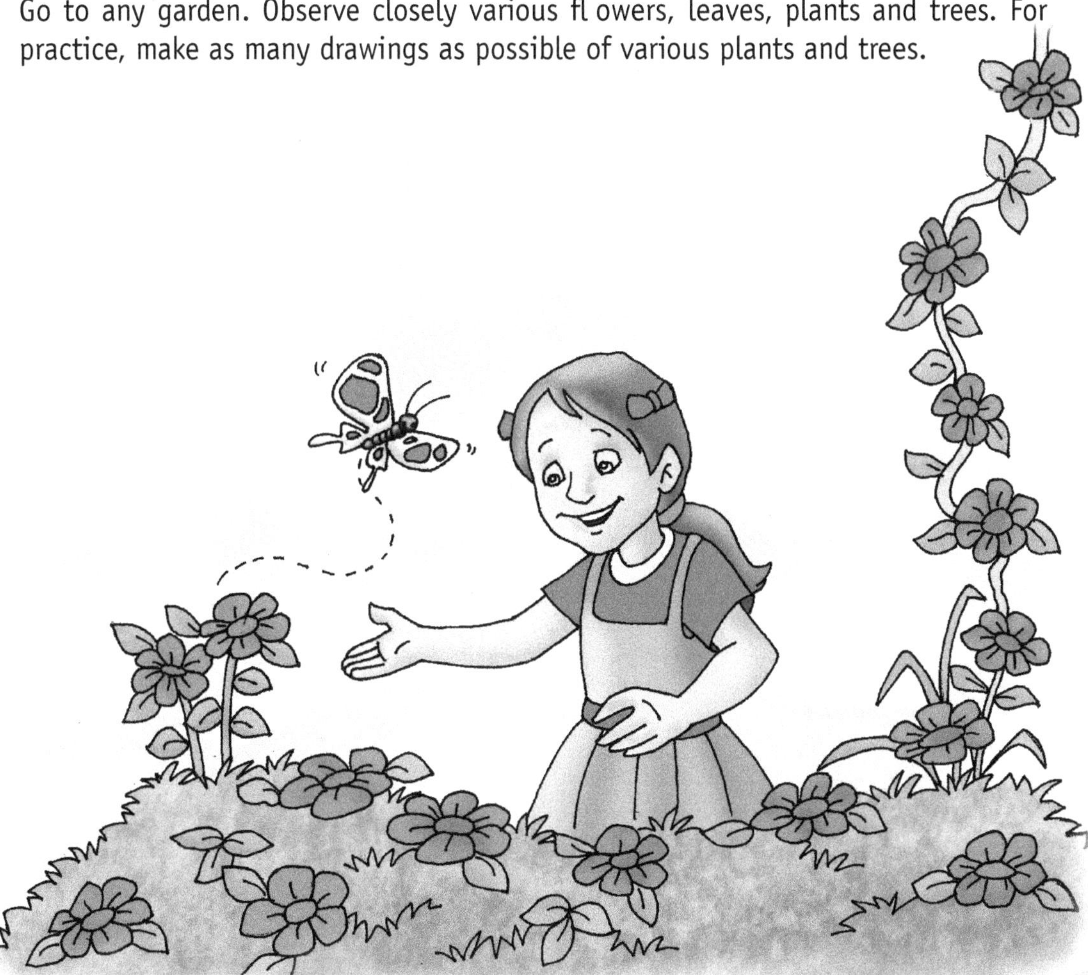

Drawing of leaves

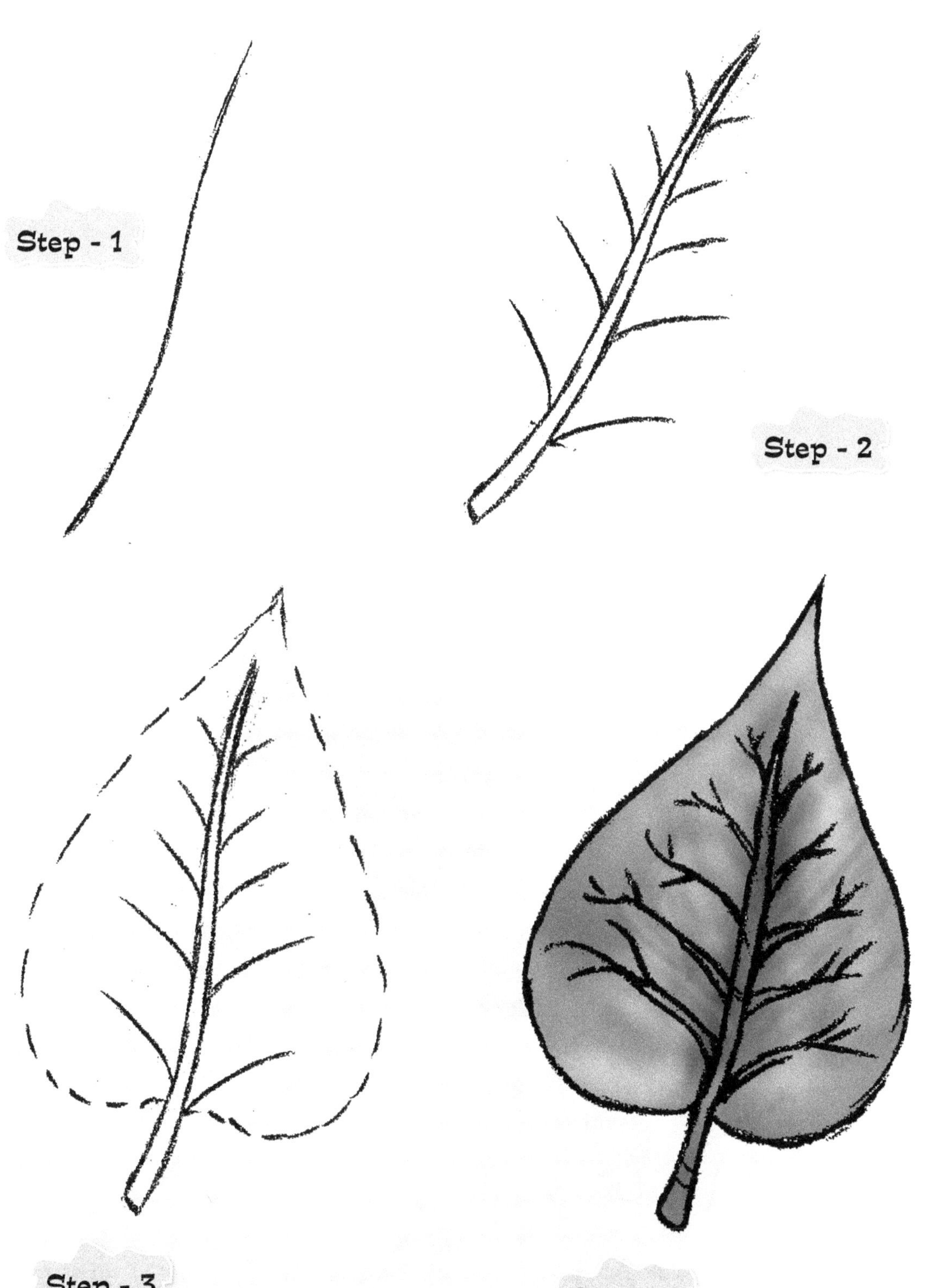
Step - 1
Step - 2
Step - 3
Step - 4

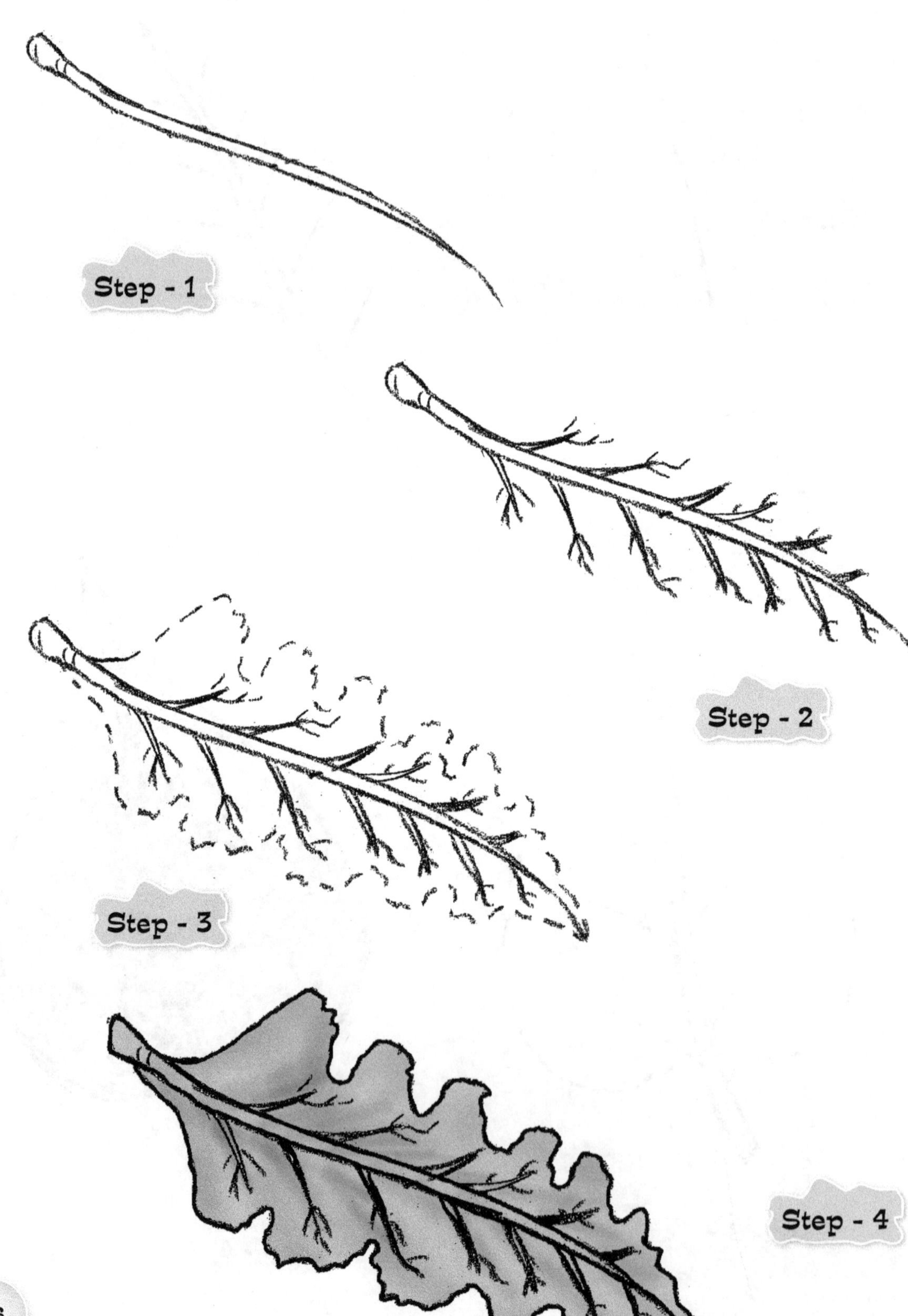
Step - 1
Step - 2
Step - 3
Step - 4

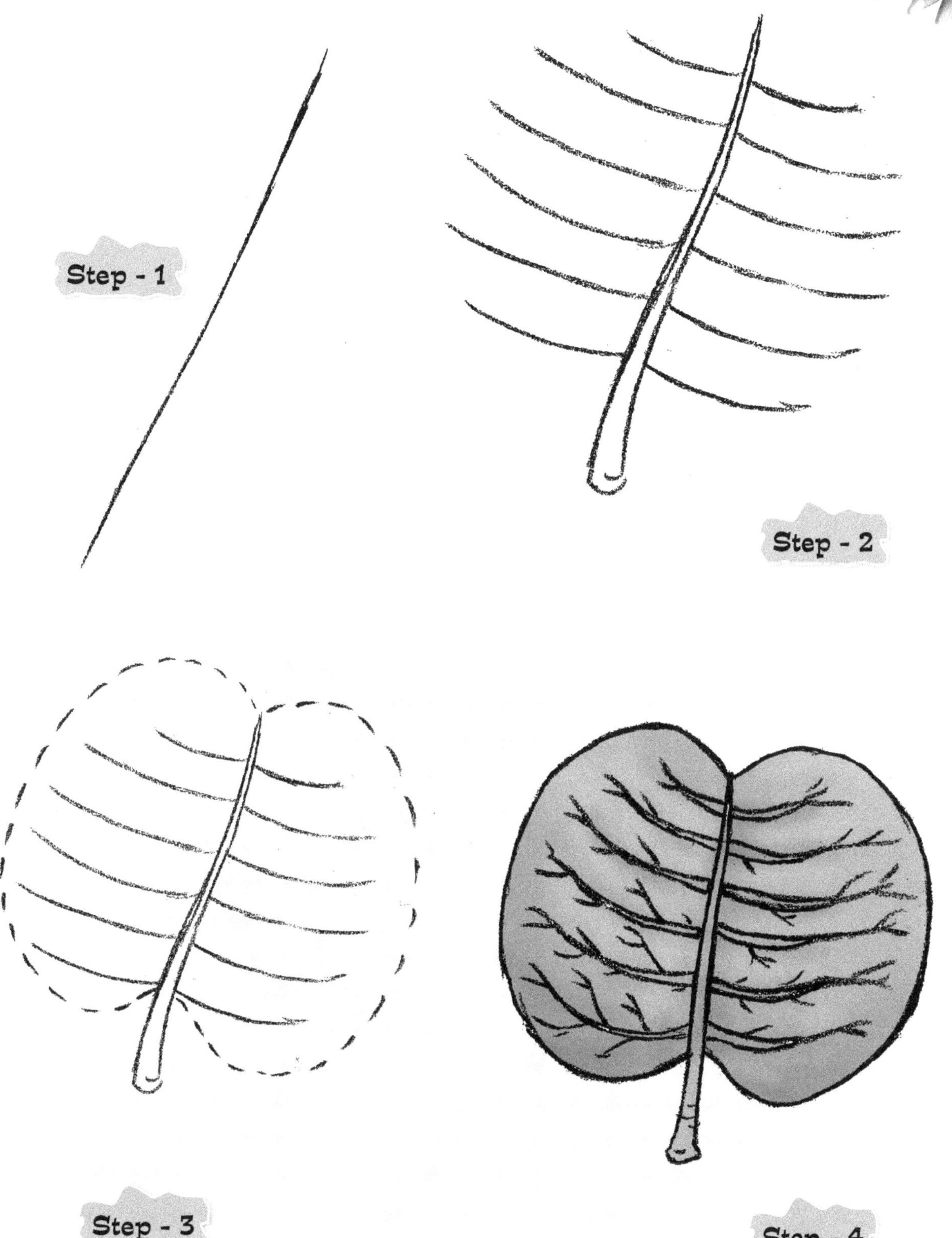
Step - 1
Step - 2
Step - 3
Step - 4

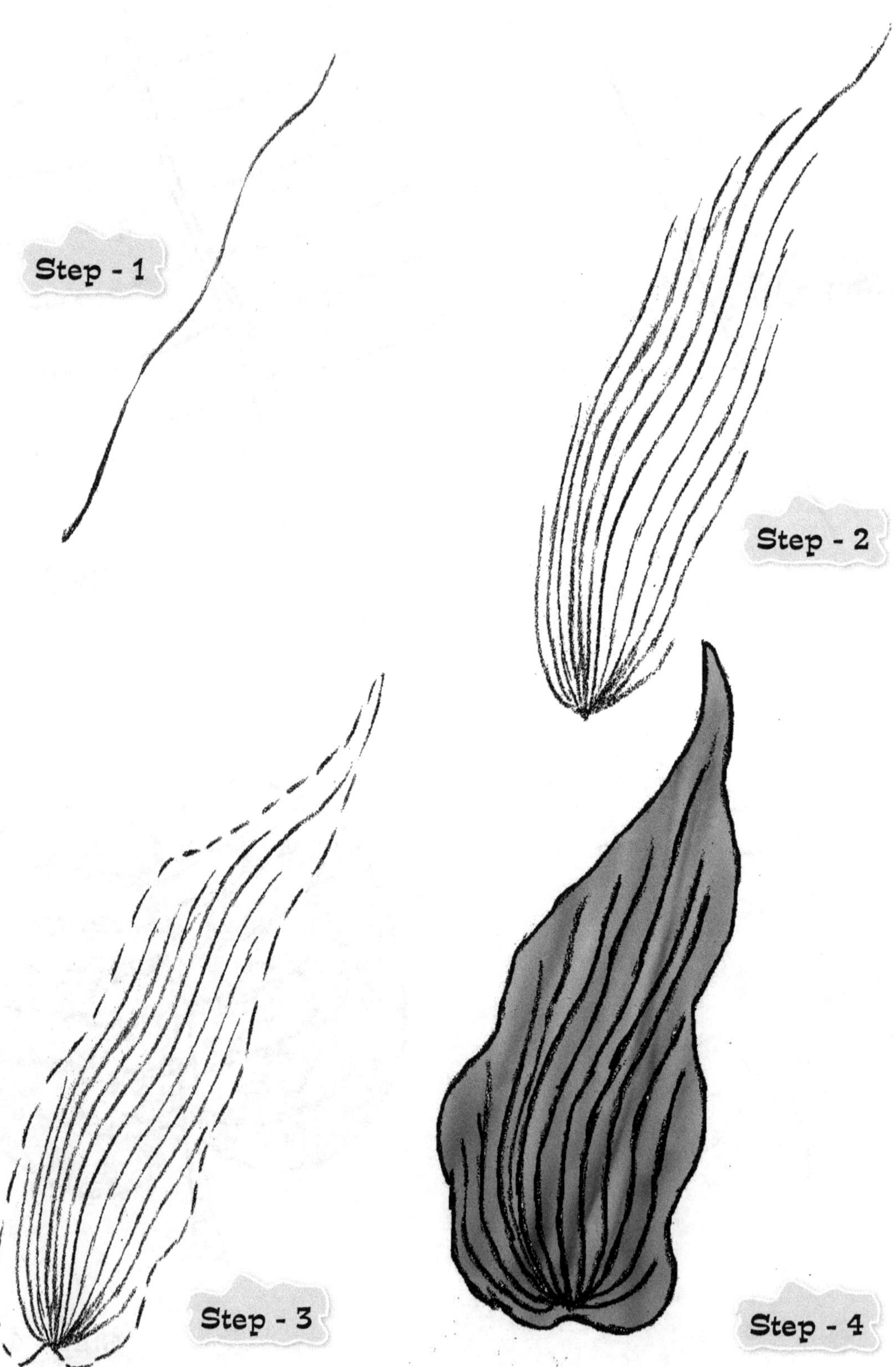
Step - 1
Step - 2
Step - 3
Step - 4

Drawing of flowers

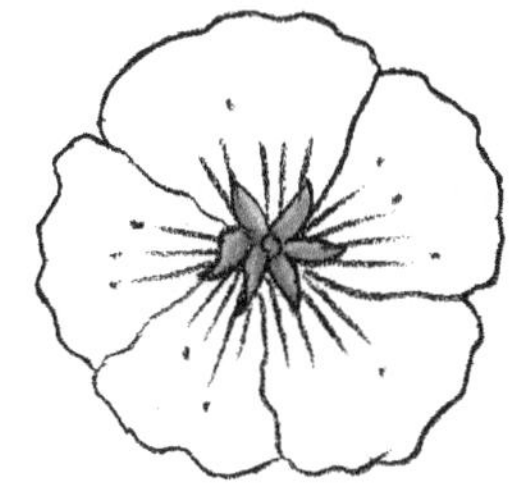
White Kaner

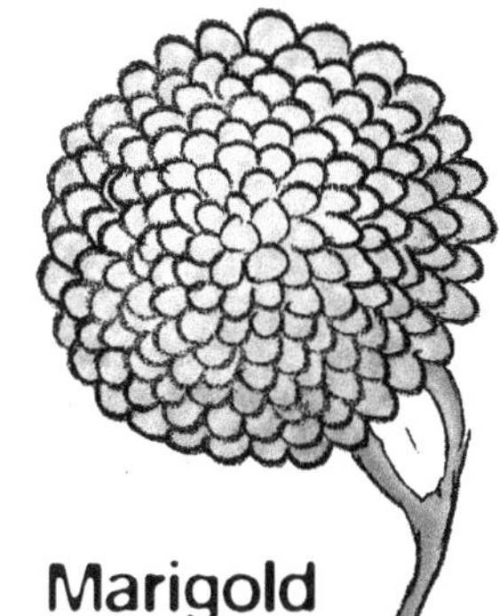
Marigold

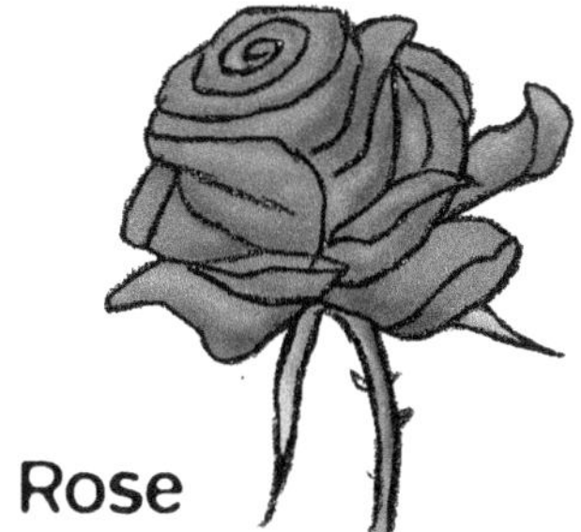
Rose

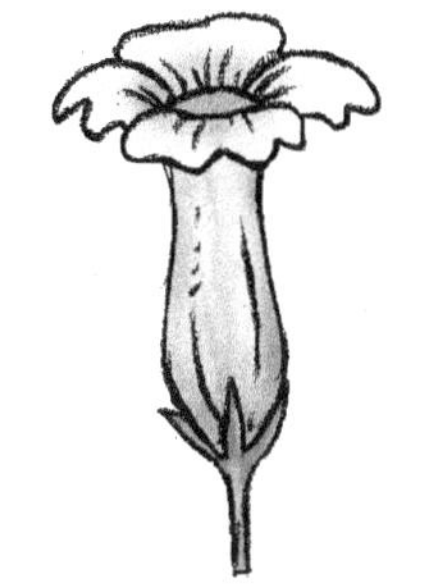
Yellow Kaner

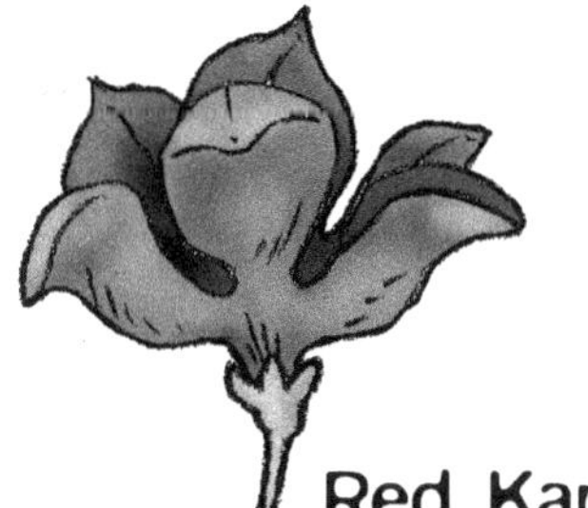
Red Kaner

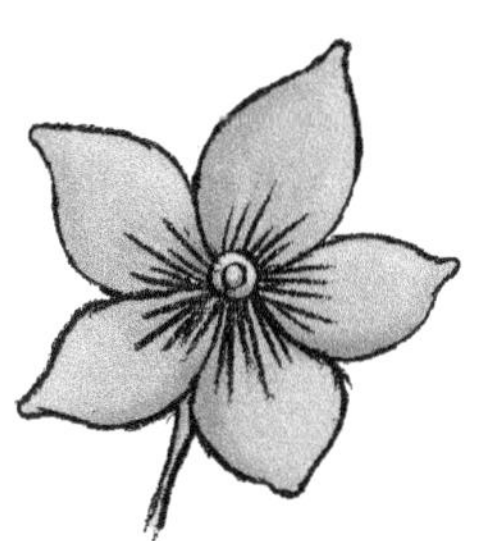
Sadabahar

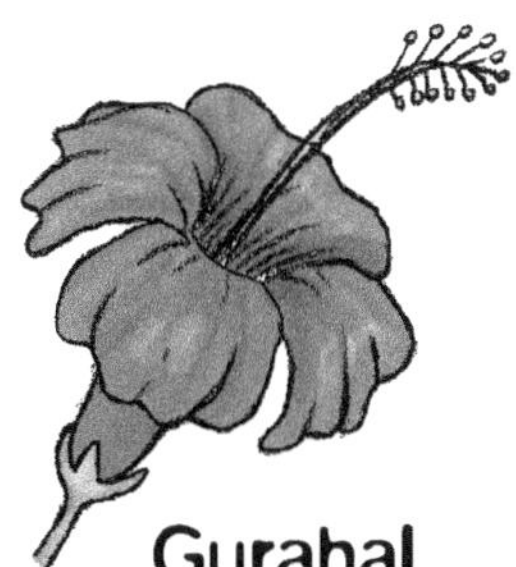
Gurahal

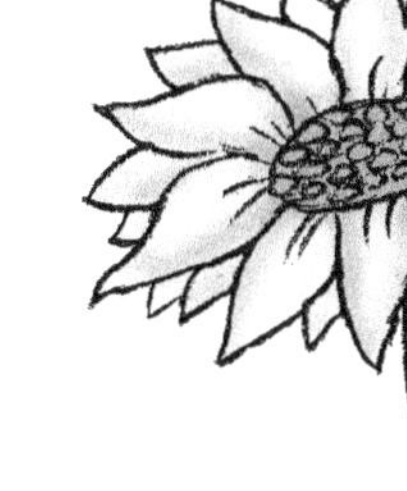
Dahlia

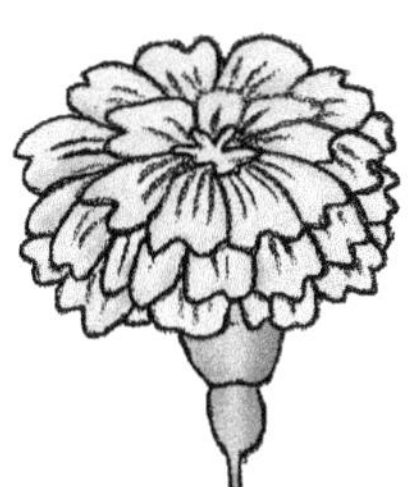
Genda Hazara

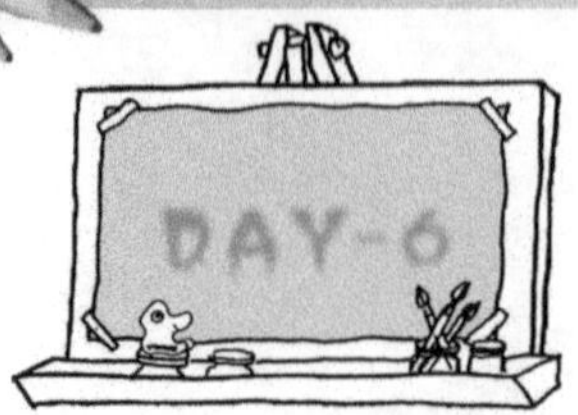

As you have done in case of flowers and leaves, examine carefully the structure of fruits and vegetables before making their drawing. Then as per their shapes—whether spherical, oval, squarish or triangular—make their outlines and fill in other details to give them the real look of fruits and vegetables. After the drawing, rub off all the unnecessary lines.

Drawing of fruits

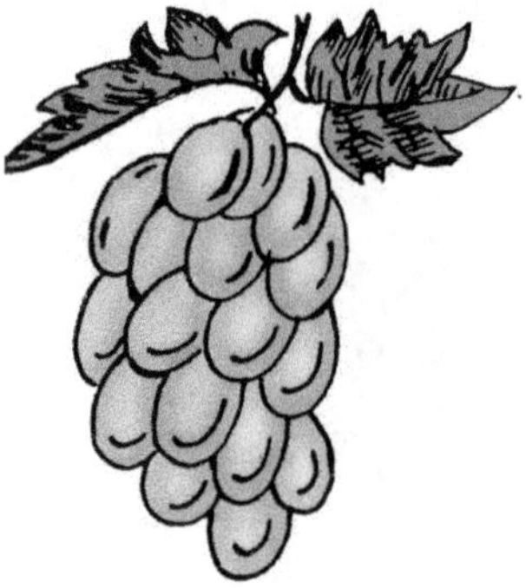

Grapes

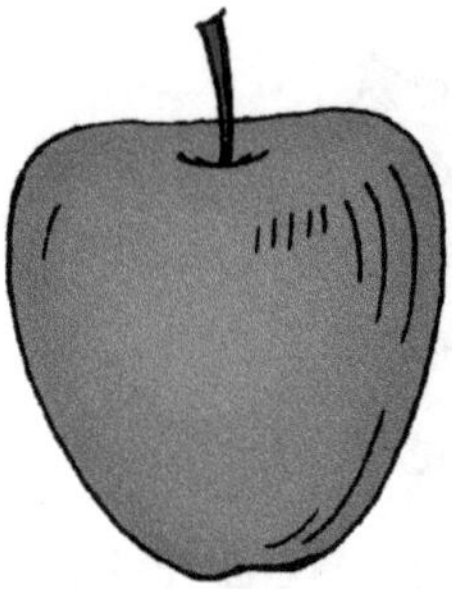

Apple

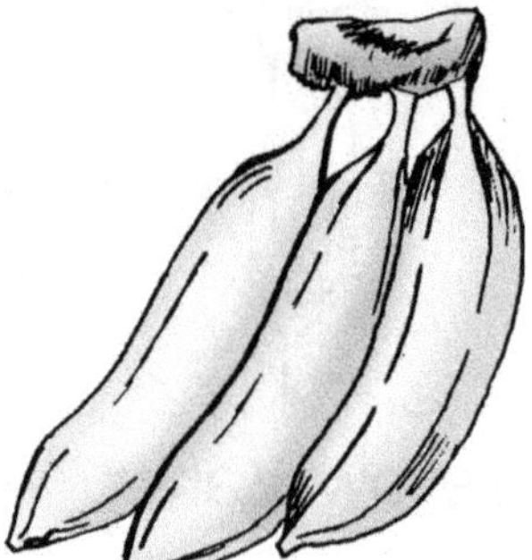

Banana

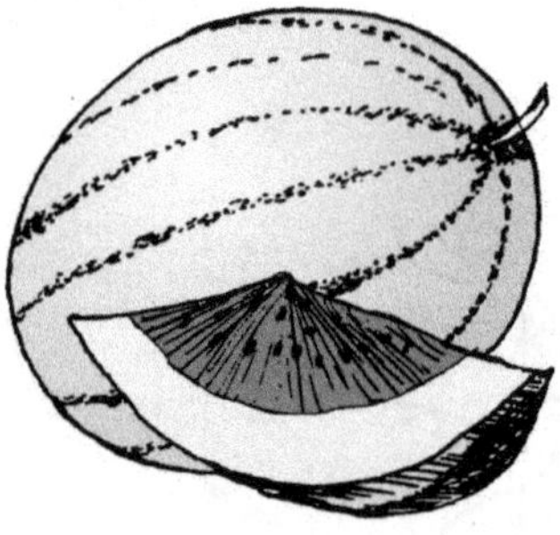

Water Melon

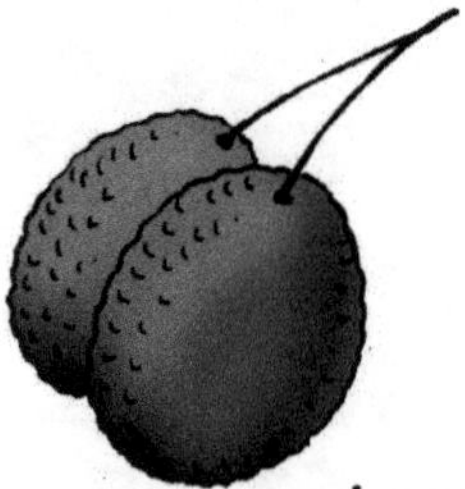

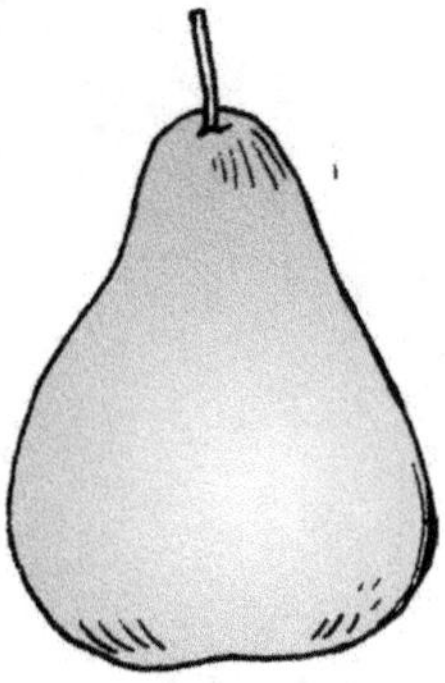

Pear

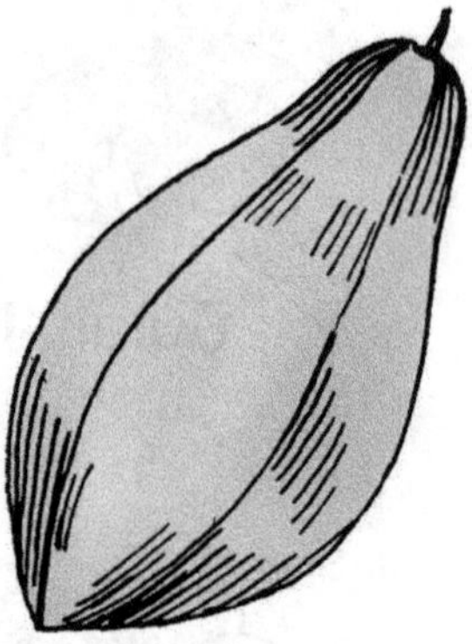

Papaya

Leechi

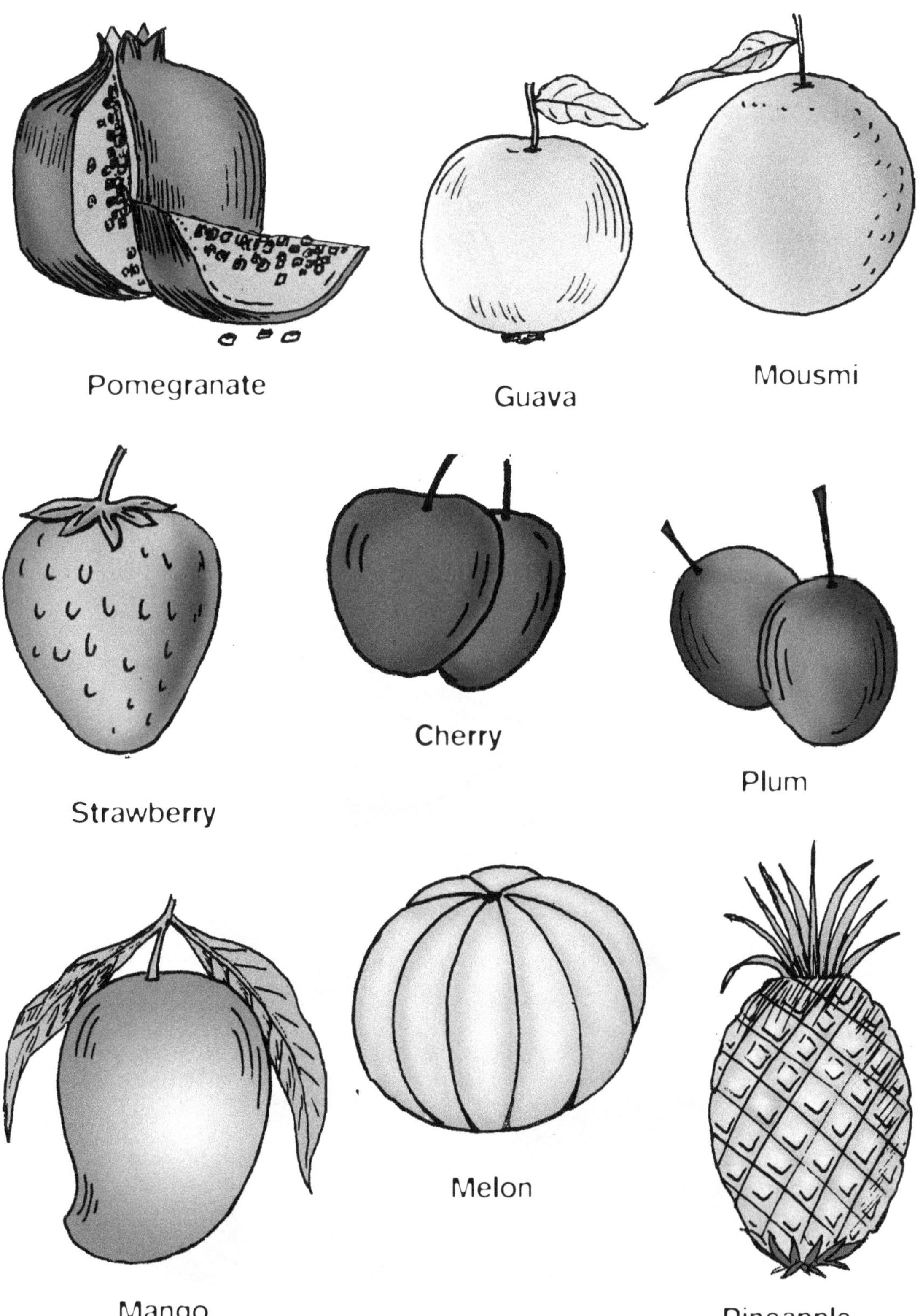
Pomegranate
Guava
Mousmi
Strawberry
Cherry
Plum
Mango
Melon
Pineapple

Drawing of vegetables

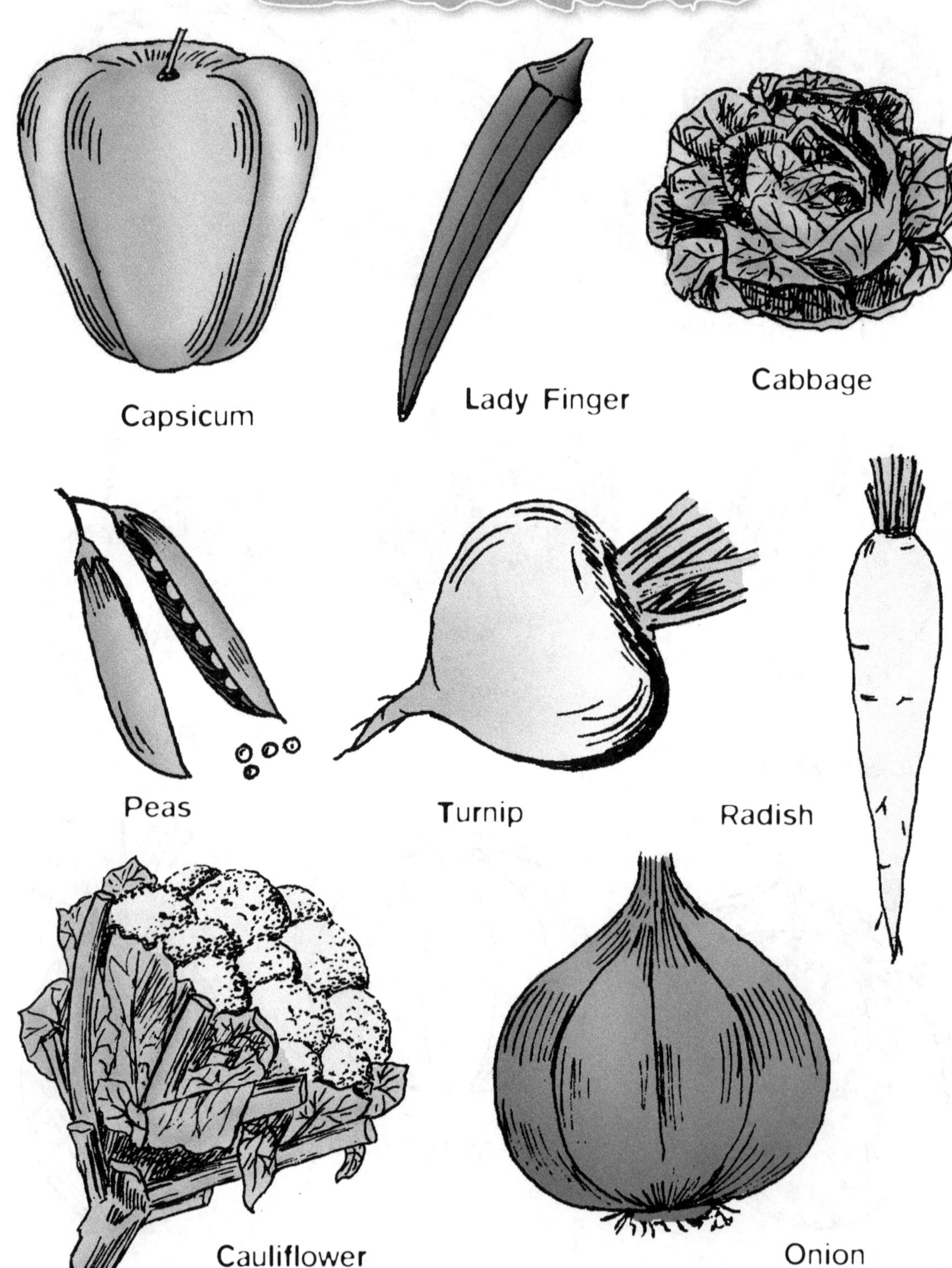

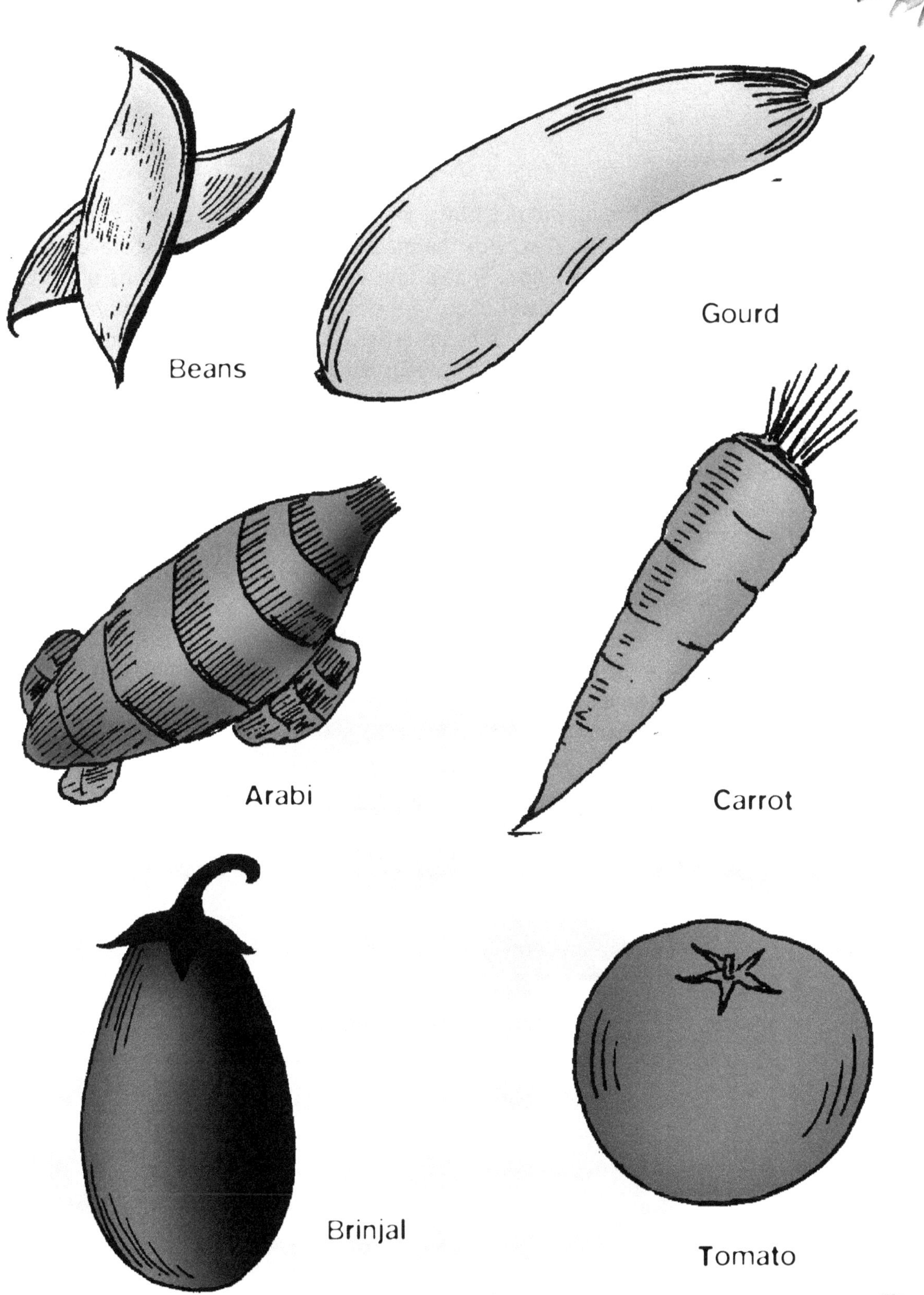
Beans
Gourd
Arabi
Carrot
Brinjal
Tomato

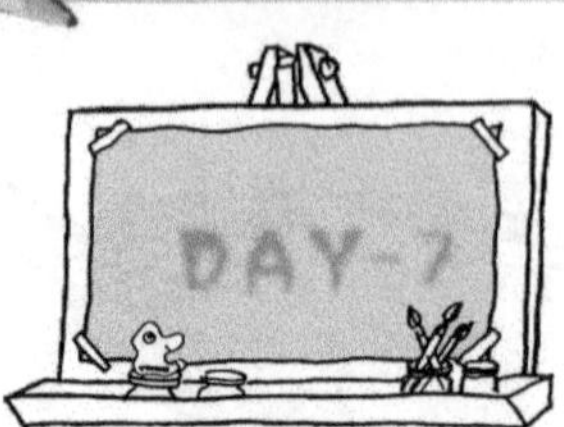

You have learnt the drawing of fruits, vegetables, leaves, fl owers, plants and trees. And we believe that with the practice of these, you must have been feeling more confi dent now. Today, join us in doing the drawings of birds. The practice of these drawings will improve the artistic faculties of your brain and you will be able to observe things as an artist. Ultimately, you will be able to impart the perfection of a good artist to your hands.

The drawing of any kind of bird can be made with the help of oval forms. The shape of a bird has three main parts—head, body and tail. Head is like a small oval, while the body resembles a big oval. When you are making the drawing of a bird, fi rst draw a small oval shape for the head and a big oval for the body. Then, as per the structure of the model bird, transform these ovals into thin, long and round shapes and join them with lines. And now create the bird's eyes, beak, wings, legs, claws, tails, etc. at the right places.

You see in your surroundings birds like parrot pigeon, crow, owl, peacock, cock, duck, crane, etc. And, you are quite familiar with their appearances. We have made here their drawings for your convenience. Observe them carefully. Isn't the method very simple? So, why waste time, take your pencil and paper and start practising these drawings. Remember, only practice can make you a good artist.

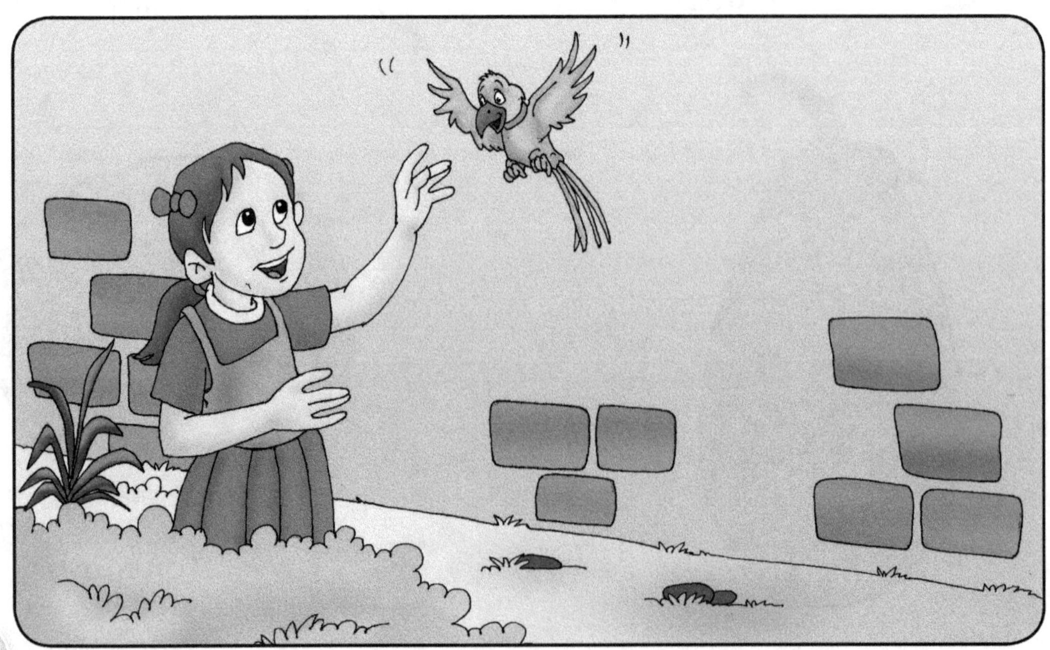

Bird

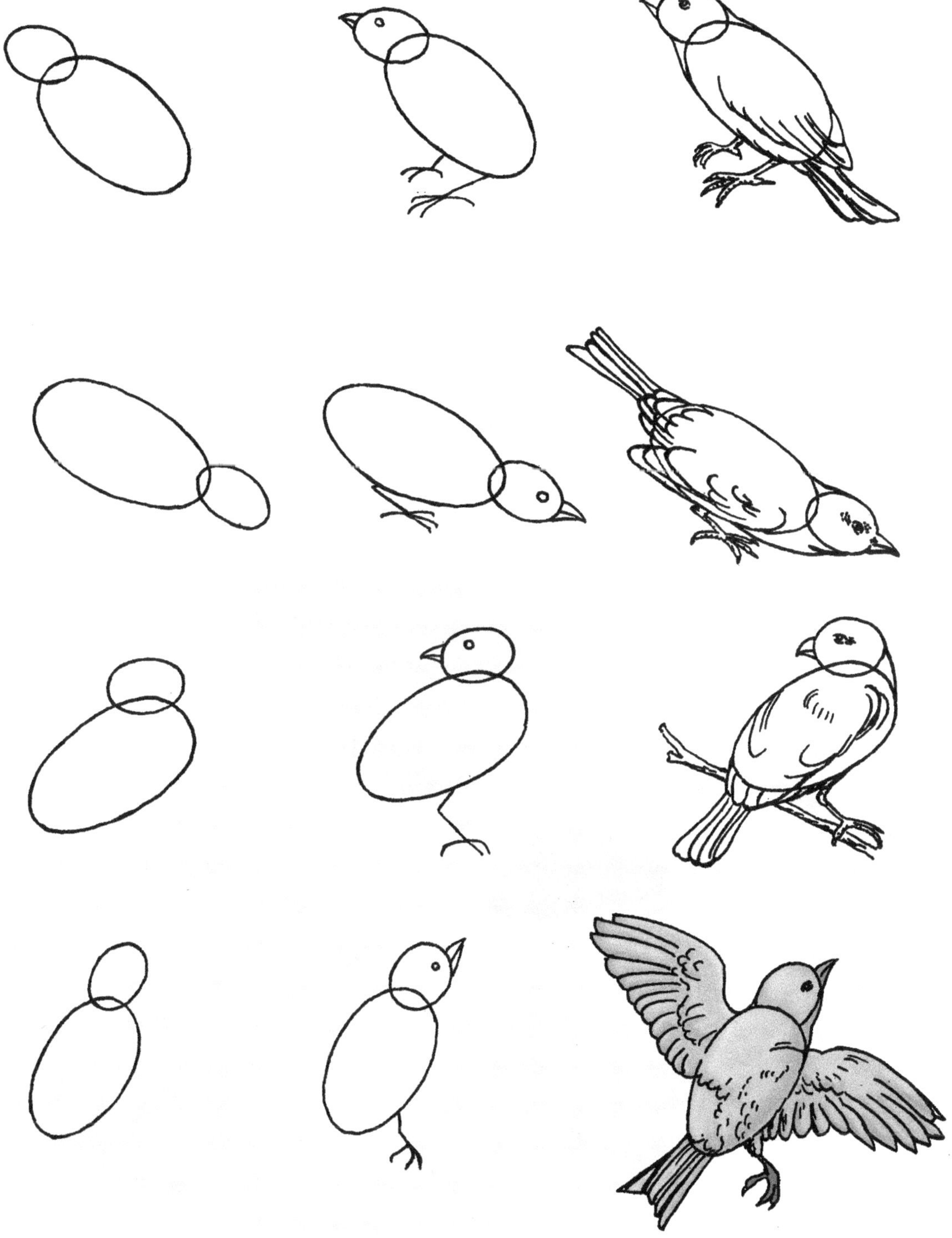

Parrot

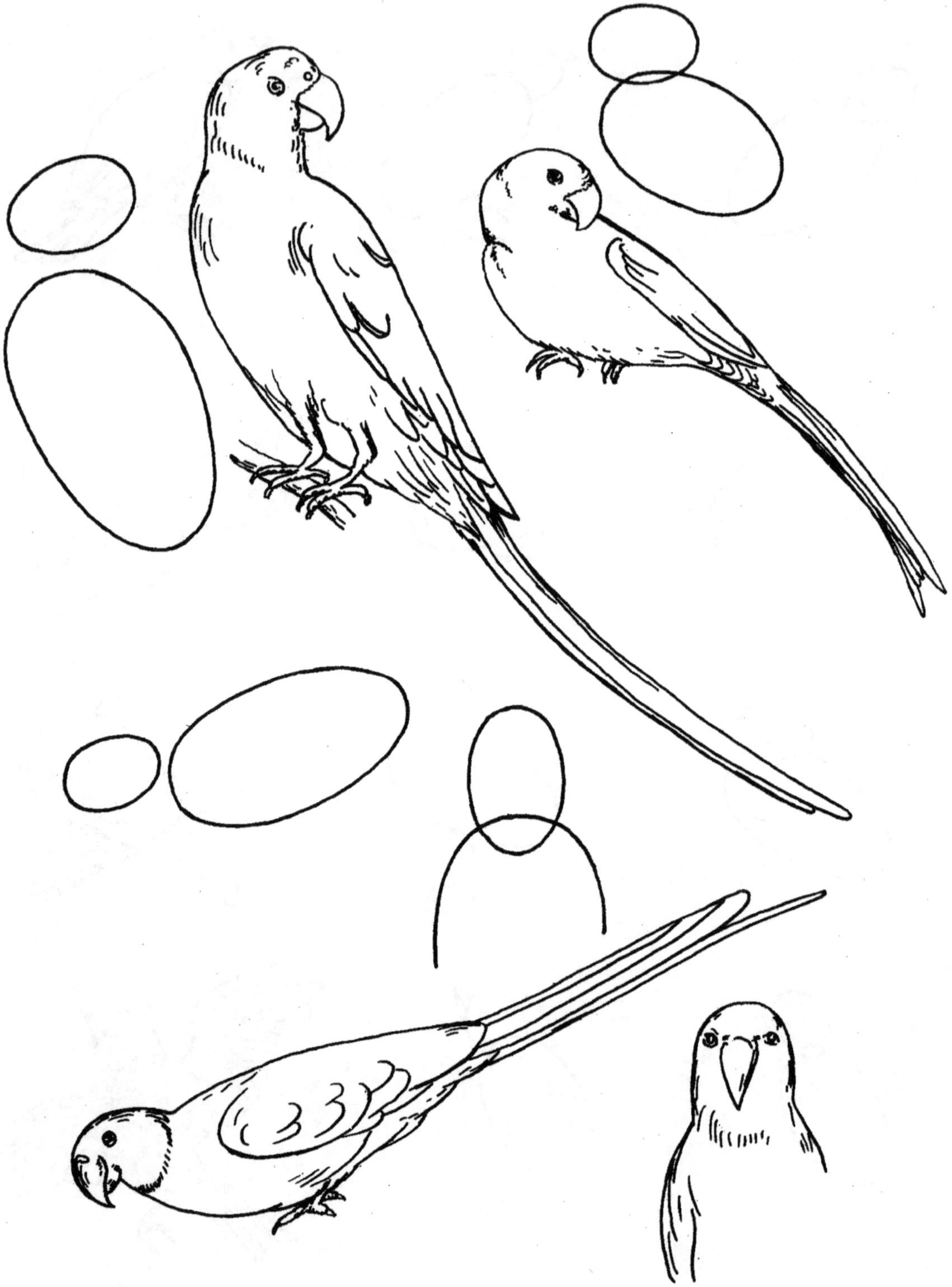

Pigeon

Cock

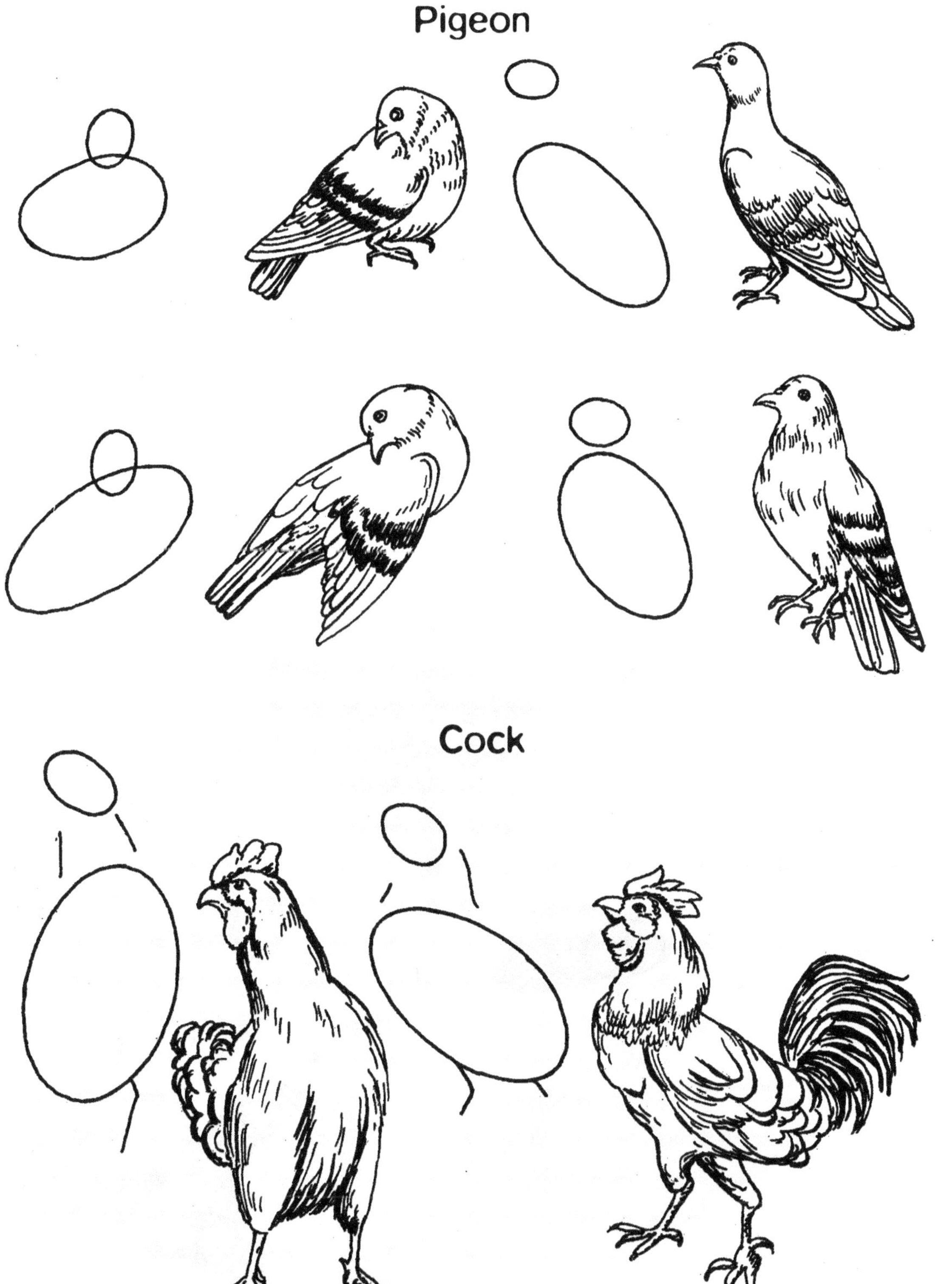

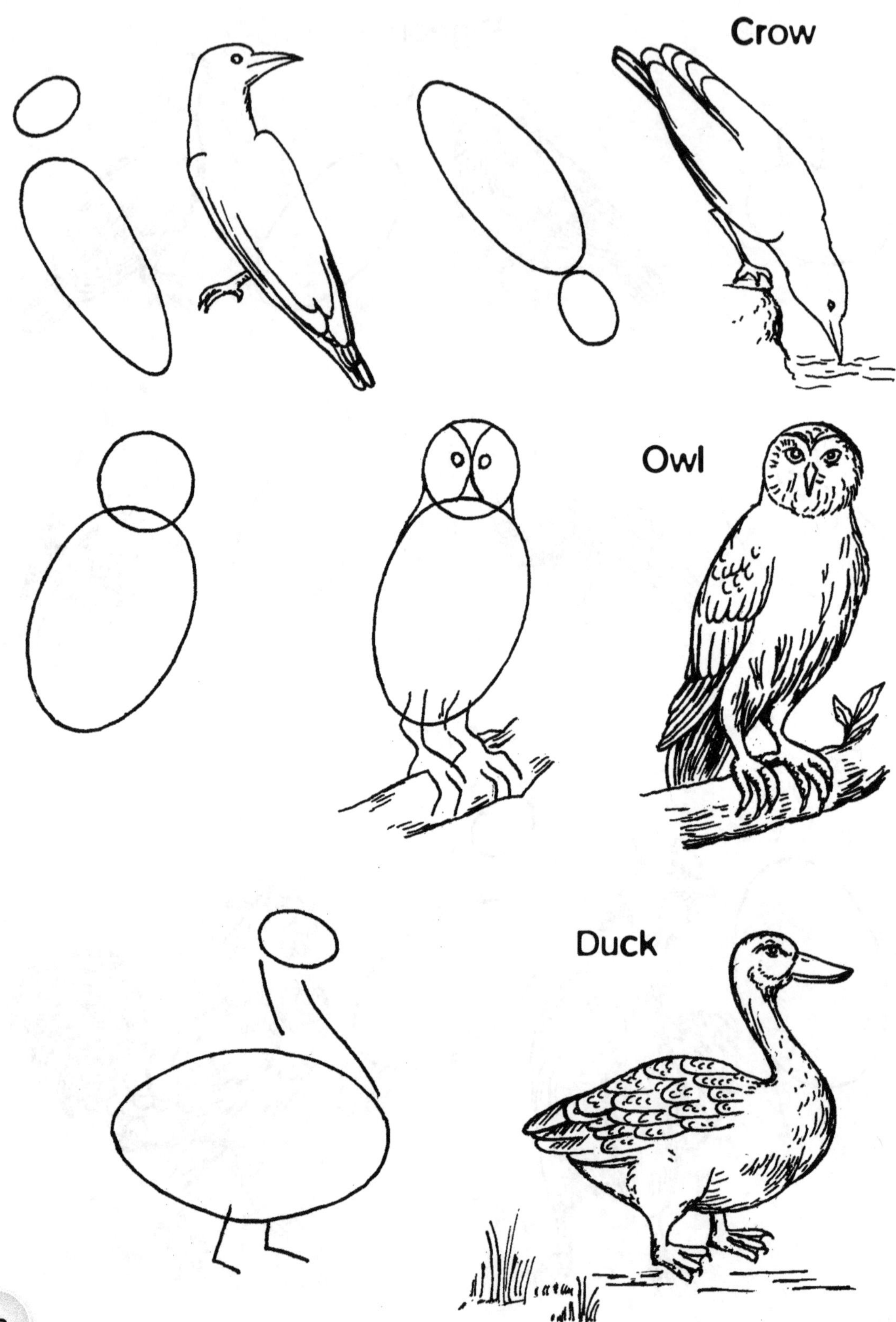
Crow
Owl
Duck

Crane

Peacock

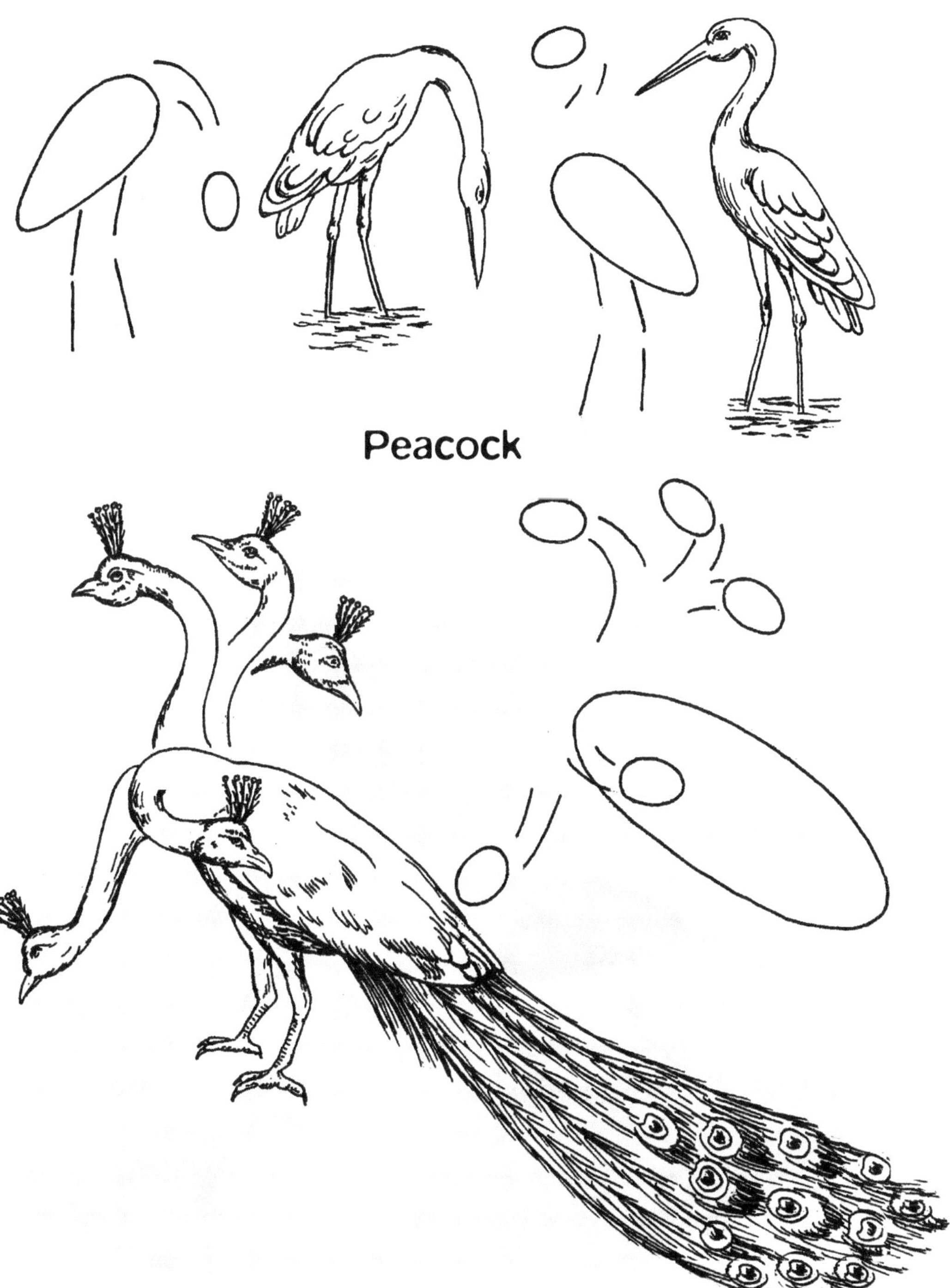

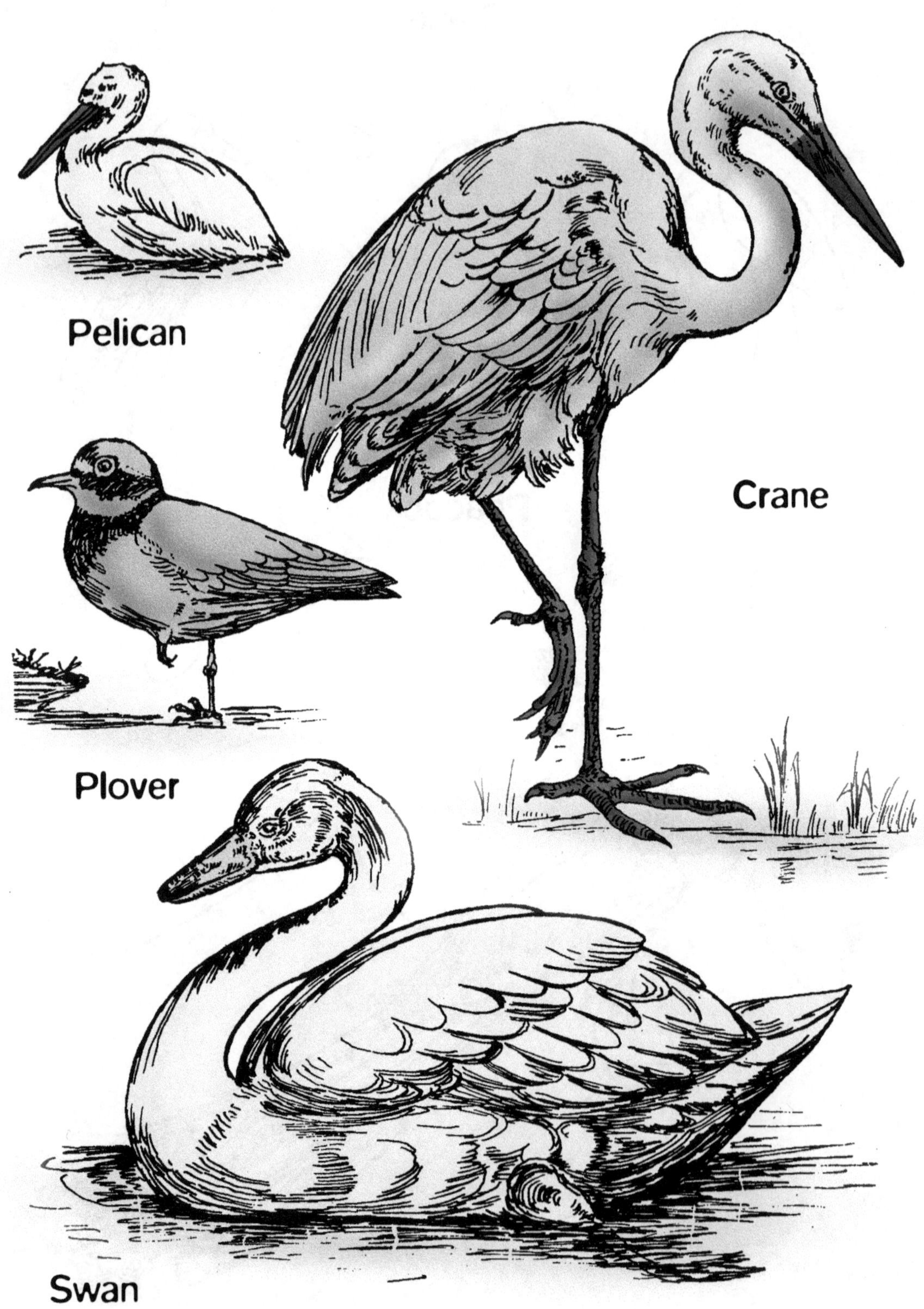
Pelican
Crane
Plover
Swan

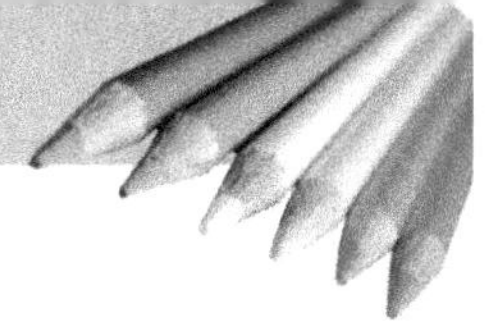

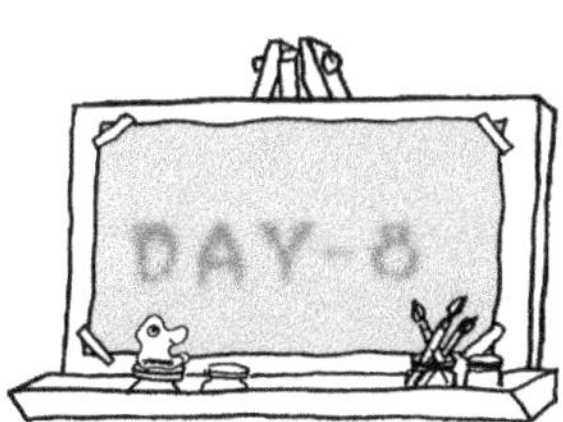

After mastering the drawing of birds, you have to learn the sketching of animals. First, try to make pictures of pet animals. When you are able to make perfect drawings of pets, then turn your attention to other animals. To make good drawings of animals, you must know about their habits and living conditions. You can go to any zoo and learn about the animals. If you live in or around Delhi, you can go to the Delhi zoo and see various animals brought from different parts of the world. Here the animals are not kept in cages, but have a forest-like environment made for them. These animals live and walk freely in the zoo, but ditches and railings are made around them to save the visitors from any possible attack by the animals.

The pictures of animals, like those of birds, can also be made with the help of oval or rectangular forms. We have made some drawings of animals for your convenience. Do their practice.

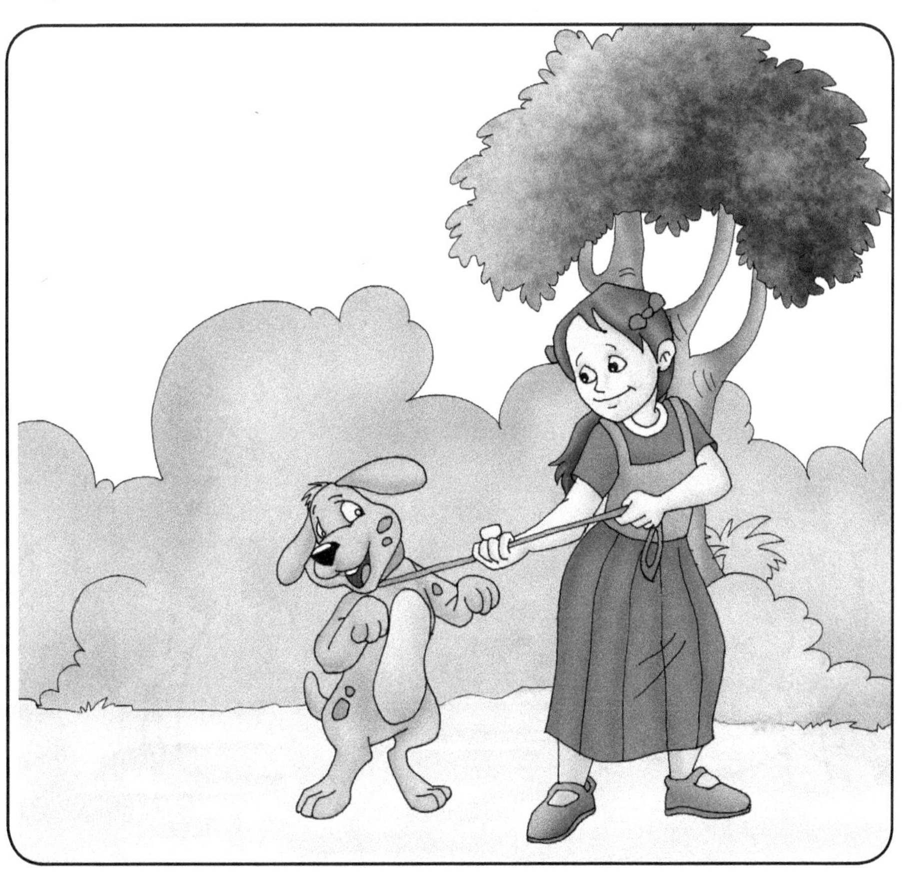

Rabbit

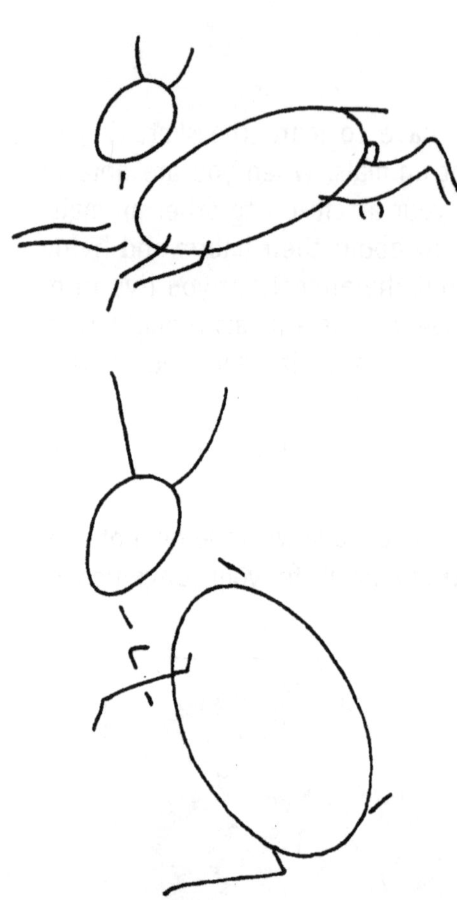

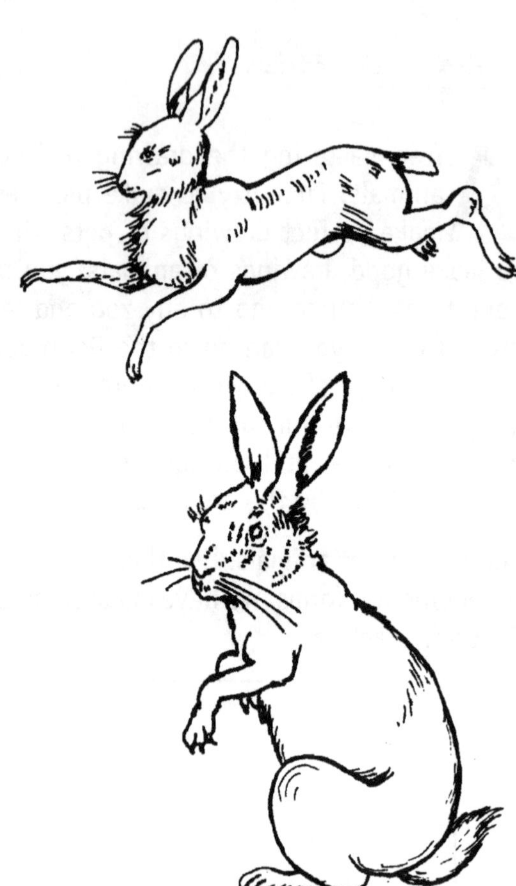

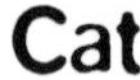

Cat

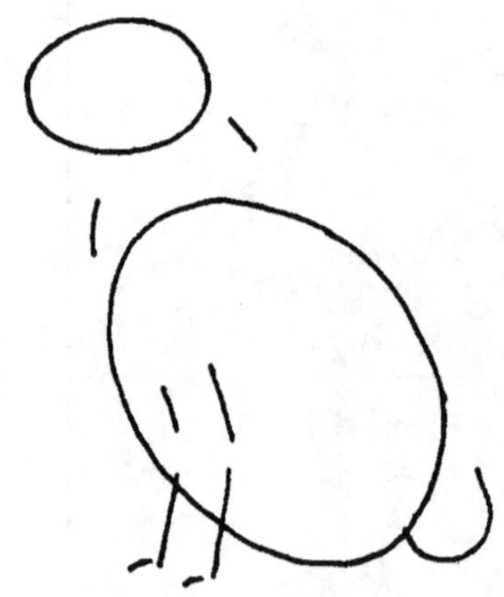

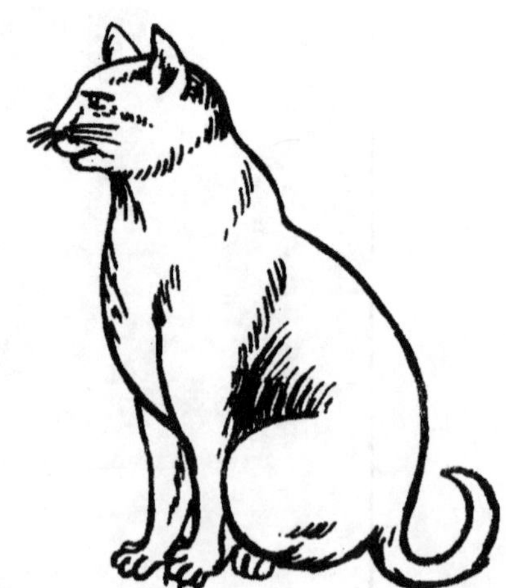

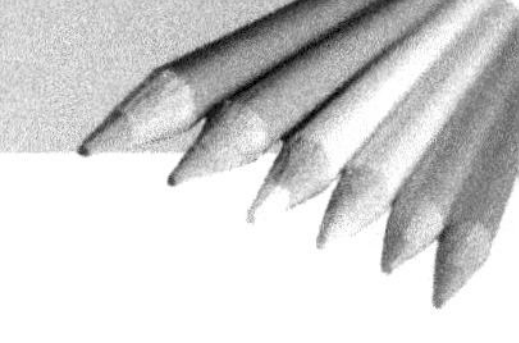

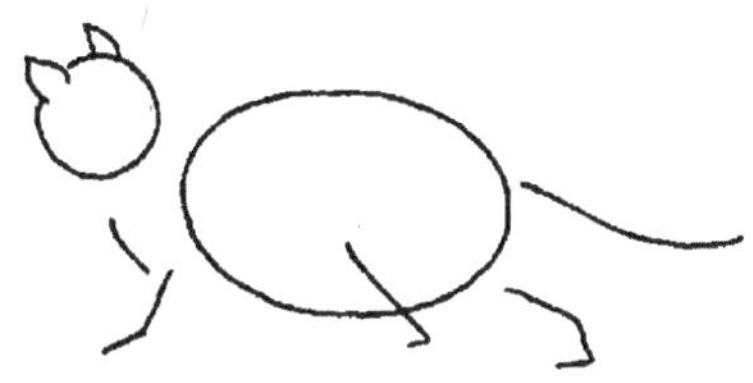

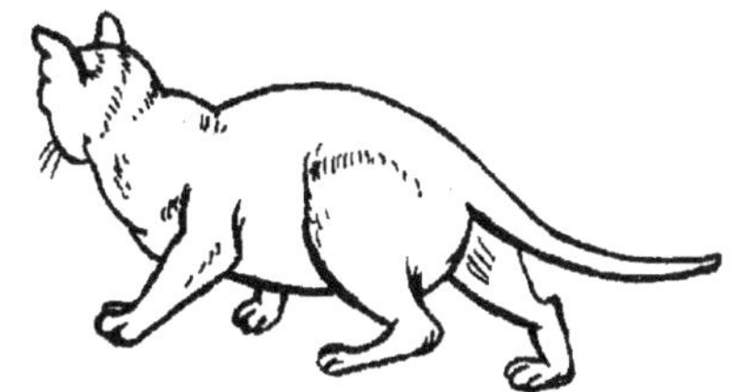

Mouse

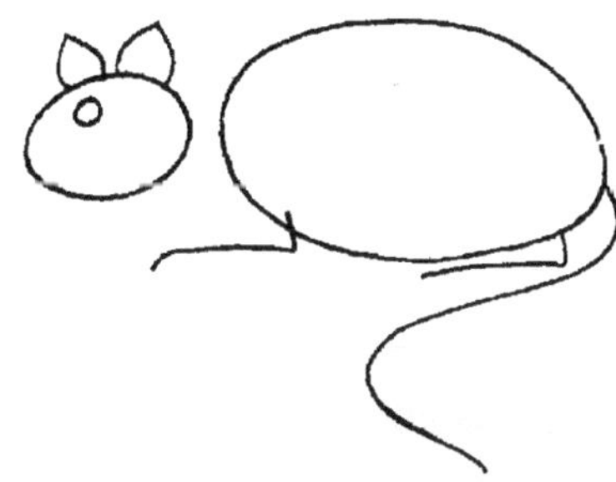

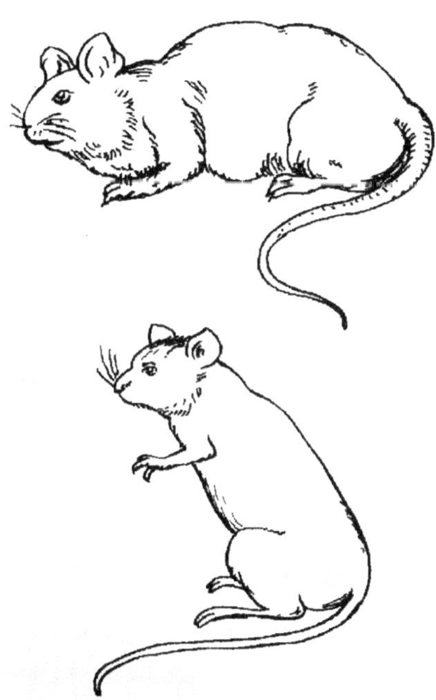

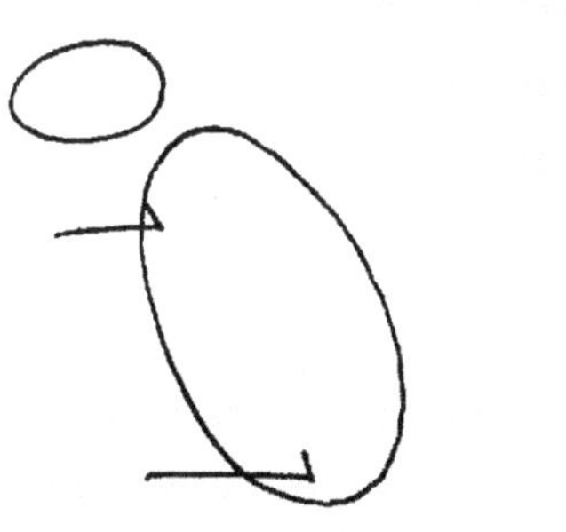

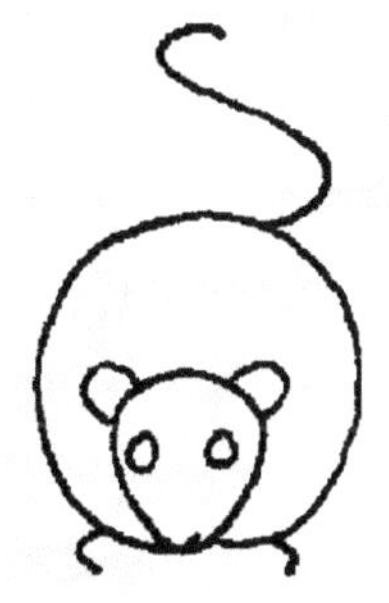

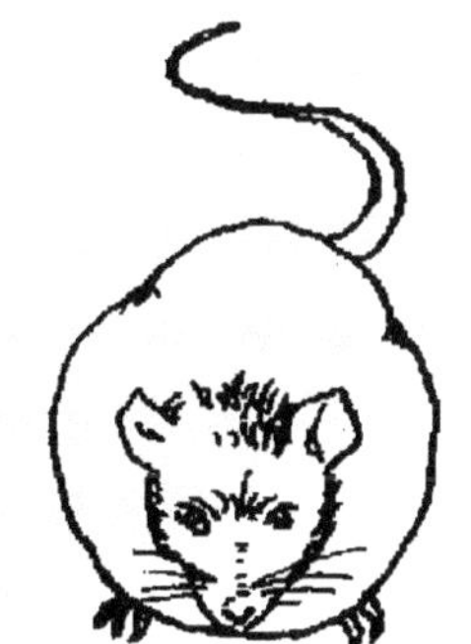

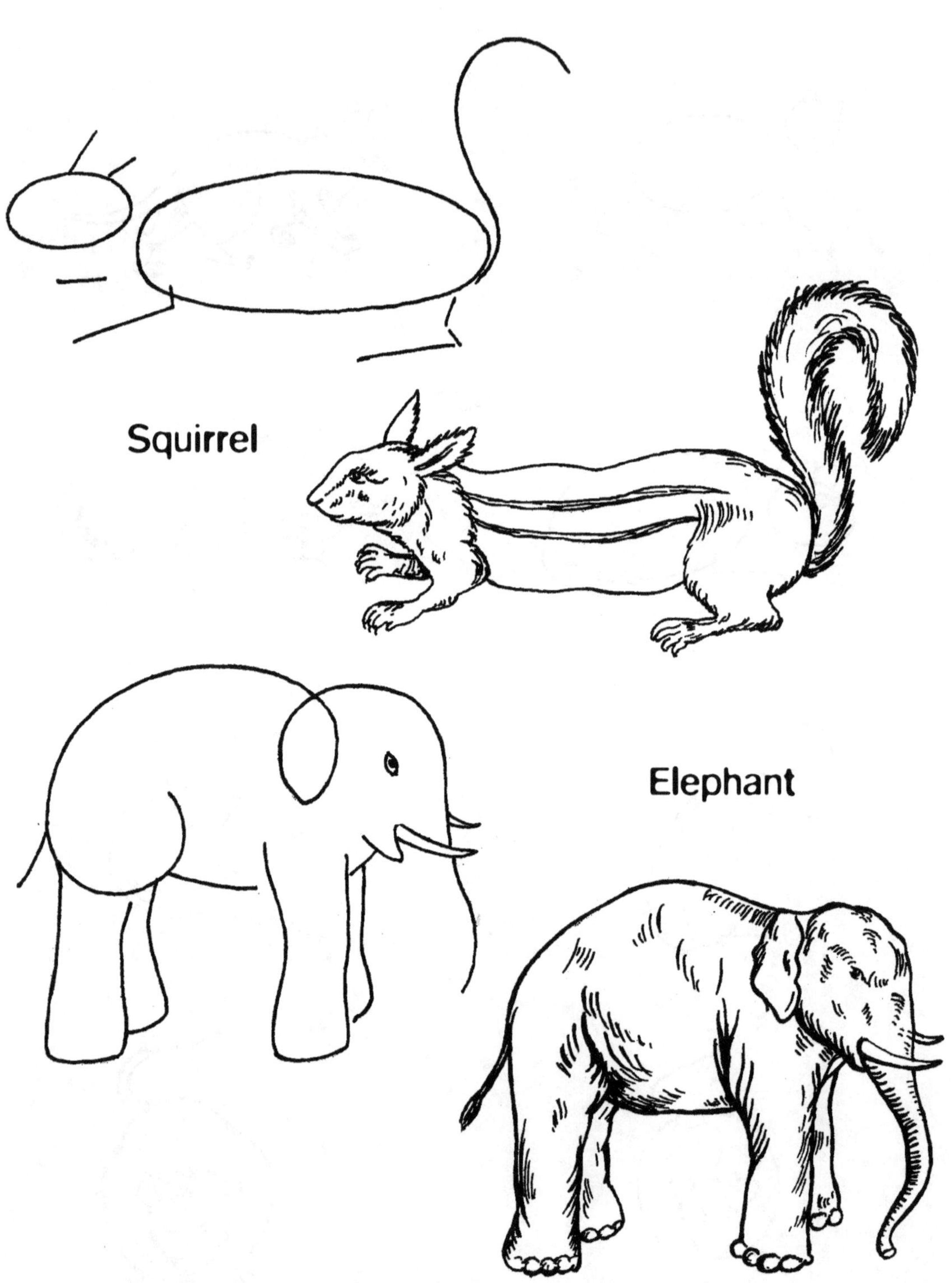
Squirrel
Elephant

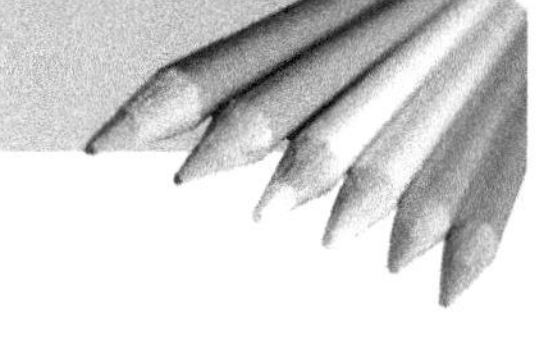

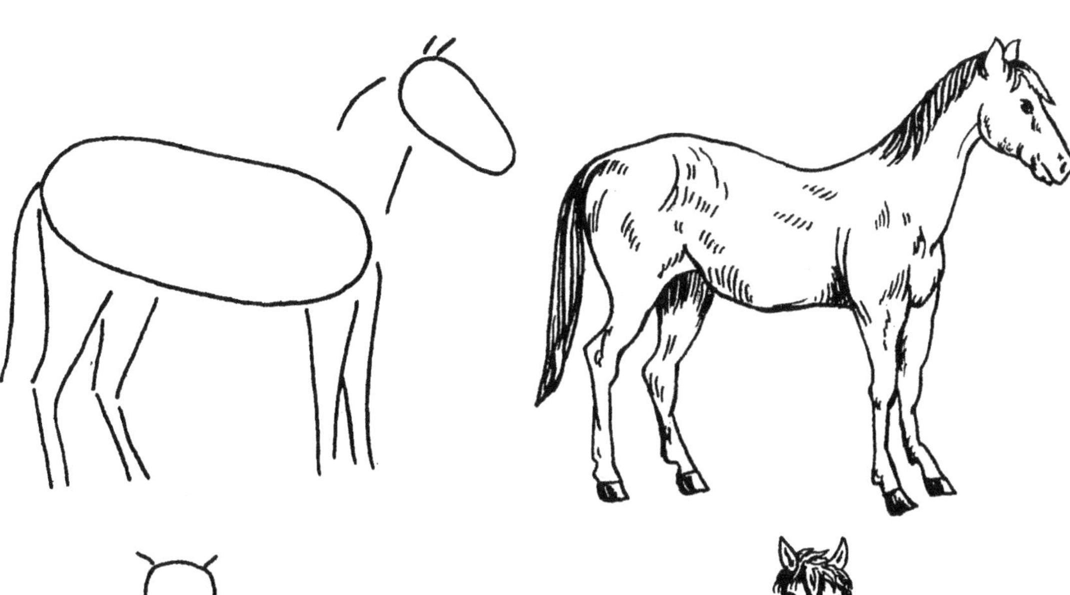

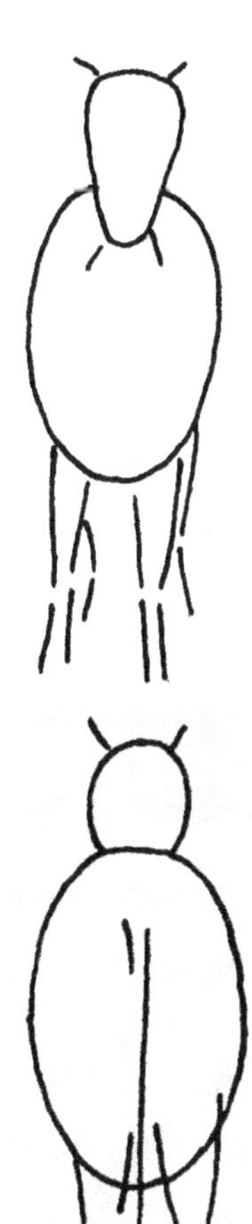

Horse

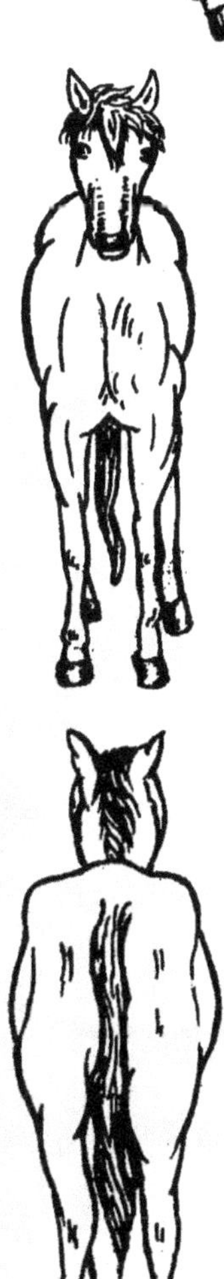

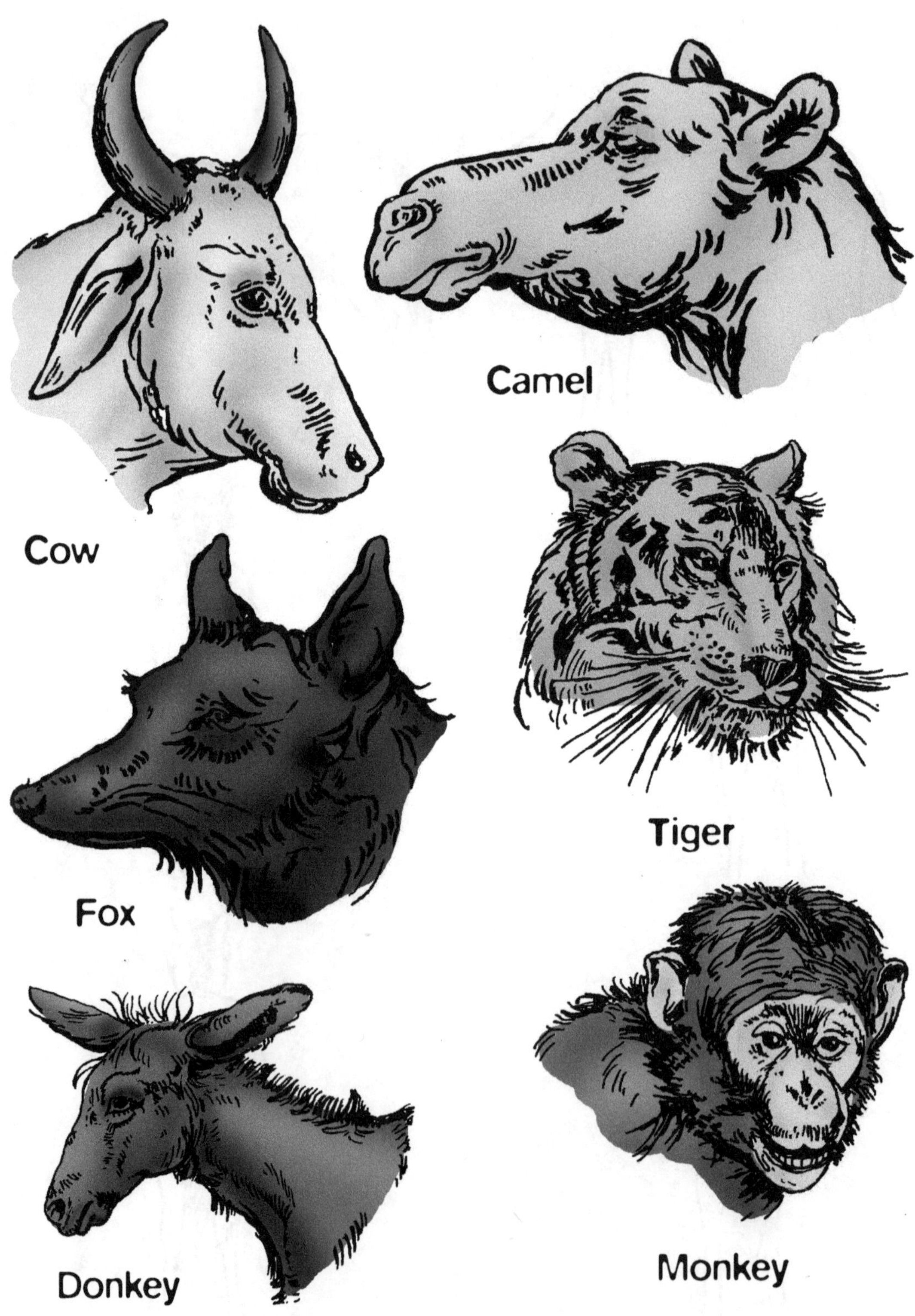
Cow
Camel
Tiger
Fox
Donkey
Monkey

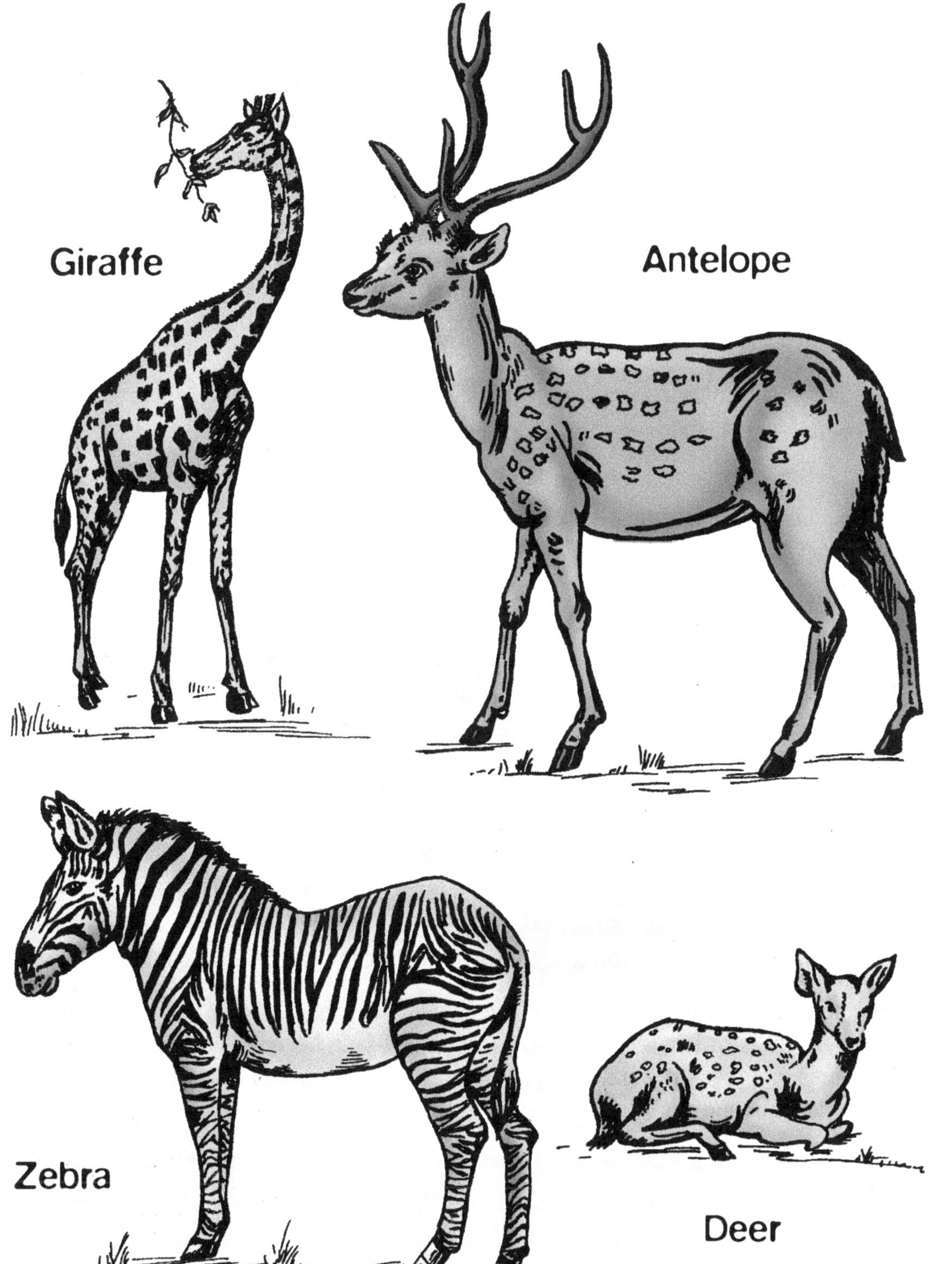
Giraffe
Antelope
Zebra
Deer

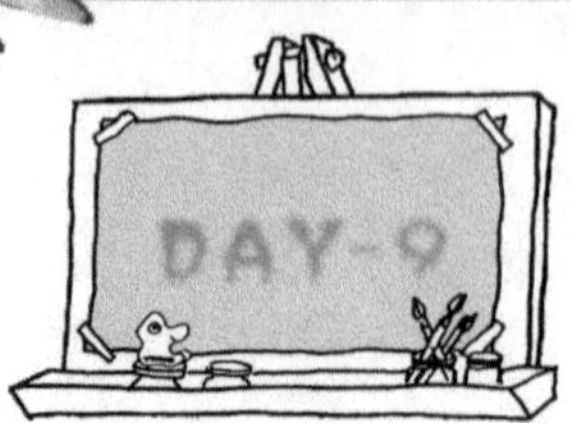

We hope that you must have practiced enough pictures of birds and animals. Today, join us to learn the drawings of man in various postures. For making the drawing of man, one must have complete knowledge of various parts of the human body and their movements. No doubt, you know about the various parts of the body, but for making their drawing you must know their proportionate sizes. The sizes and proportions of various human body parts should be learnt by heart.

Sizes and Proportions of Different Parts of Body

1. Height or length of the face is 9 inches.
2. Length of the torso—22½ inches (2½ times the face)
3. Length of legs :
   (a) From hip joint to the knee—18 inches (2 times the face)
   (b) From knee to the ankle—18 inches (2 times the face)
   (c) Length of feet—10 inches (little more than face)
4. Length of arms :
   (a) From shoulder to elbow—13½ inches (1½ times the face)
   (b) From elbow to the wrist—13½ inches (1½ times the face)
   (c) Length of hands—7inches (a quarter less than the face)
5. Width of the two shoulders—18 inches (2 times the face)
6. Width of the two thighs—13½ inches (1½ times the face)
7. Width of waist—10 inches (a little more than face)

So, now you can quickly tell that the height of a man's body is 7½ times his face. A new-born baby has a height 4 times its face because its head is big and the arms and legs are small. With growth, the baby's various body parts assume their right proportions.

We have told you about the measurements of human body parts and their relative proportions. Now, fi rst, you make the drawings of men doing different works, with the help of lines, and also outline their shapes. Thereafter, try to give them the shape of man's appearance. Make an oval in the place of head. Show the two hands with two lines and make the arms above and below the elbow. Now make the torso with one line, and below it make the two legs with two lines. The line above the knee represents thigh, and below the knee, the line becomes leg. After sketching these lines, draw the oval shapes, taking every line as the centre. And, lastly, try to create in the drawing a realistic appearance of man.

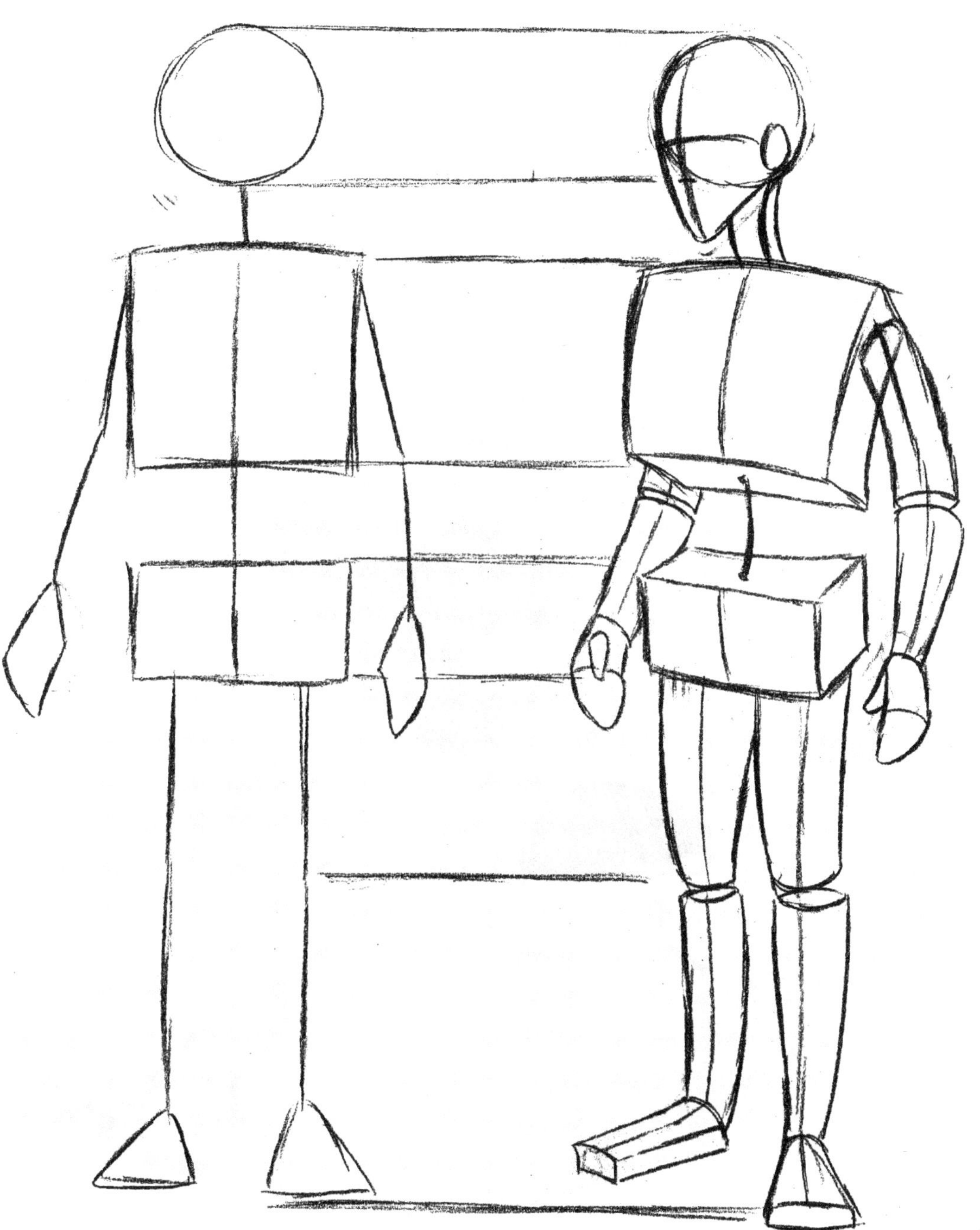

Proportion of parts of a man's body

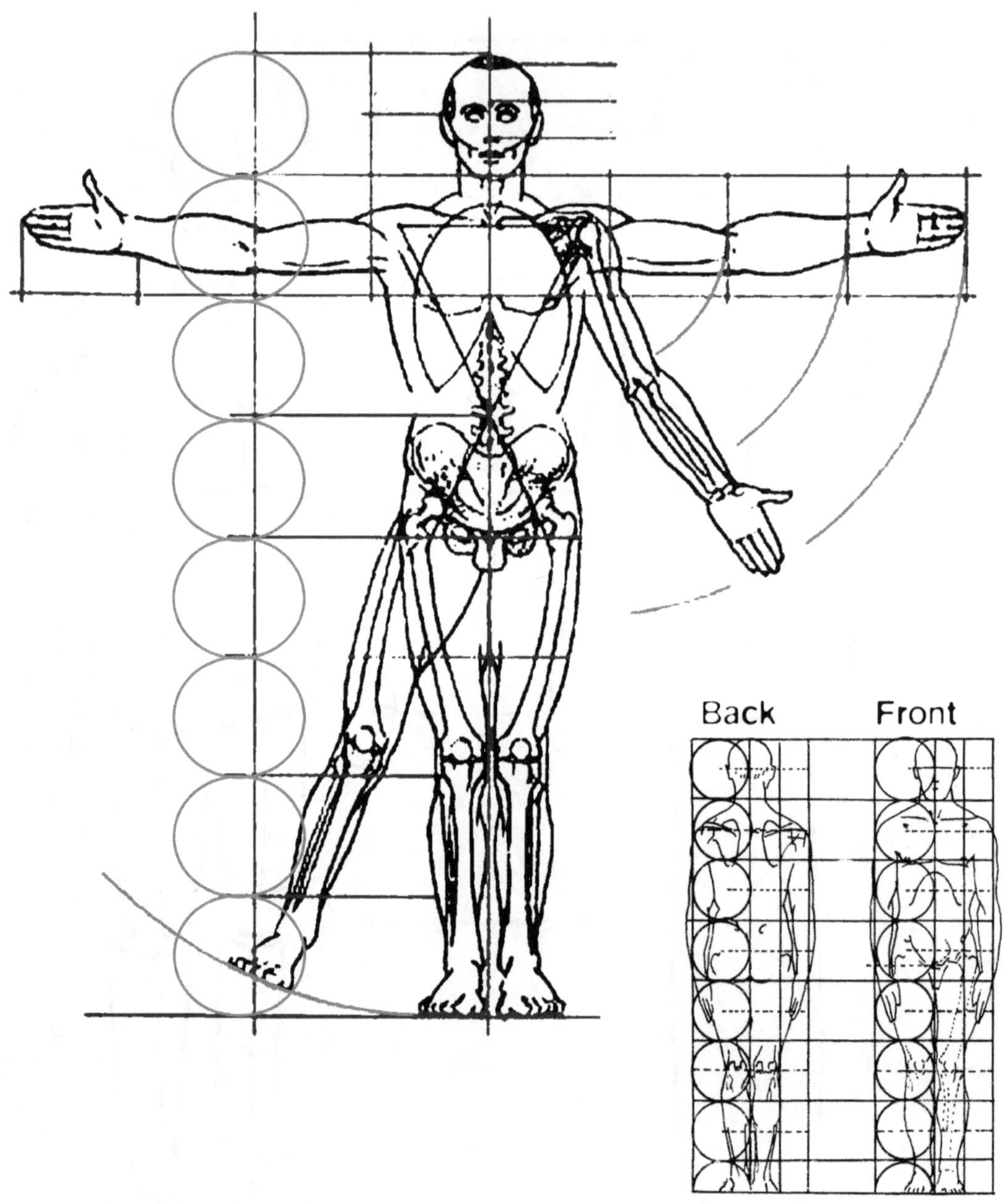

Proportion of parts of a woman's body

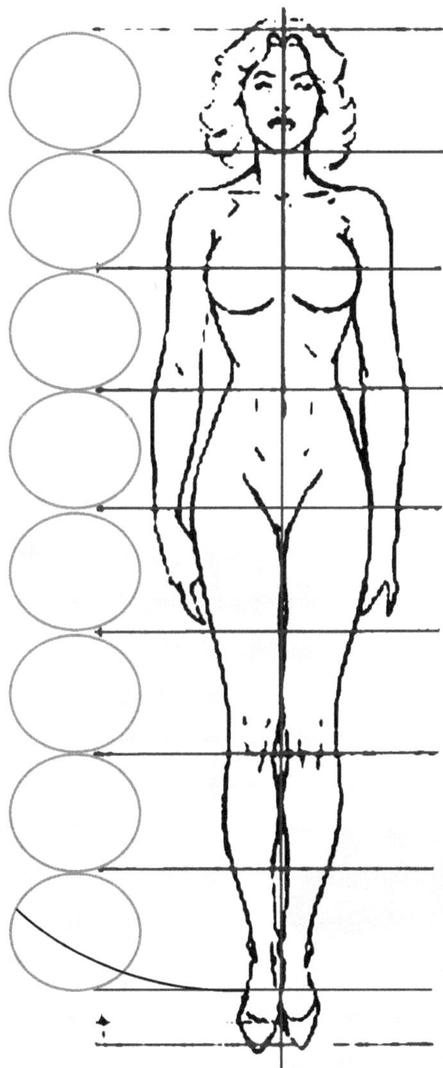

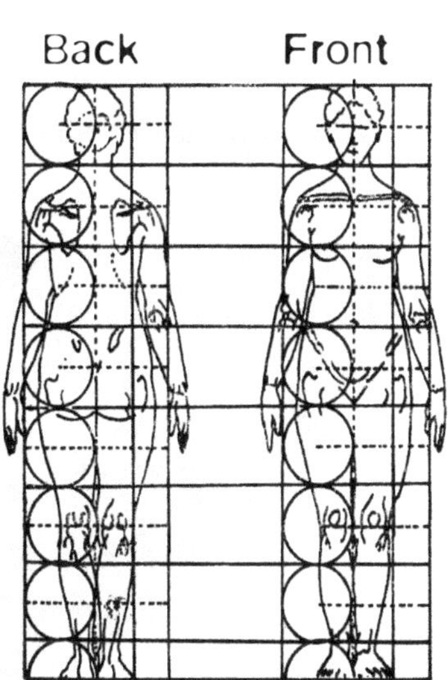

Different gestures of man's body

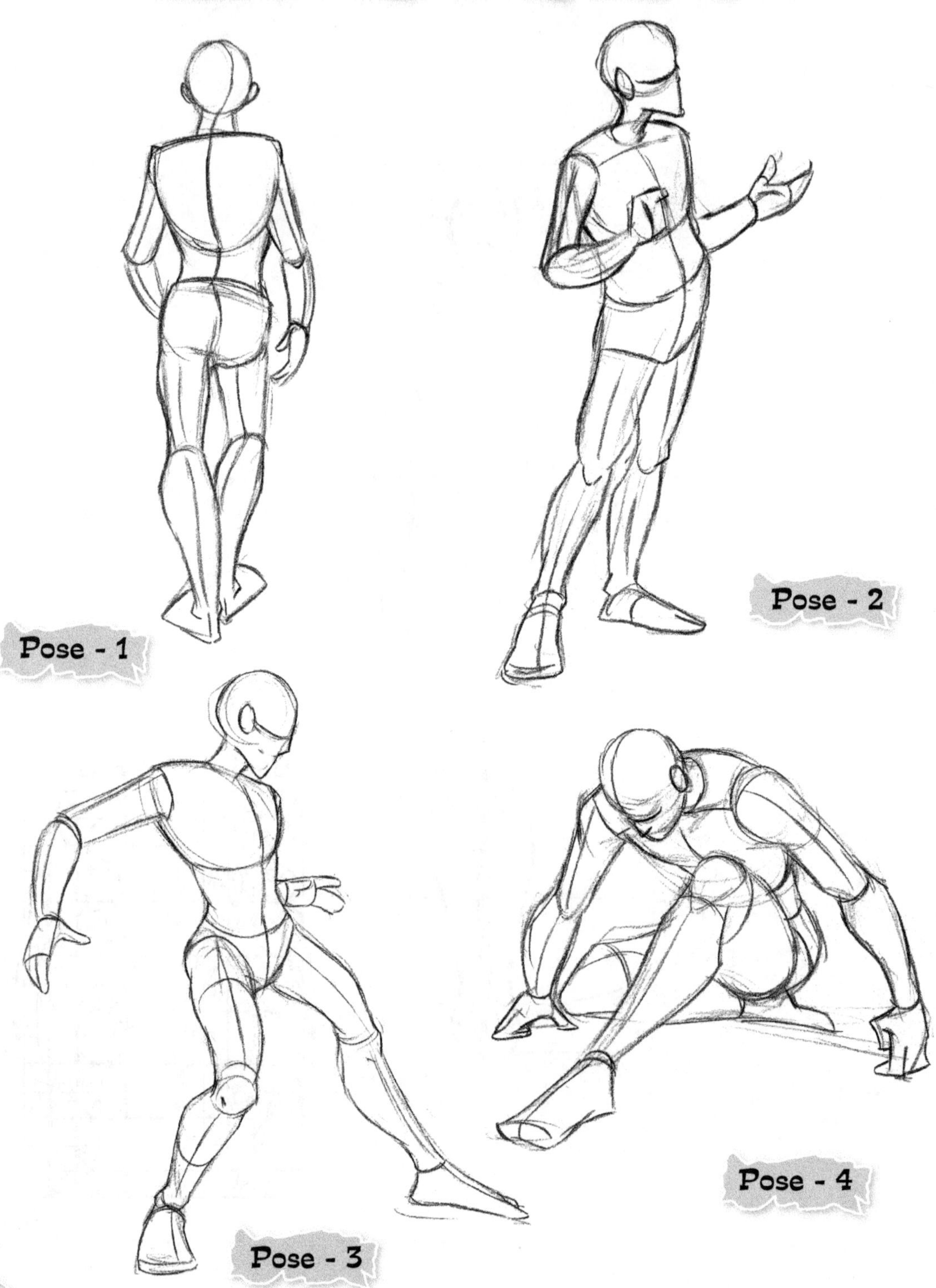

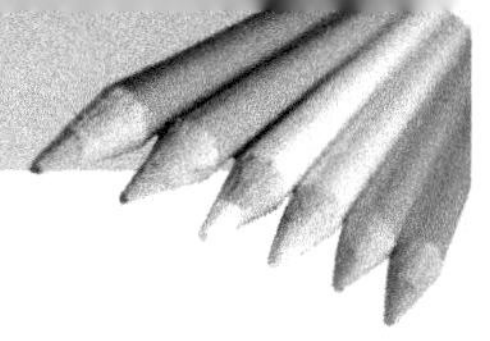

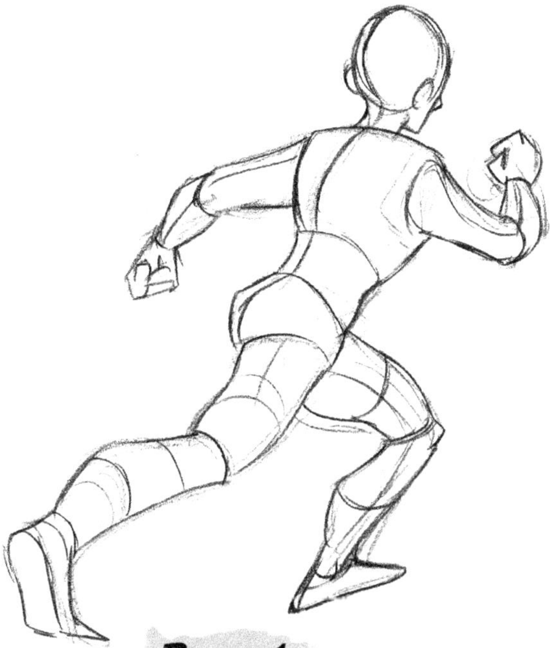

Pose - 1

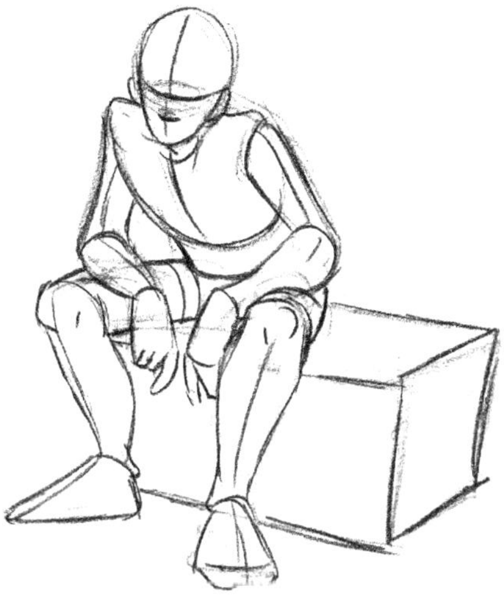

Pose - 2

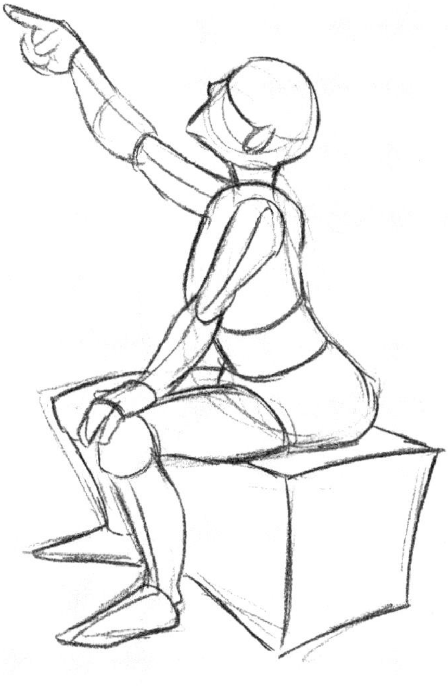

Pose - 3

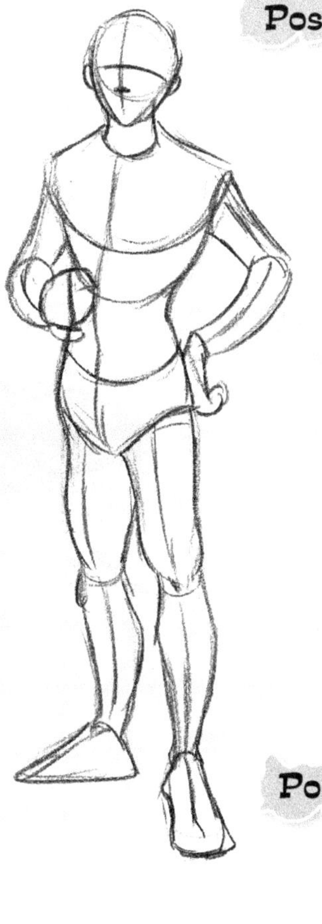

Pose - 4

Different gestures of woman's body

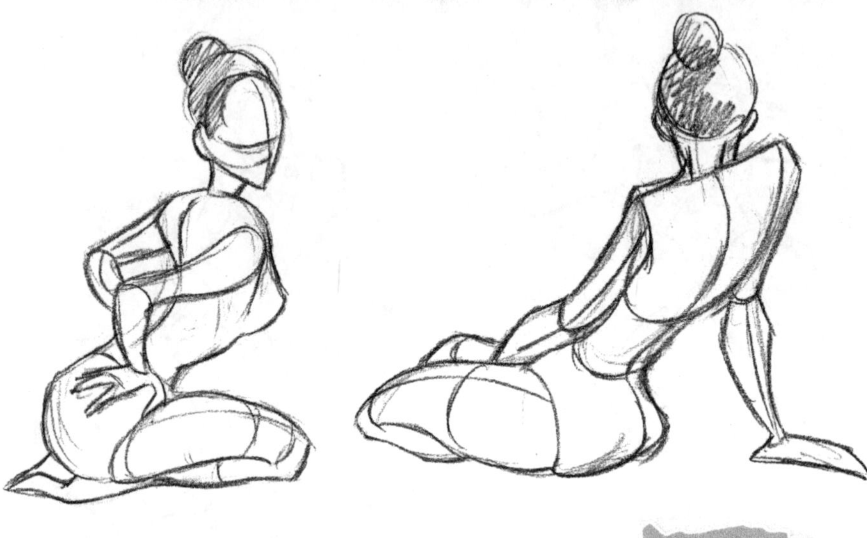

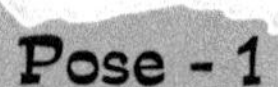

Pose - 2

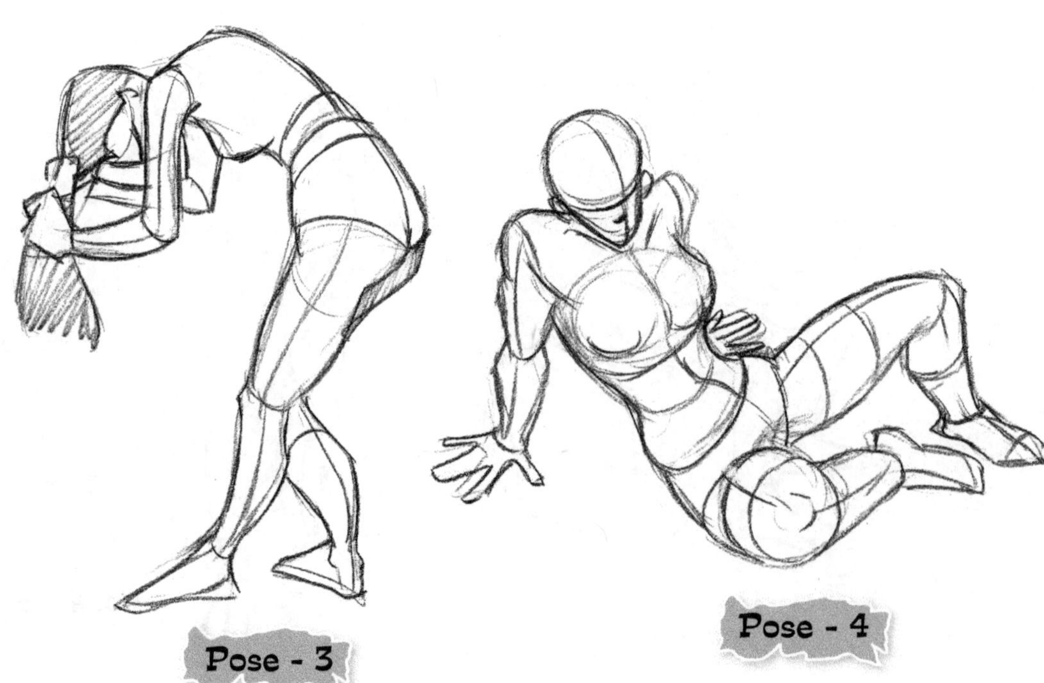

Pose - 3

Pose - 4

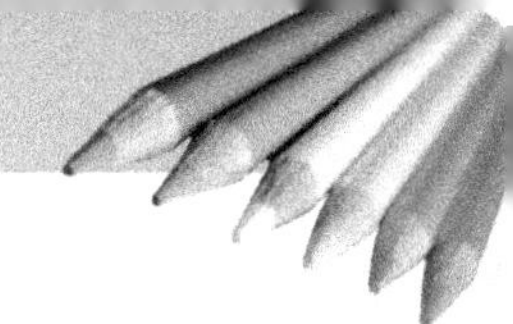

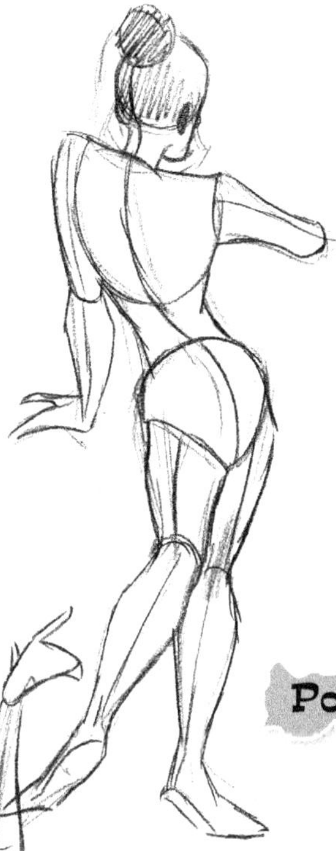

Pose - 1

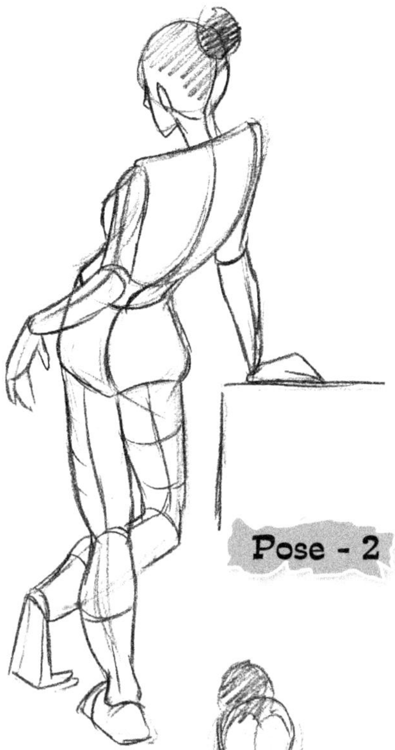

Pose - 2

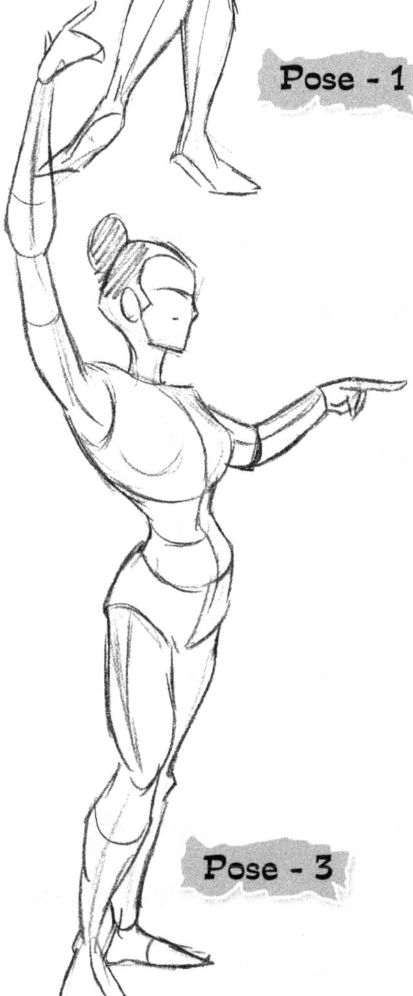

Pose - 3

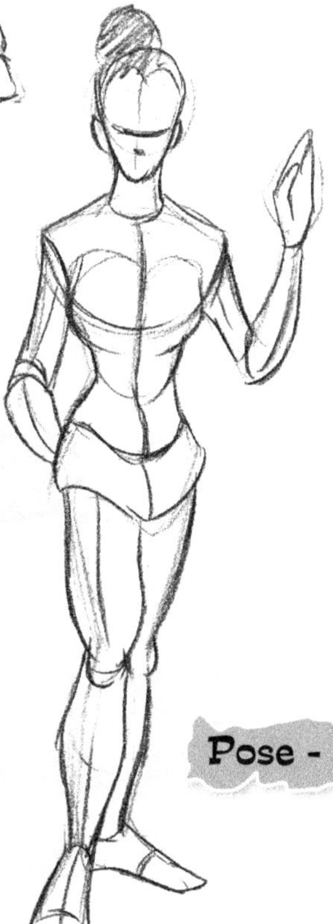

Pose - 4

Different gestures of child's body

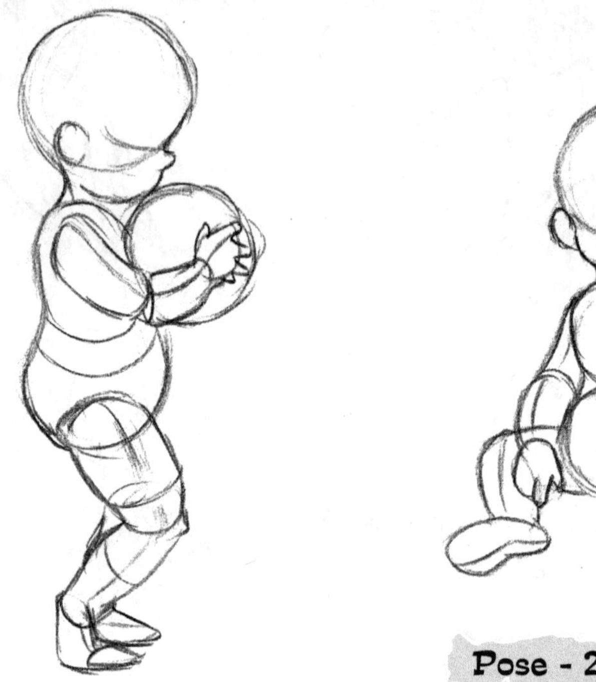

Pose - 1

Pose - 2

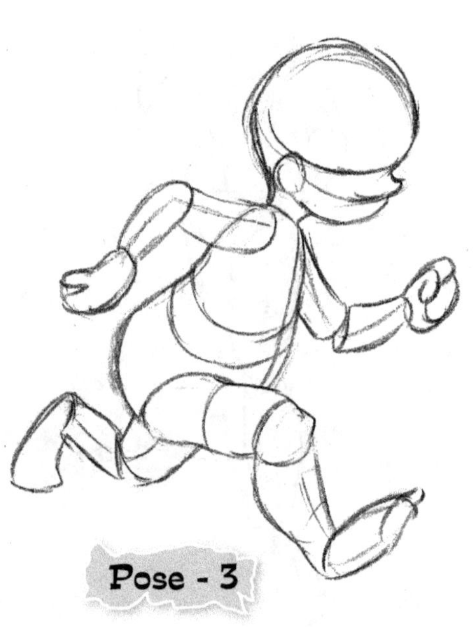

Pose - 3

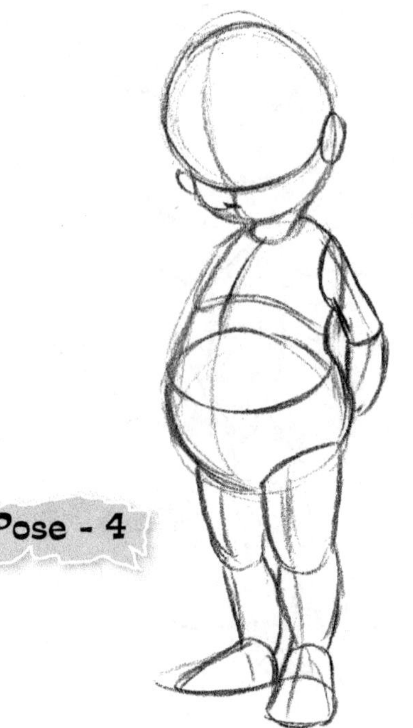

Pose - 4

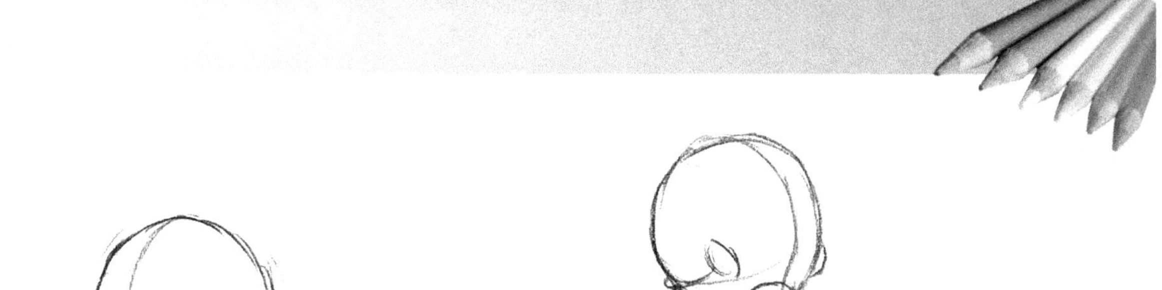

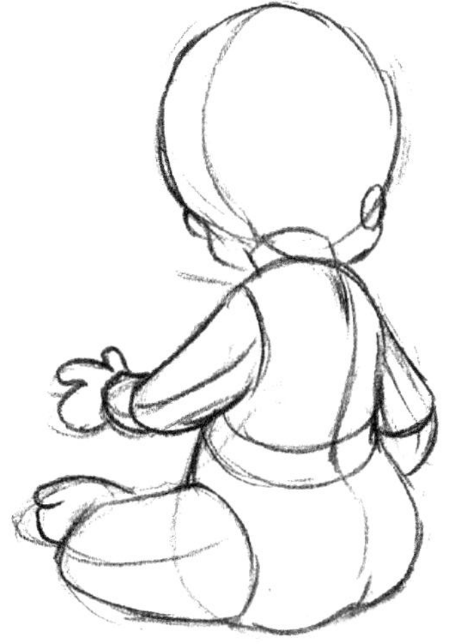

Pose - 1

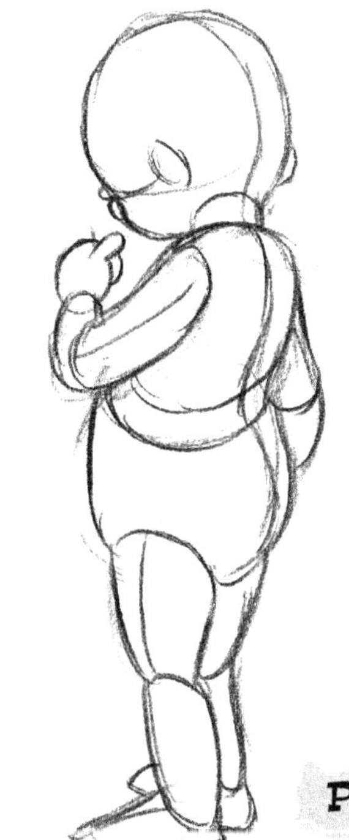

Pose - 2

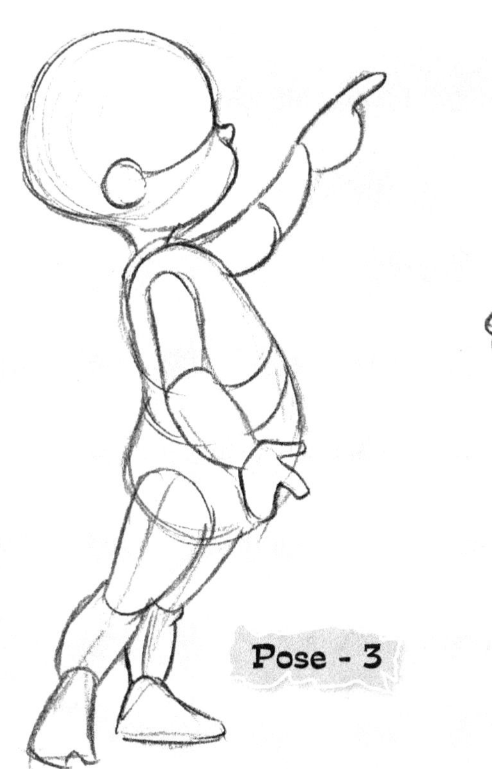

Pose - 3

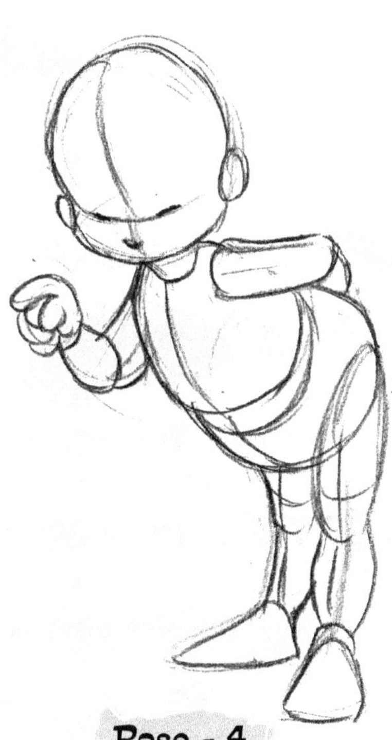

Pose - 4

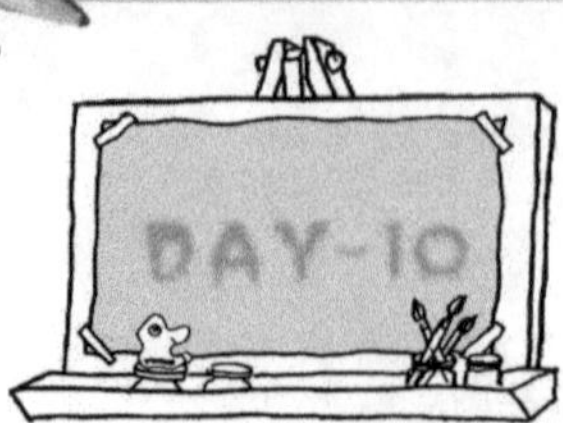

Yesterday you had done exercises in drawing man doing various works with the help of oval shapes and lines, keeping in mind the measurements and relative proportions of various human body parts. Now, let us proceed further. While drawing human fi gure, you must have faced the problem—which part to make fi rst. You may remember that earlier we had told you to always draw a line from top to bottom. And, you know that the top part of human body is head. Therefore, following the top-to-bottom rule of the line drawing, you must draw the face first.

Drawing face or head is most diffi cult in the whole human fi gure. If you can draw the head without any problem, then certainly you have mastered important task in drawing a human fi gure.

Pay attention to the fact that eyes look different in different persons. Similarly, forehead, eyebrows, cheeks, nose, mouth and chin, etc., are of different types.

Among different parts of the face, the head, forehead, eyebrows, eyes, nose, ears, lips, chin, beard-moustache and hair are the most important. Small variations in the facial parts of various persons give different appearances to different faces. You know the different parts of the face, but for drawing, you must remember their order.

1. Head—It includes all the parts of face.
2. Forehead—It consists of the lower area of head and the uppermost part of the face.
3. Eyes—These include eyebrows, eyelashes, lids and inner structure of the eyes.
4. Nose—It is situated below the forehead and between the eyes.
5. Cheeks—These are on both sides of the nose.
6. Lips—Two lips—upper and lower–lie in between the nose and the chin.
7. Chin—It is the lowest part of the face.
8. Moustache-beard—These are parts of man's face.

Out of the above listed parts, the eyes, nose, ears and lips should be practised specially.

Eyes

The outer shape of eyes is egg-like, but the eye corners are almond-shaped. A human being is recognized by his eyes. While drawing eyes, you should carefully observe to which age group and which race do they belong. The eyes of man and woman also look different. While drawing different positions of eyes—like looking left or right, upwards or downwards—remember that the structure of eyeballs and eyelashes is made differently. In the drawing of eyes special attention should be paid to the eyeballs. They should be of same size for both the eyes. The eyebrows should also be practised while drawing eyes.

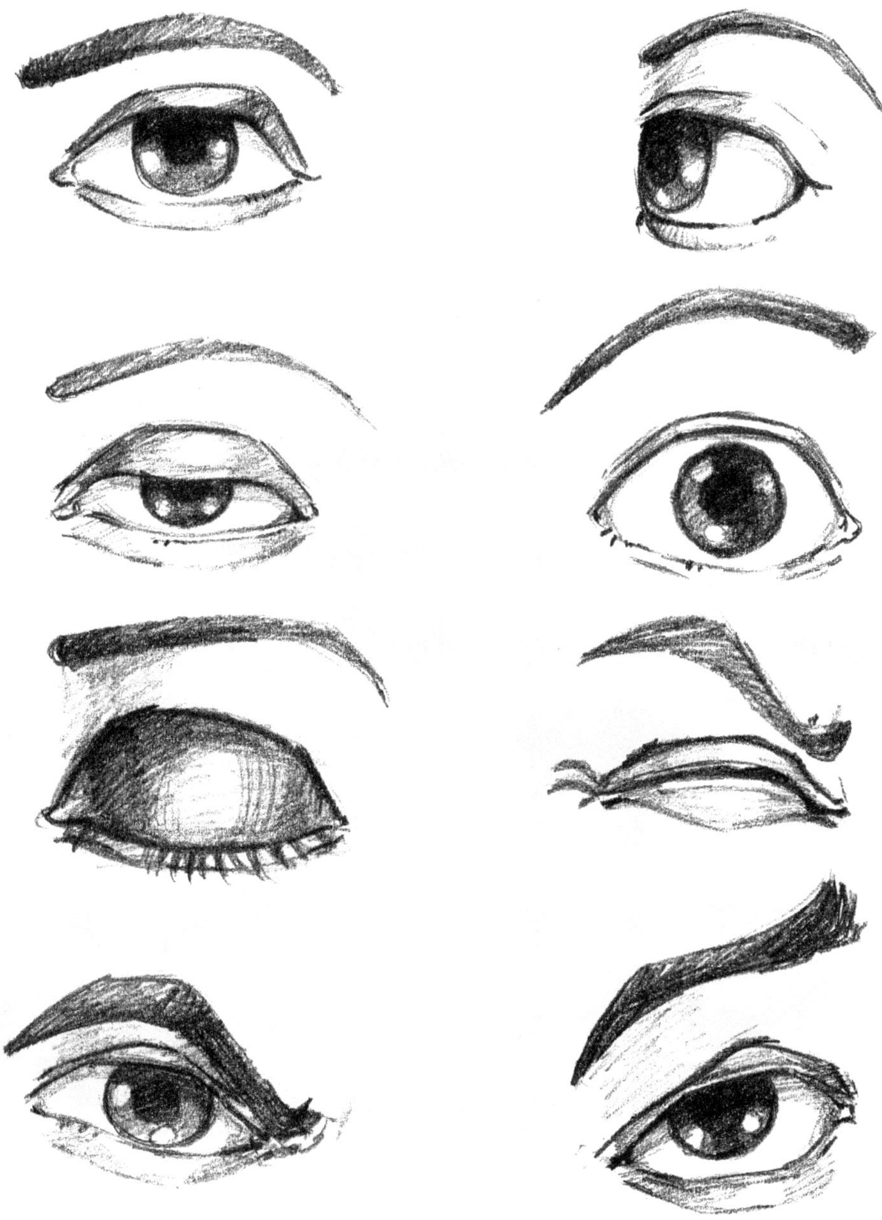

Nose

Every person's nose appears different from those of others. The upper depression of a man's nose is more, and the nose is higher and pointed. Whereas a woman's nose is not so high, is a little broad, round and a bit smaller.

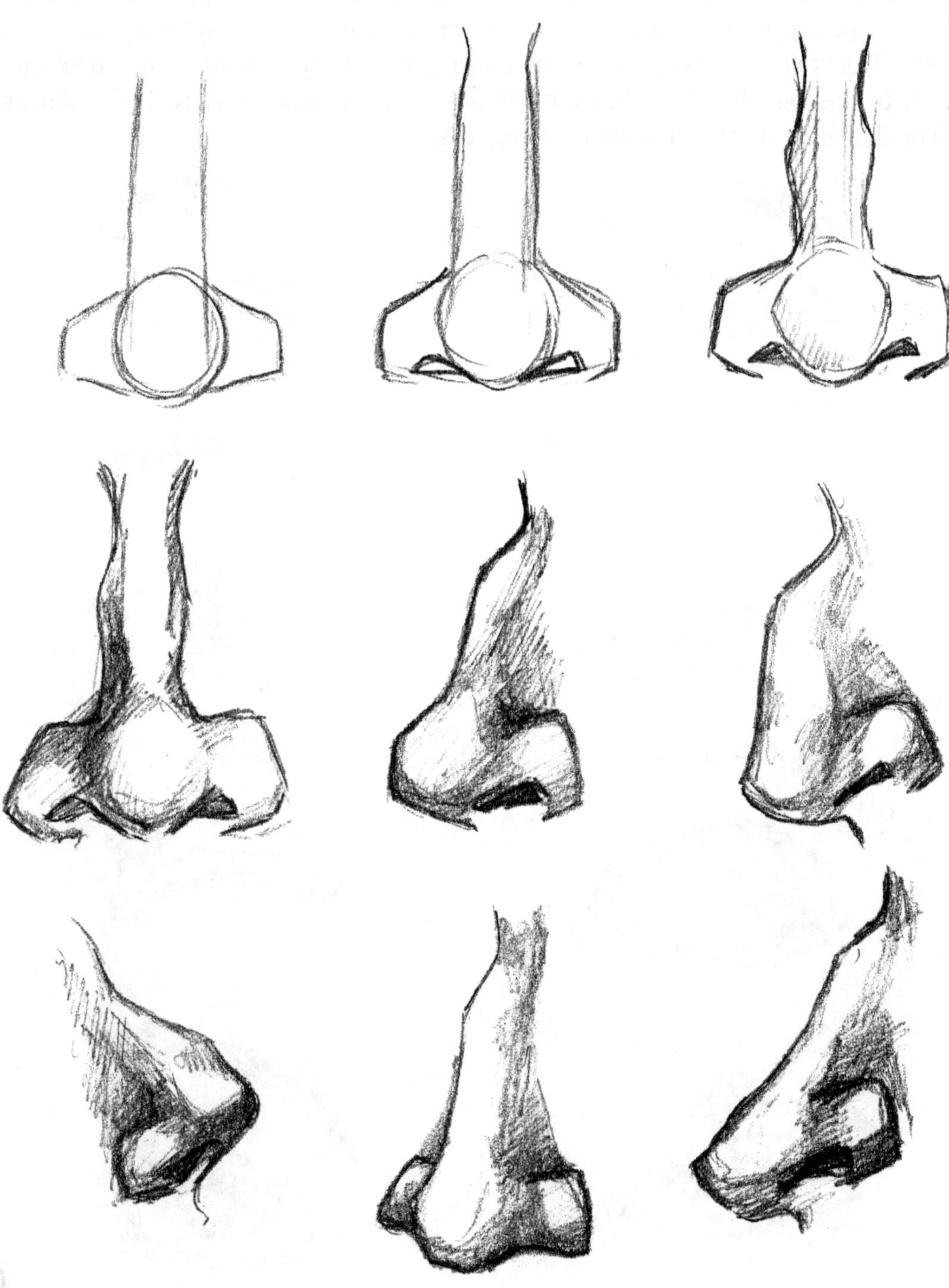

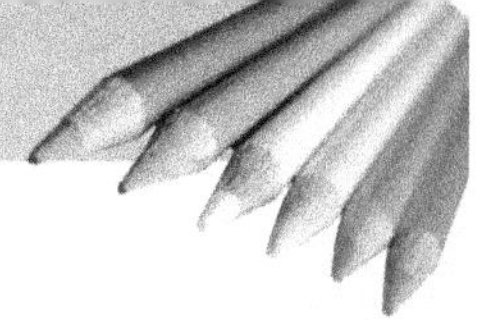

Lips

The lips of any two persons are always different in appearance. Sometimes this difference is not recognizable, still the lips give a different look to the face. When you make the lips, be careful about the line between them. This line can express the movement of the lip, the expression of face, etc. It can also identify the race of a man. In ordinary faces this line is straight, but it changes while the face is laughing, smiling, crying or getting angry.

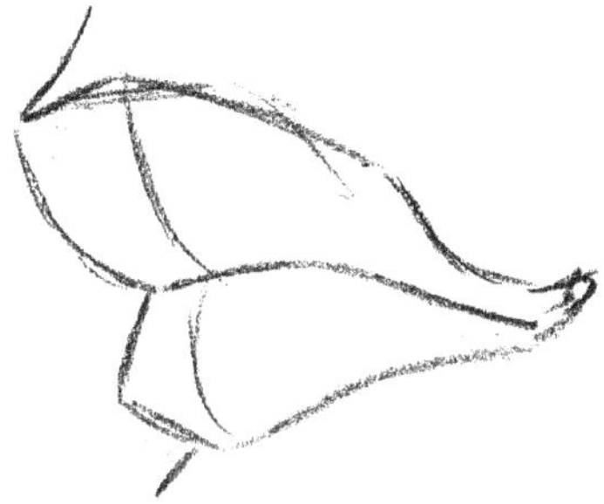

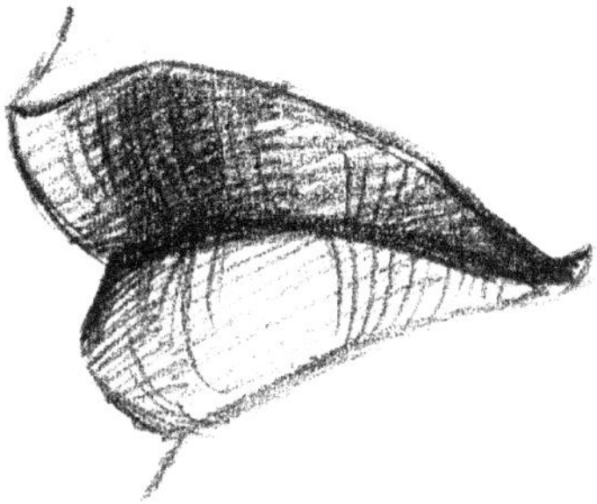

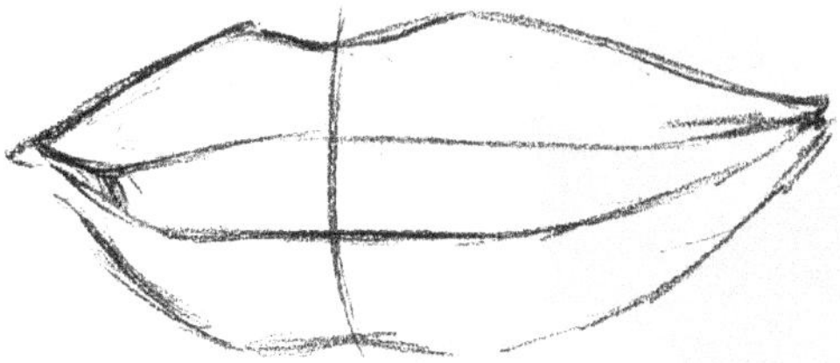

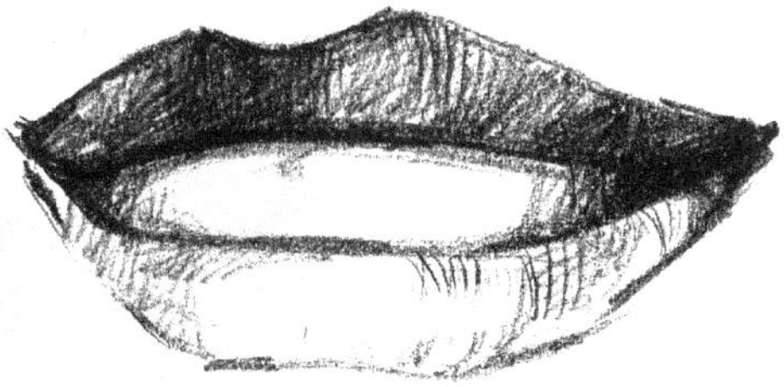

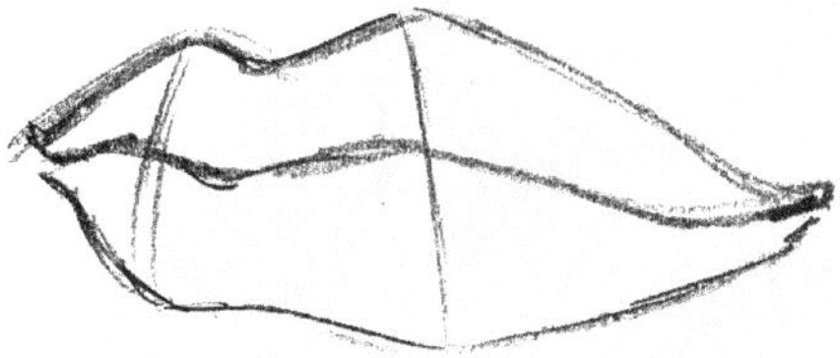

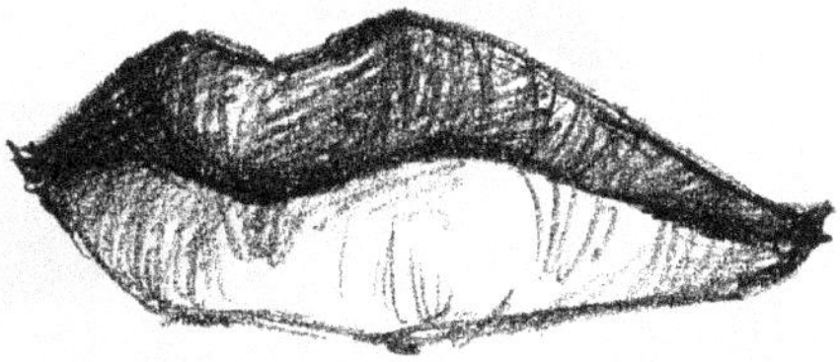

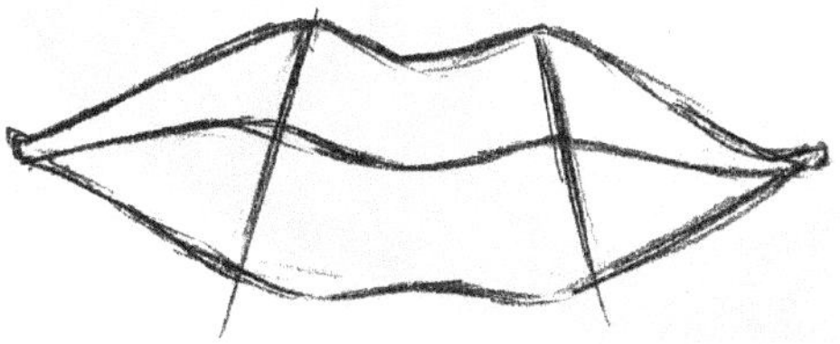

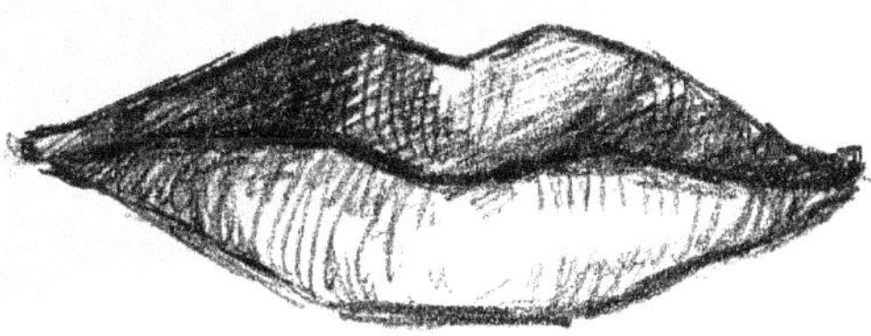

Ears

The structure of ears differs from man to man. Ears look like sea-shells in appearance. If you look at the ears carefully you will fi nd fi ve joints in the plain lines. The length and width of ears depend on the state of face, the age of the person and his race.

For your convenience we have given here some drawings of eyes, nose, lips and ears. Observe them carefully and do their exercise.

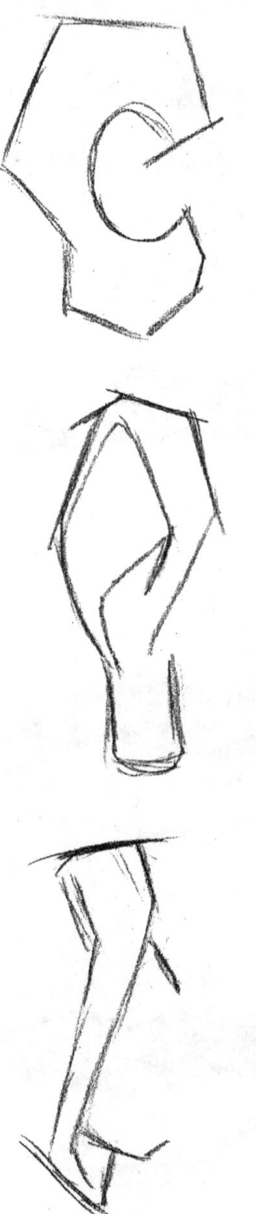

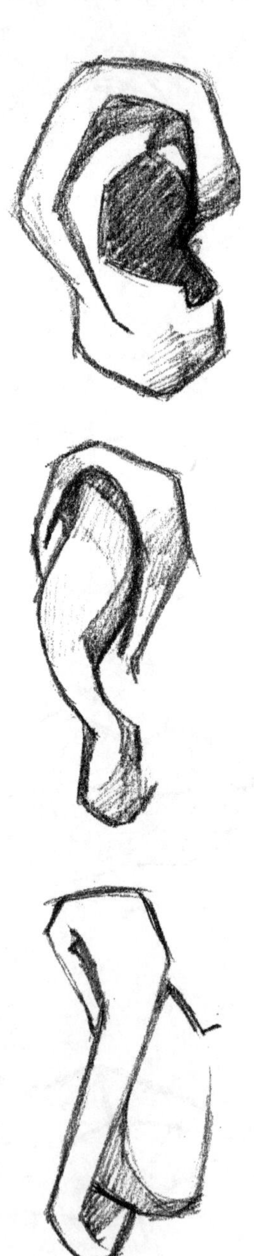

Face

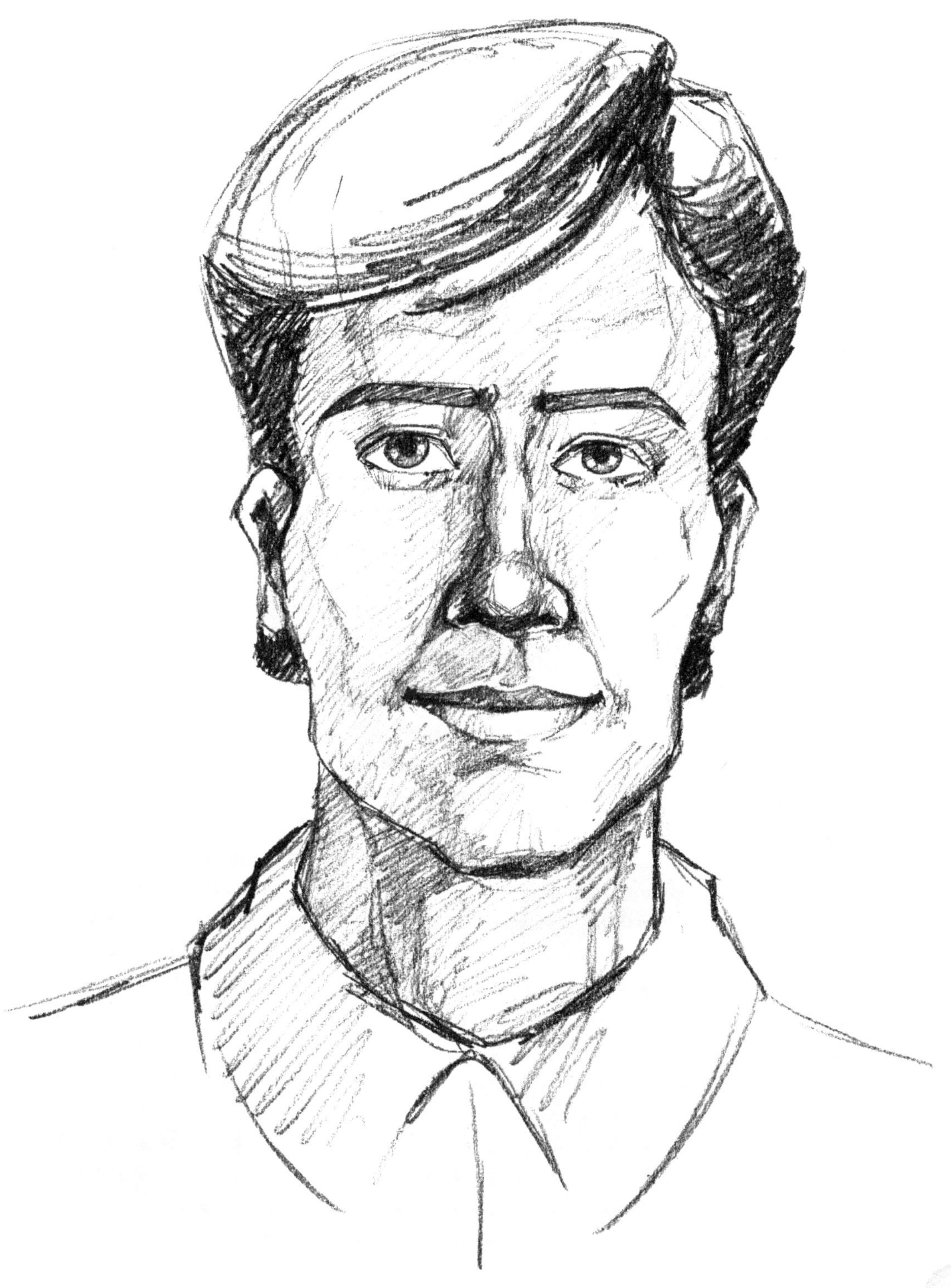

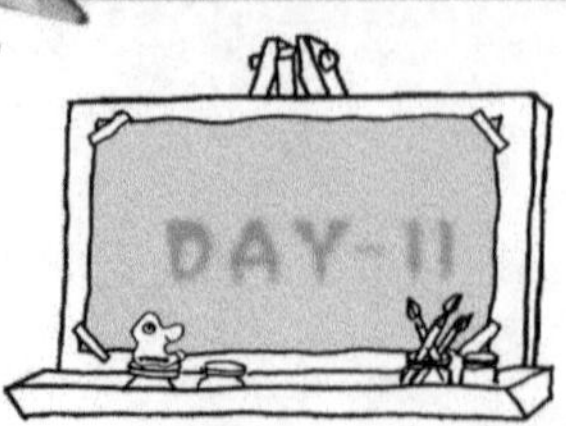

We have told you about various kinds of faces. Actually, drawing a face or a head is very interesting. Various expressions come upon the face, and to show them through drawing is a creation of an artist. So come on, let us know how to create facial expressions.

Profile of Head or Face

Let us start from the side view of head. If you work with your right hand, then you must start the face drawing from the left side. And, if you are a left-hander, then start the face-drawing from the right side. But, after regular practice, you can start from any side. Here we tell you a six-point method for the drawing of face (head). This will help you a lot and your speed will also increase.

1. First of all, following the illustration make an X, then fi nd out the length of nose and mark it.
2. Draw two parallel lines inwards, from eyebrow and nose points. Then make a mark for the ear on these lines, and draw a line parallel to the nose.
3. Draw a vertical line, touching the line of the ear, as shown in the picture. This is the centre of head.
4. The distance between the vertical line and the line of ear will show you the centre of head and the line of the eye. The width of ear is   of this length.
5. From the centre of head and the two lengths of nose, you will come to know the chin and the upper part of head. The height of head is four times the length of nose.
6. With the help of the line of nose and the centre of head, you will be able to know the back of head. The collar is on the line beside the mouth. The mouth is   of the distance between nose and chin.

For the drawing of face, this method is followed in most of the art schools. By this method, you can draw more than 100,000 various kinds of head. You know, as we have told you earlier, that the drawing of face or head is very diffi cult. Therefore, you will have to do a lot of exercise to become successful in drawing a face or a head. Try to draw the faces of children, young and old people. We have for your convenience given some drawings. First, as a practice you can copy them. But, later on, you must be able to draw them from memory.

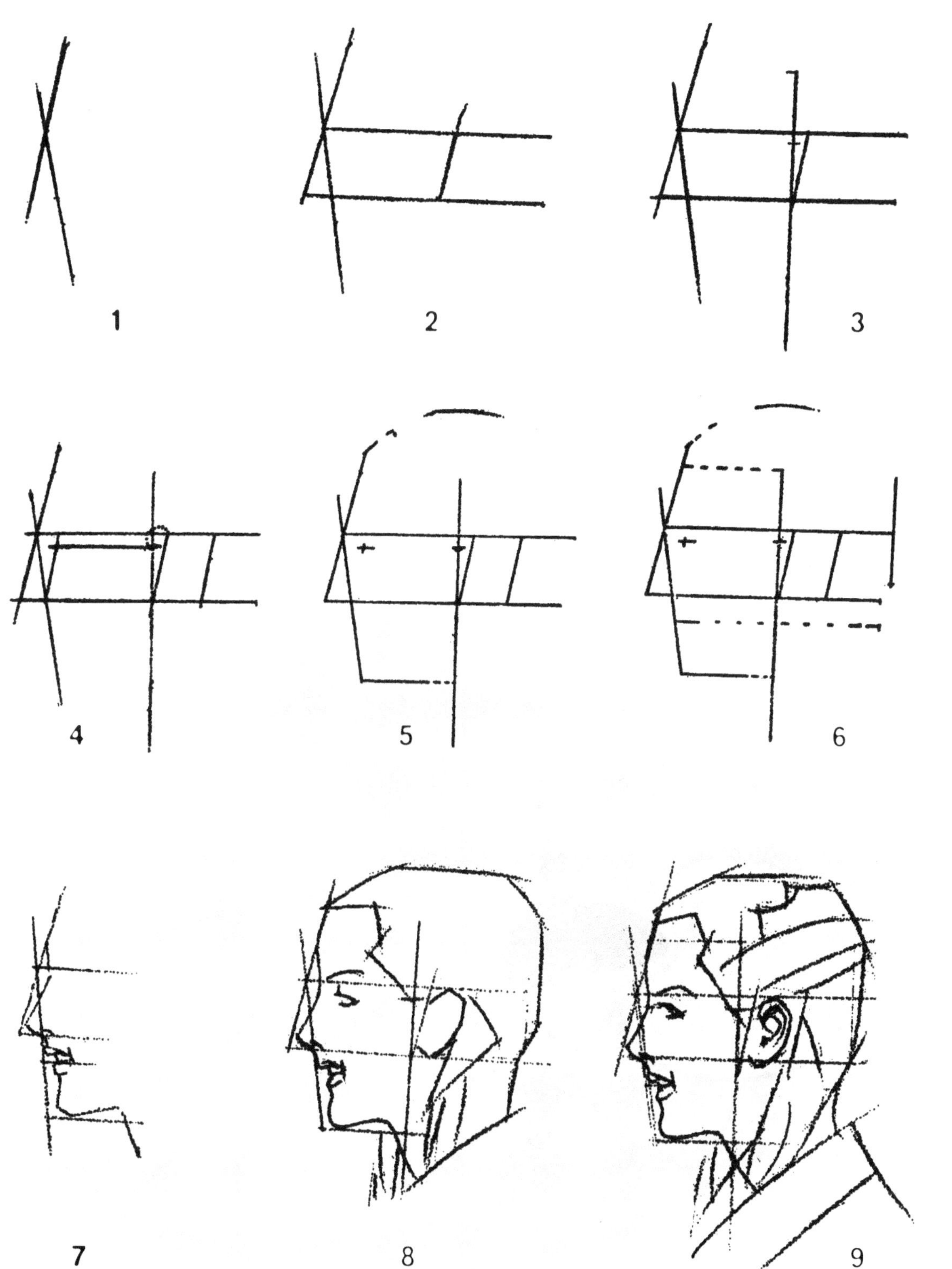
1
2
3
4
5
6
7
8
9

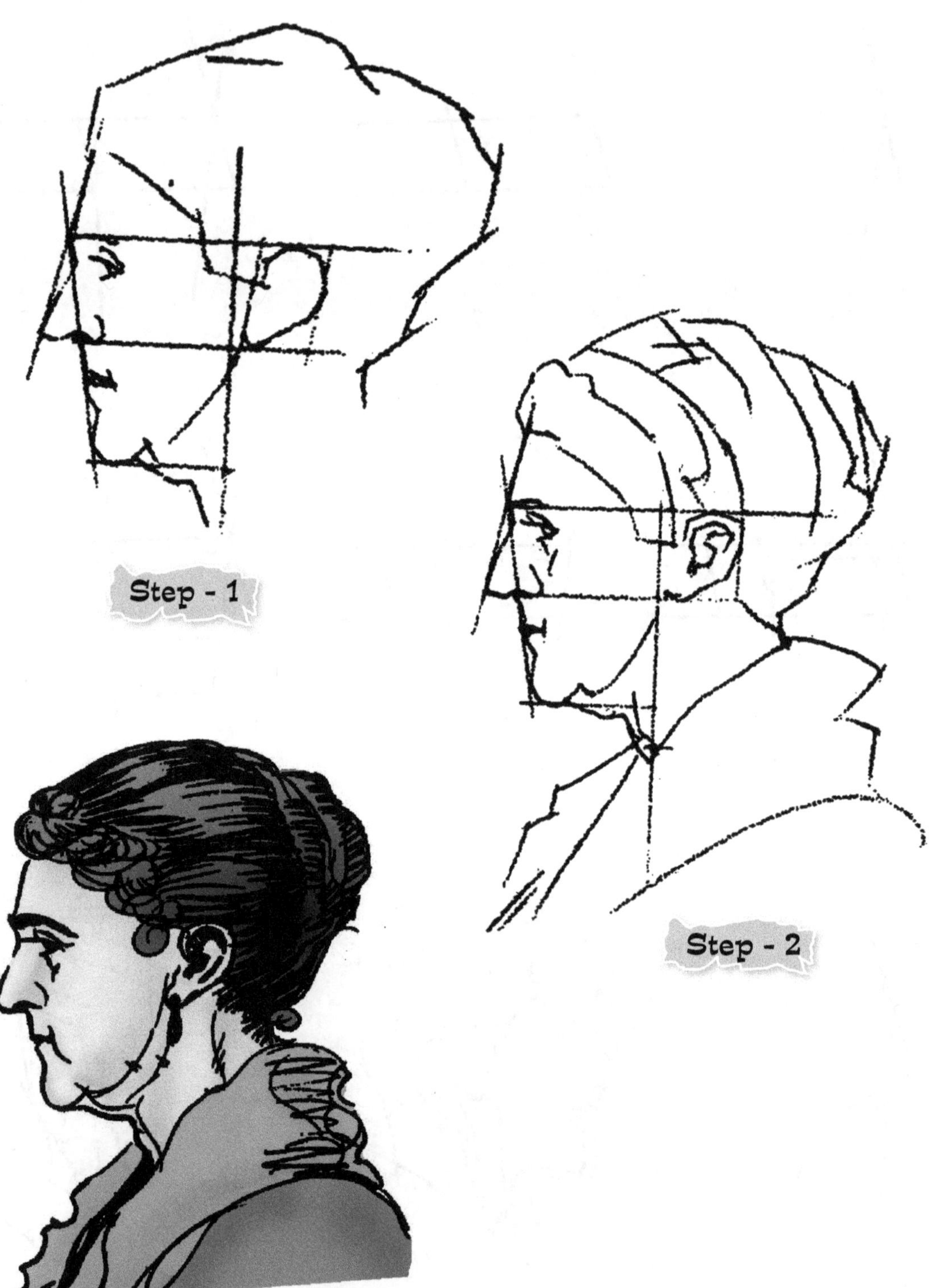

Step - 3

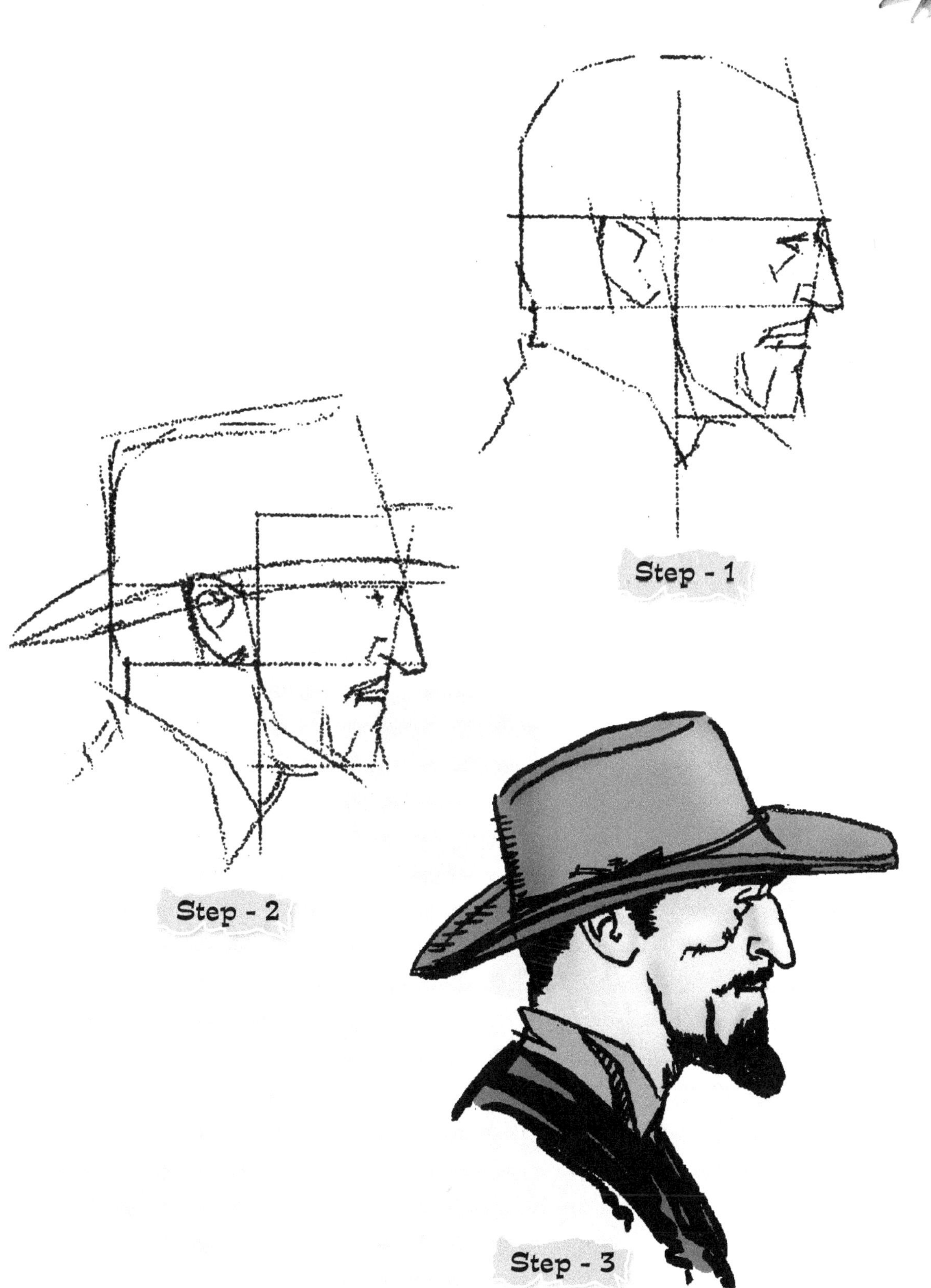
Step - 1
Step - 2
Step - 3

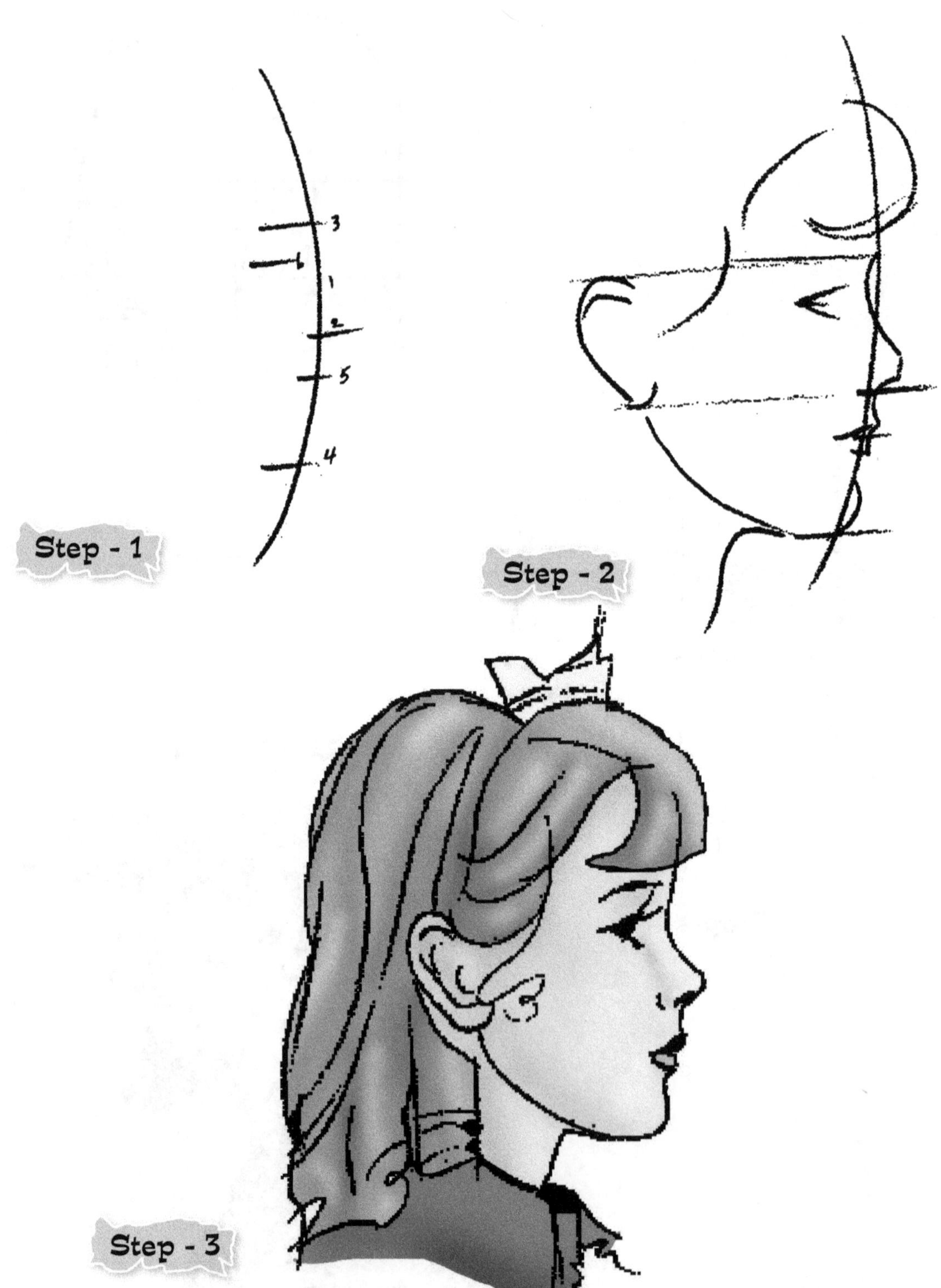
Step - 1
Step - 2
Step - 3

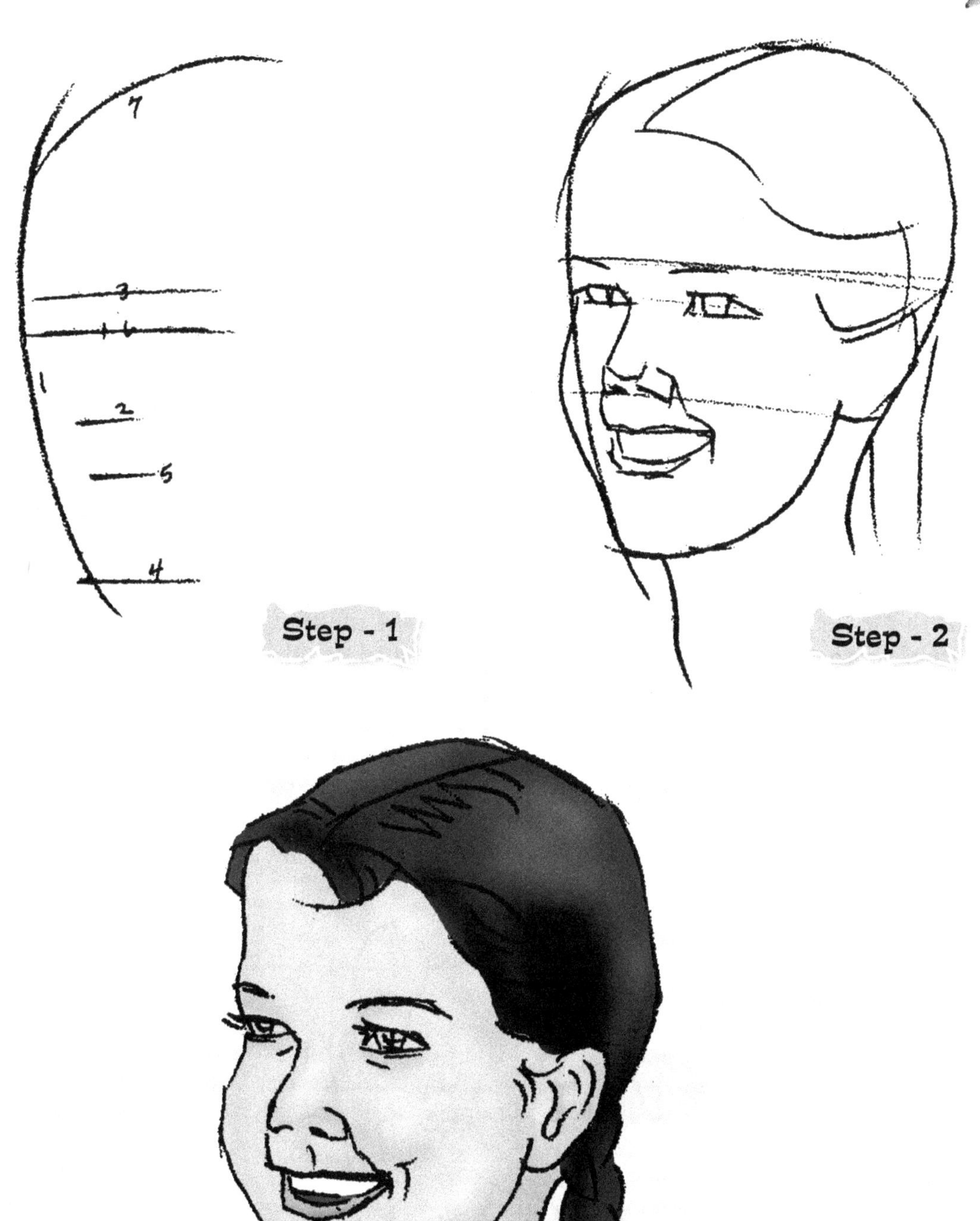

Step - 3

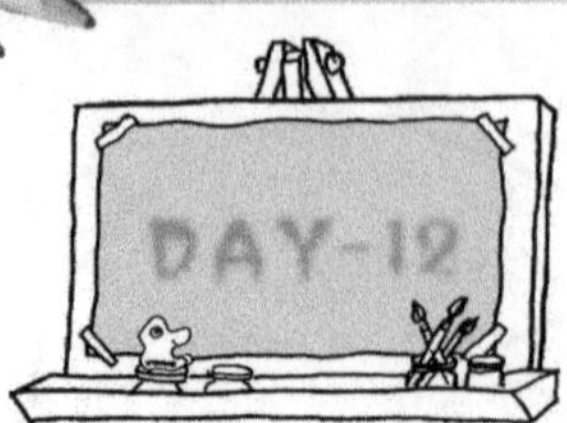

We had told you about how to draw the profi le of a head or a face. And, to make such faces, we had given you a six-point method. We hope, now you must be feeling at ease while drawing a head or a face. To make you a confident and perfect artist is our aim. Now, after gaining perfection in the six-point method, take another step towards becoming a good artist.

Front Position of Head

You have made the profi le of the head. Now, here is the method to draw the front position of head. This kind of drawing may be a bit diffi cult. But you should not worry at all. You already know the right proportions of various parts of the face. With the help of these proportions, you can make the front part of the face. See carefully the front and side positions of the head in the illustration. Here you can easily see the right position of every part of the face.

Following the illustration, try to draw a face with the help of structural lines. We have also made some other drawings for your convenience. Some of these pictures are not exactly front poses but also show some part of the side face. For practice, you can copy them. But, later on, you must be able to draw them from memory.

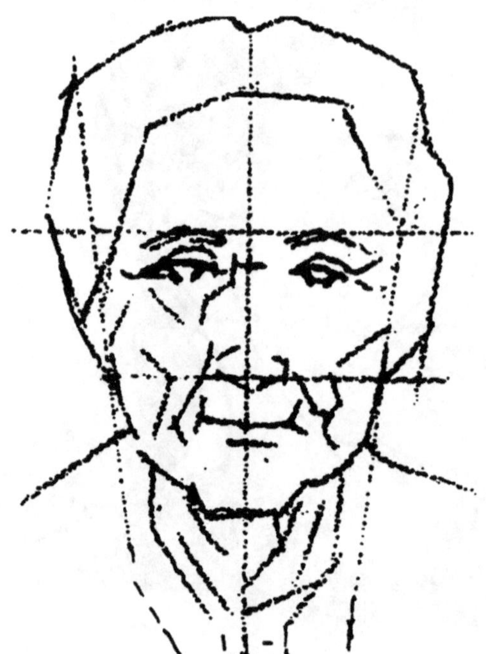

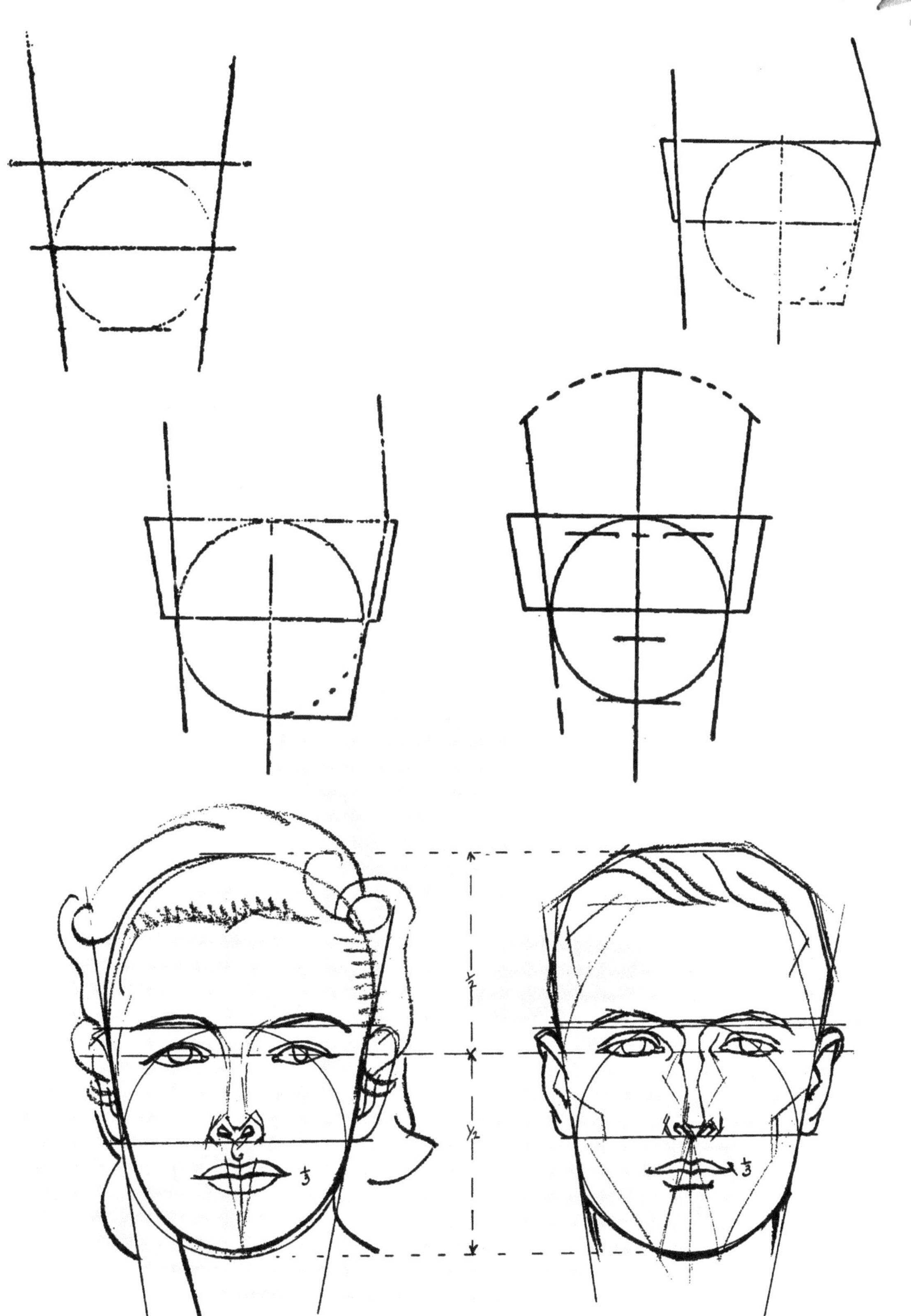
1/2
1/2
1/3
1/3

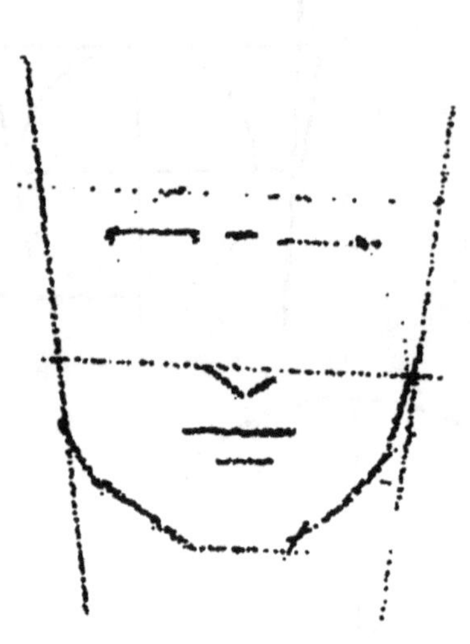
Step - 1

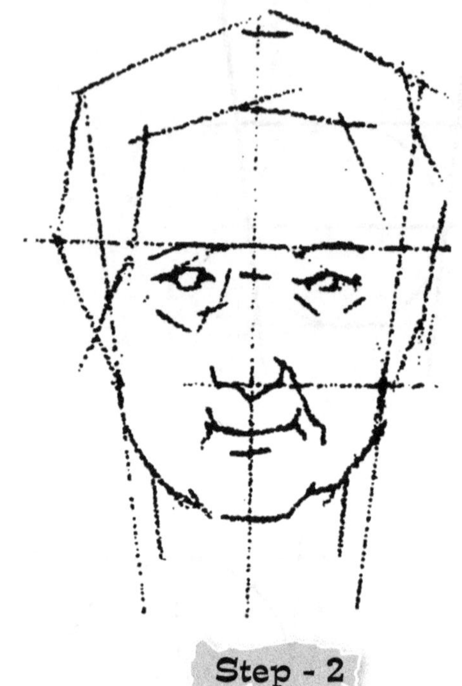
Step - 2

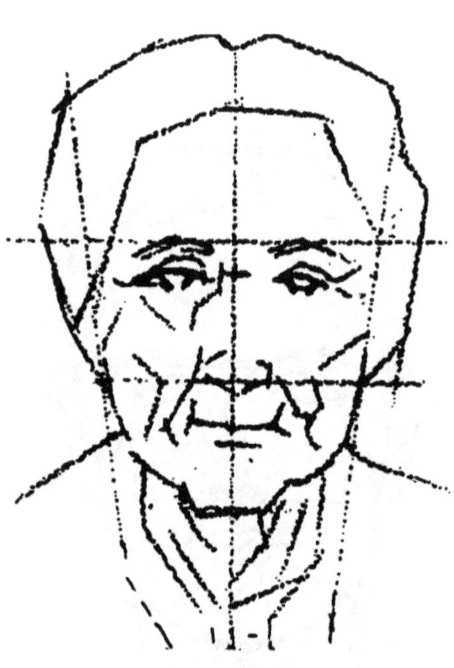
Step - 3

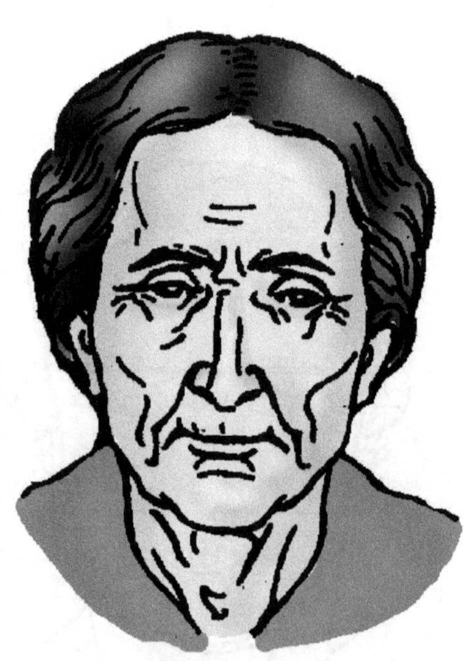
Step - 4

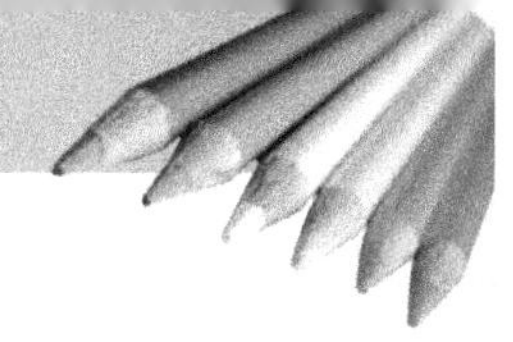

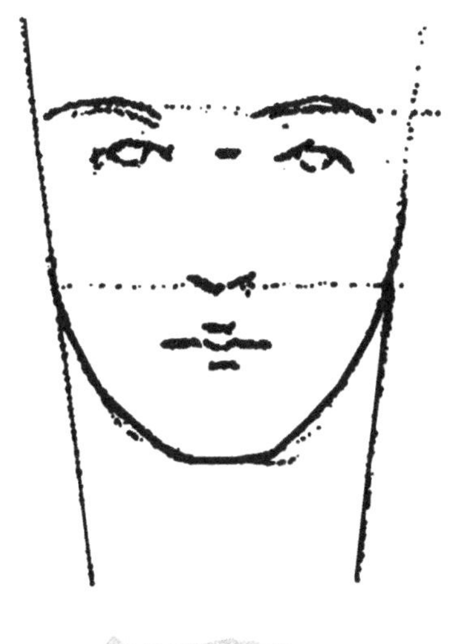

Step - 1

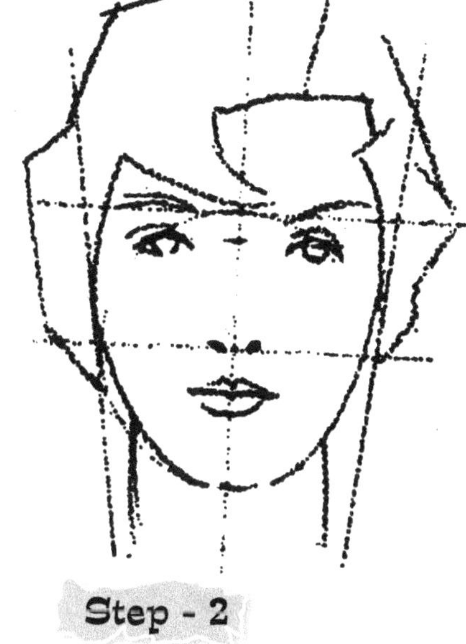

Step - 2

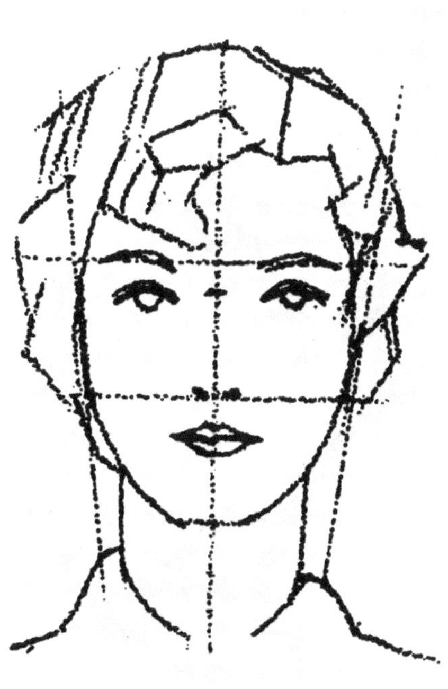

Step - 3

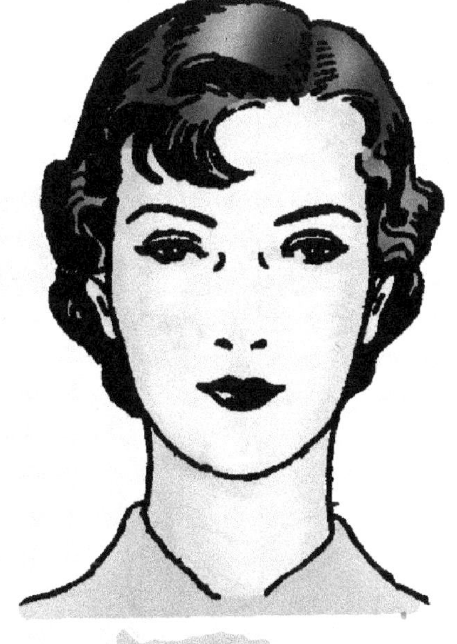

Step - 4

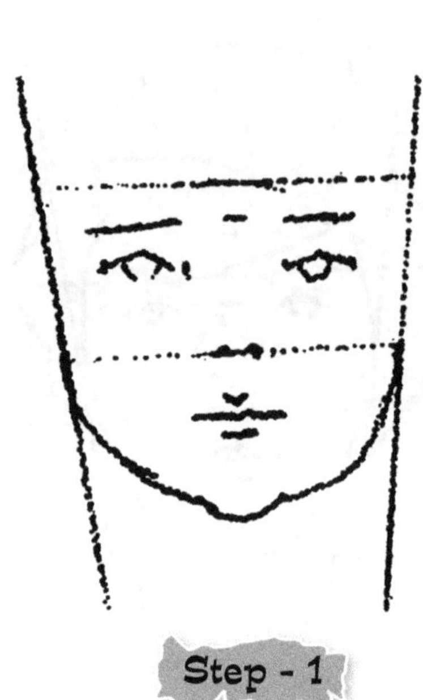
Step - 1

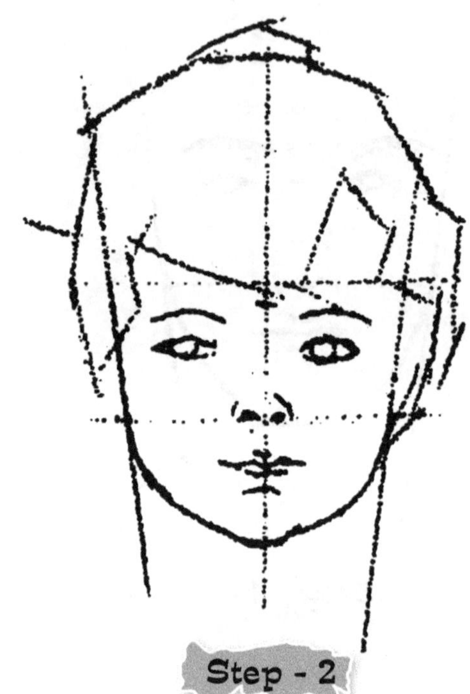
Step - 2

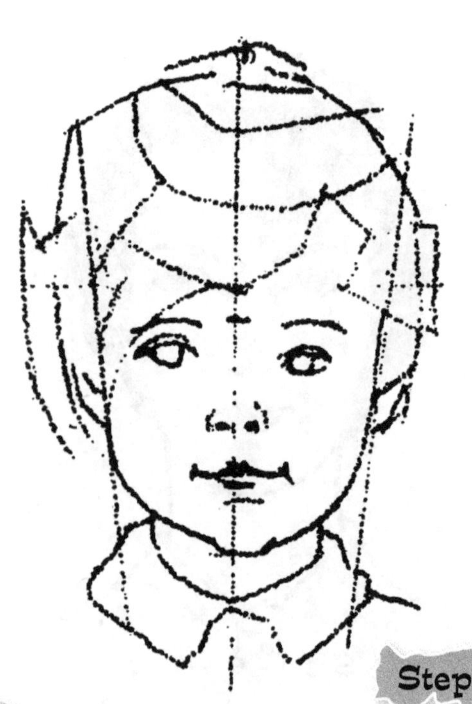
Step - 3

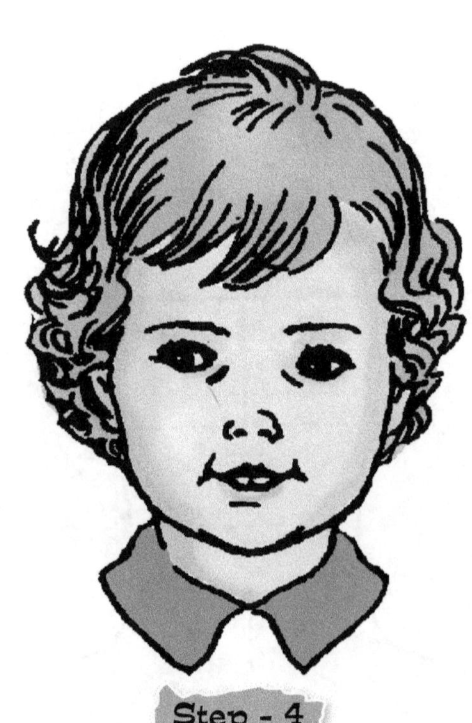
Step - 4

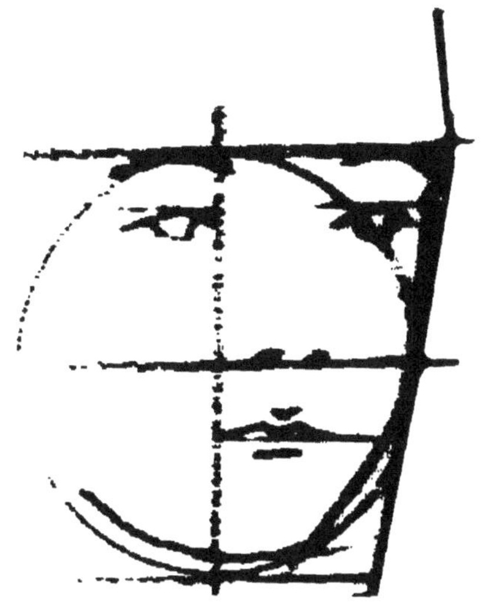

Step - 1

Step - 2

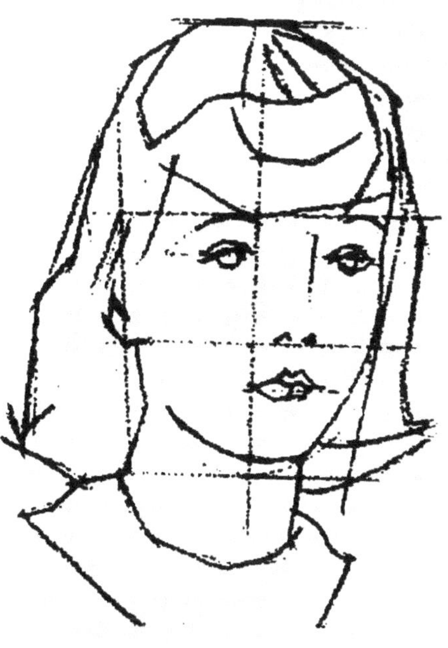

Step - 3

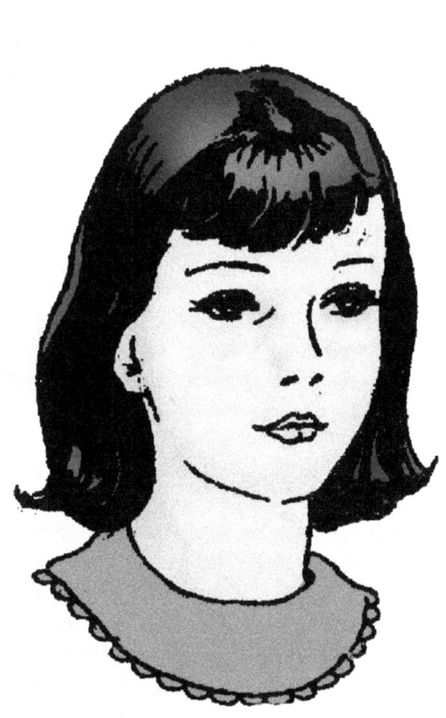

Step - 4

Expressions

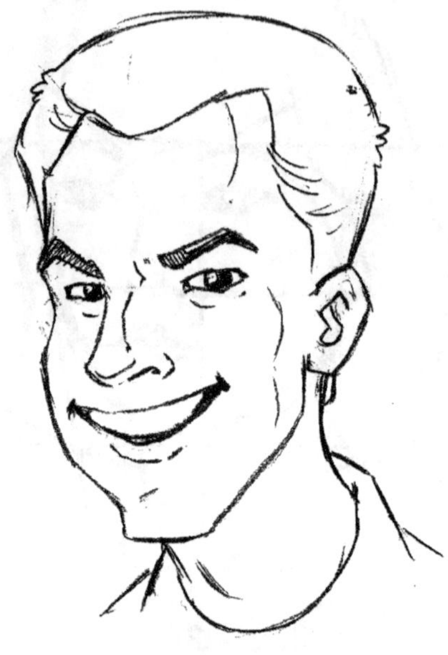

Happy

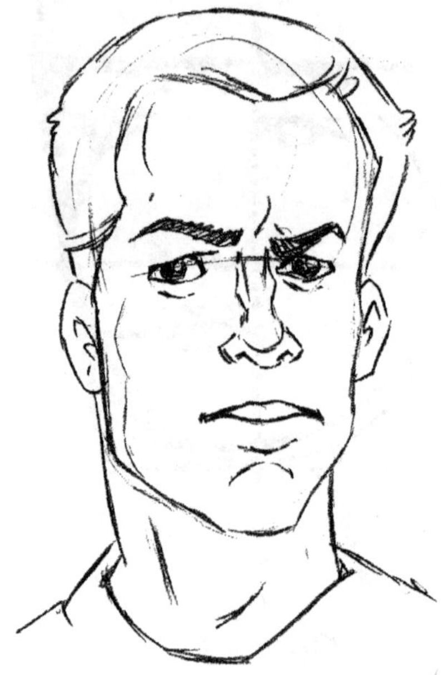

Anxious

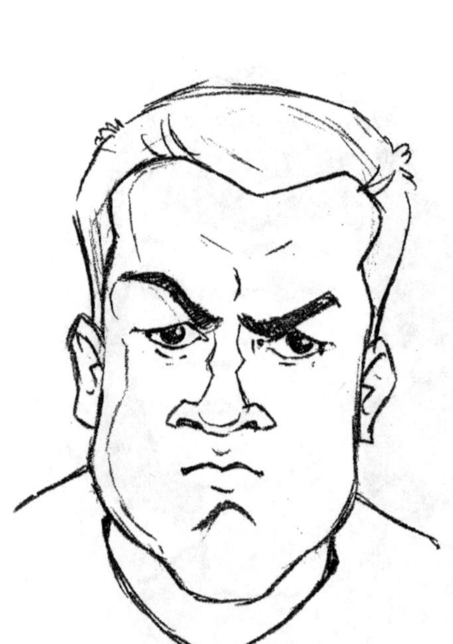

Grumpy

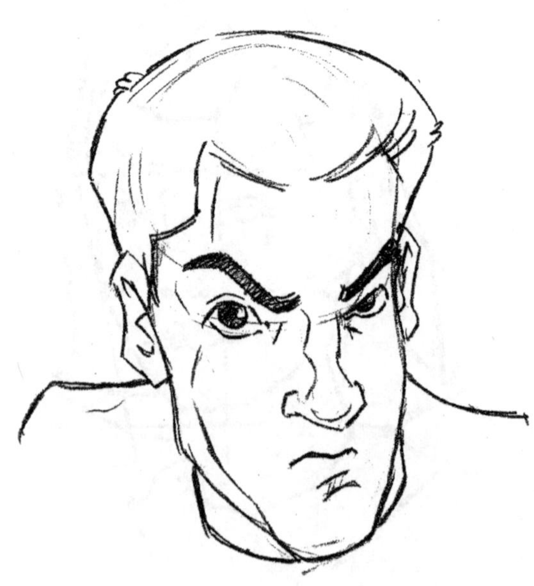

Angry

Expressions

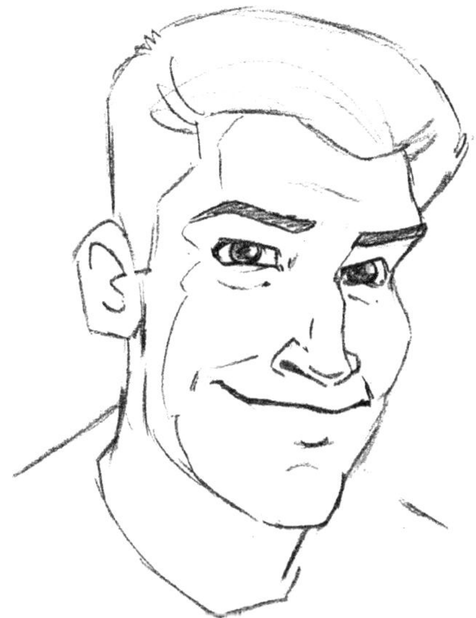

Smiling

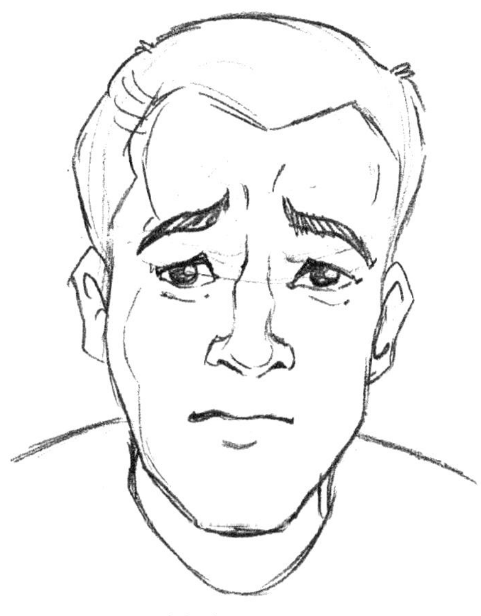

Unhappy

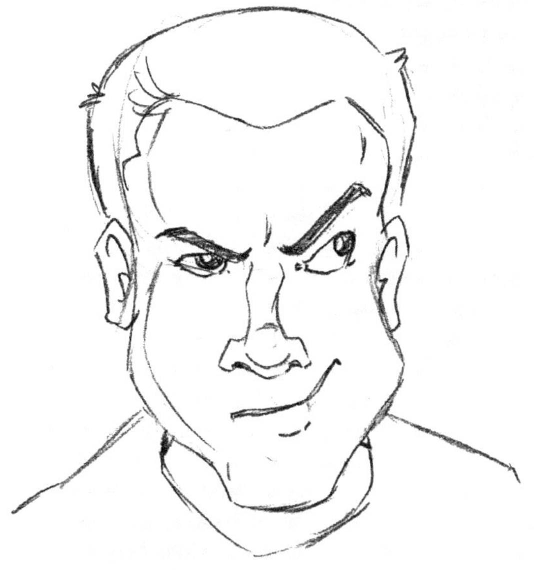

Suspicious

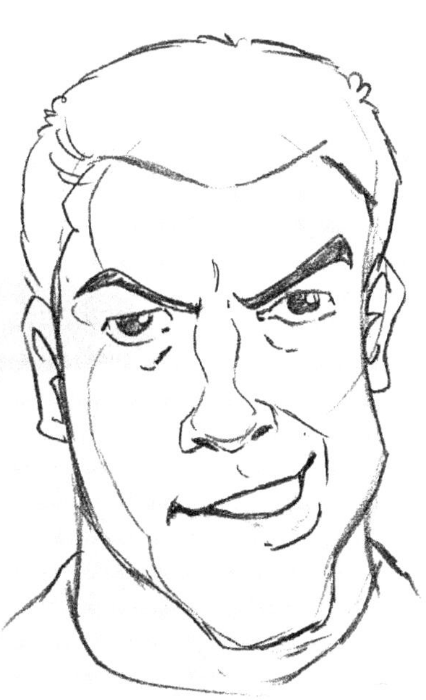

Cheesy Smile

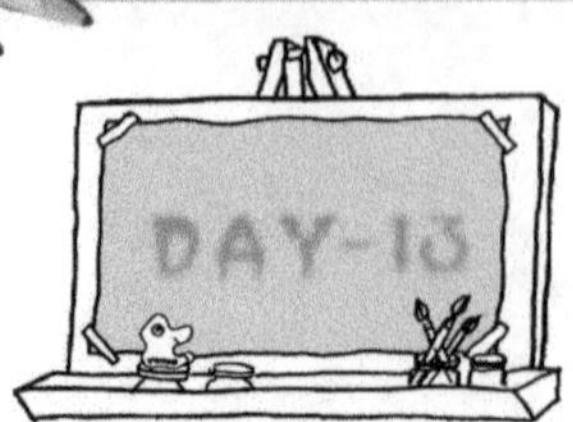

As you know, in the drawing of the human fi gure, the face is the most diffi cult. We hope, by now you must have become perfect in drawing various faces. Now there is nothing diffi cult for you. With the help of simple and straight lines, you can complete the drawing of the human fi gure. Now, think of the other body parts that should be drawn after face drawing. If you are unable to decide, then we'll tell you. The hands and feet are next in importance to face. You will be able to draw them easily after some practice.

Drawing of Hands and Postures

See your hand carefully. What are the differences between right and left hands? From where does the thumb start; what is the distance between the thumb and other fi ngers and what is their position. Try to understand the structure of thumb, and the length and breadth of fi ngers and nails, and their proportions. Apart from the breadth and thickness of the palm, special attention must be paid to the lines on the hand and its structure.

The length from the joint of wrist to the centre fi nger is according to the age. The average length is 7½ inches. In comparison to a man, a woman's hand is small, thin and delicate and the fi ngers are specially long and pointed. The hands of children are well-shaped and in proportion as per their age. The effects of race and profession can also be seen on the hands. One can't ignore the differences between the hands of an artist and a peasant.

For the drawing of human fi gure, the various postures of hand should be known. Try to make drawings of hands holding objects of daily use in various postures. For your convenience, we have made some drawings of hands in various postures. Observe them carefully and do regular practice of their drawings.

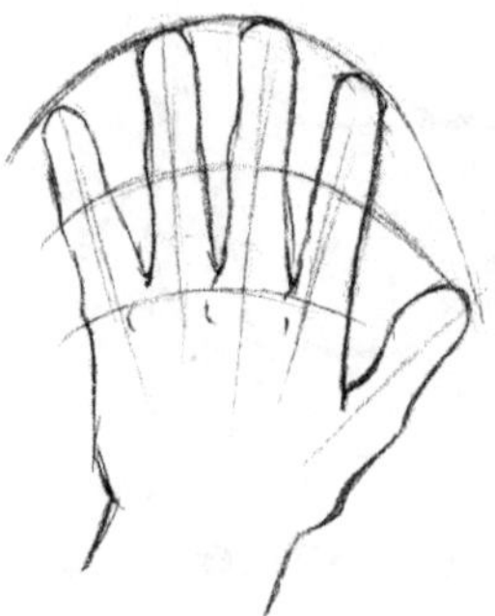

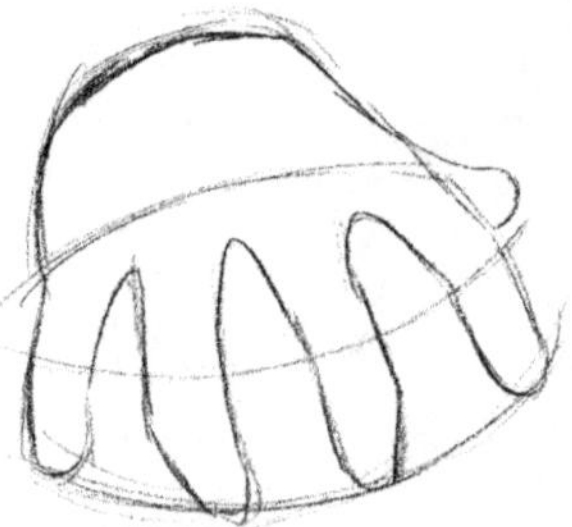

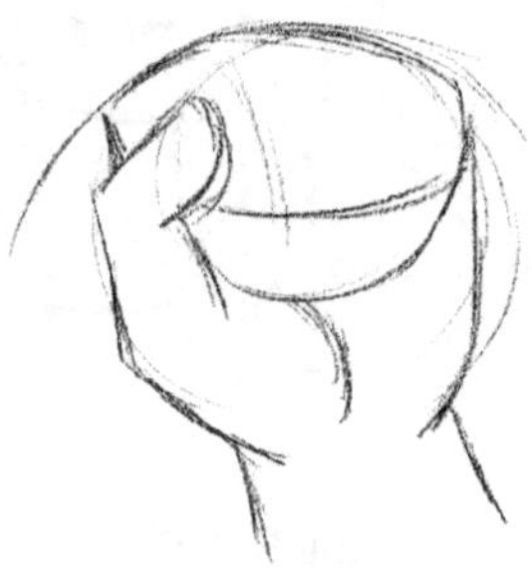

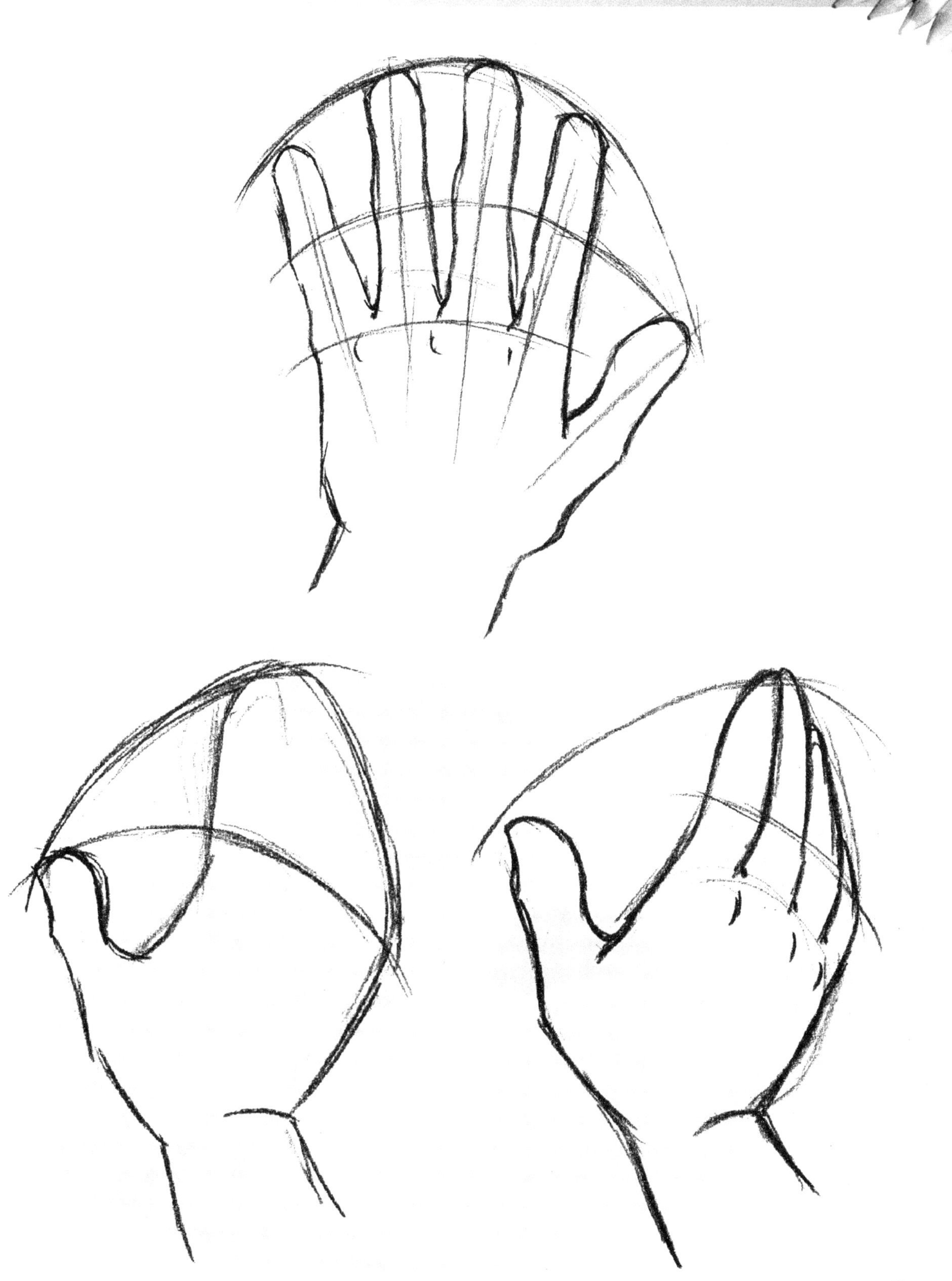

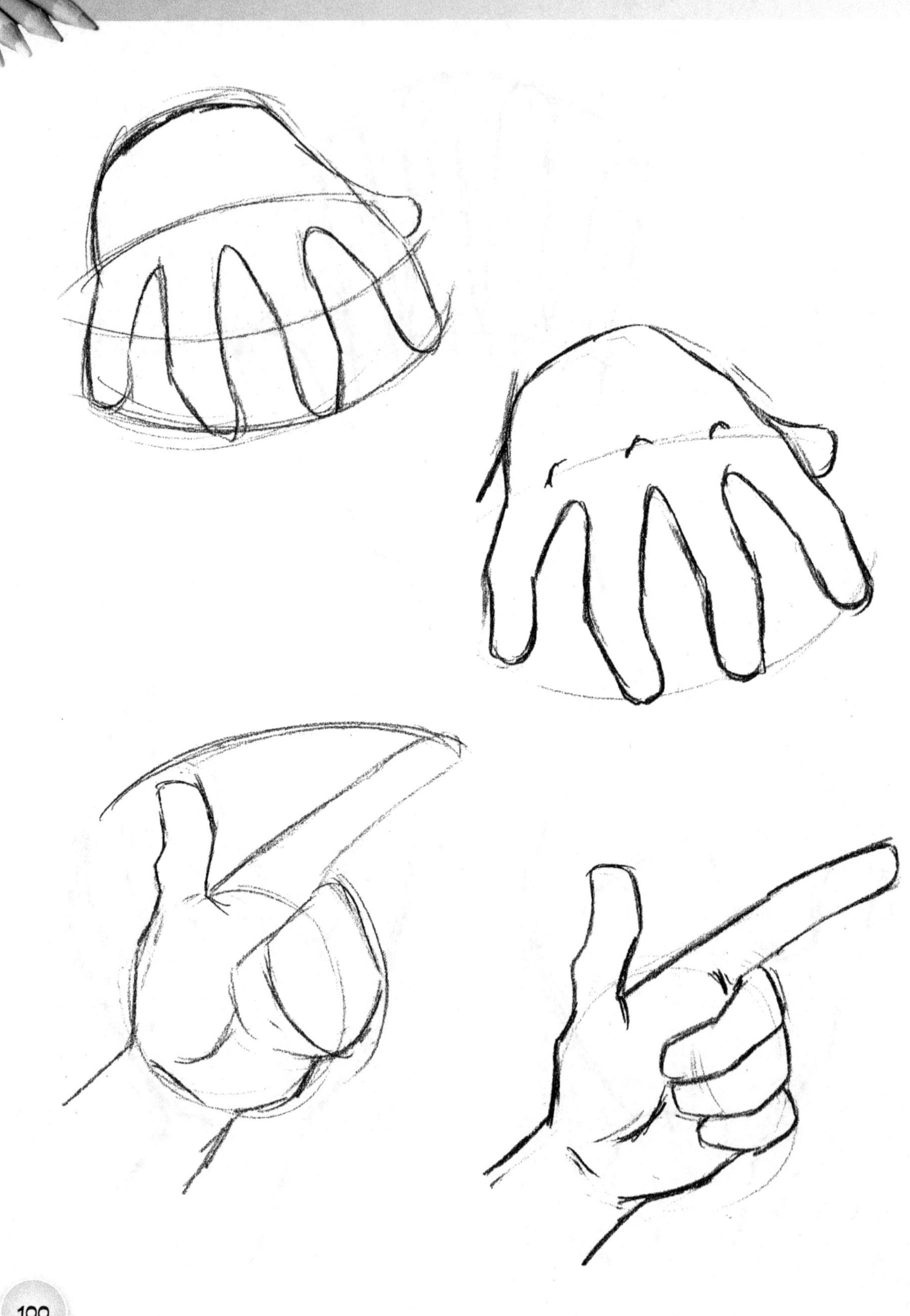

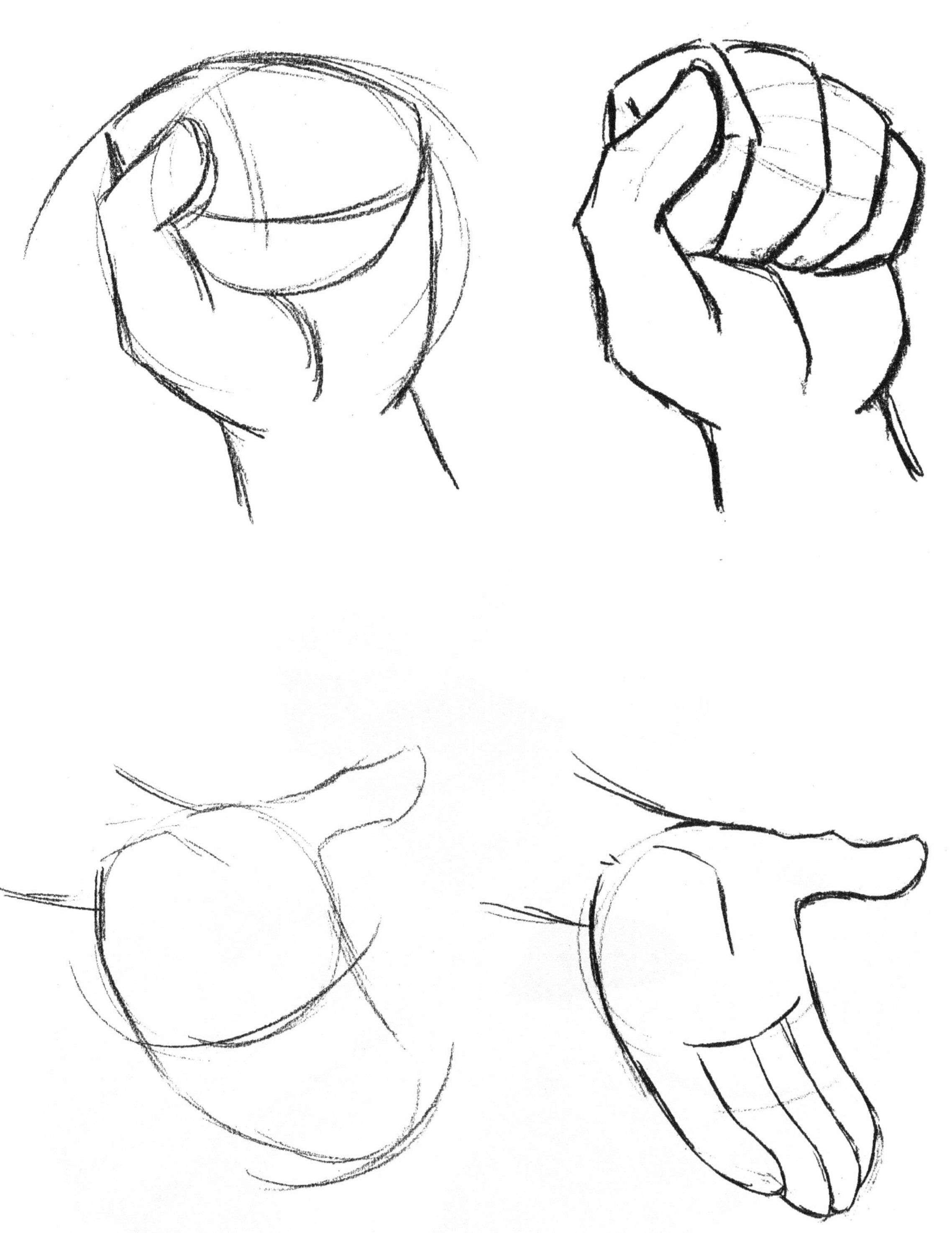

Structure of Feet and Postures

Like hands you must also know the structure of feet. You must be knowing the difference between the structures of the right and the left foot. You must take care of the difference in proportions of the toe and its fi ngers. The length of the foot of an ordinary man is 10 inches, from toe to ankle. Just like hands, the feet of a woman, in comparison to man's, are small and delicate. The feet of children are according to their age. The effects of race and profession are also visible on the structure of human feet.

According to the movement, we have given here a few postures of the feet. See and practice them. Apart from this, a few samples of shoes and sandals have also been given for your convenience. You should be able to draw shoe-wearing feet, because these days feet are mostly shown in shoes.

Drawing of Other Parts of Body

In the drawing of the human fi gure, special care should be taken at the ratio of proportion among various parts of the body. The drawings of neck, shoulders, chest, waist, hip, hand, legs, etc., should be made as per the fatness of the body. A woman's body structure, in comparison to that of a man, has to be kept different. There is a marked difference between the chest of man and woman. The wrist and calf of a woman, as compared to a man's, are round and shapely. There is also a clear difference between their hips.

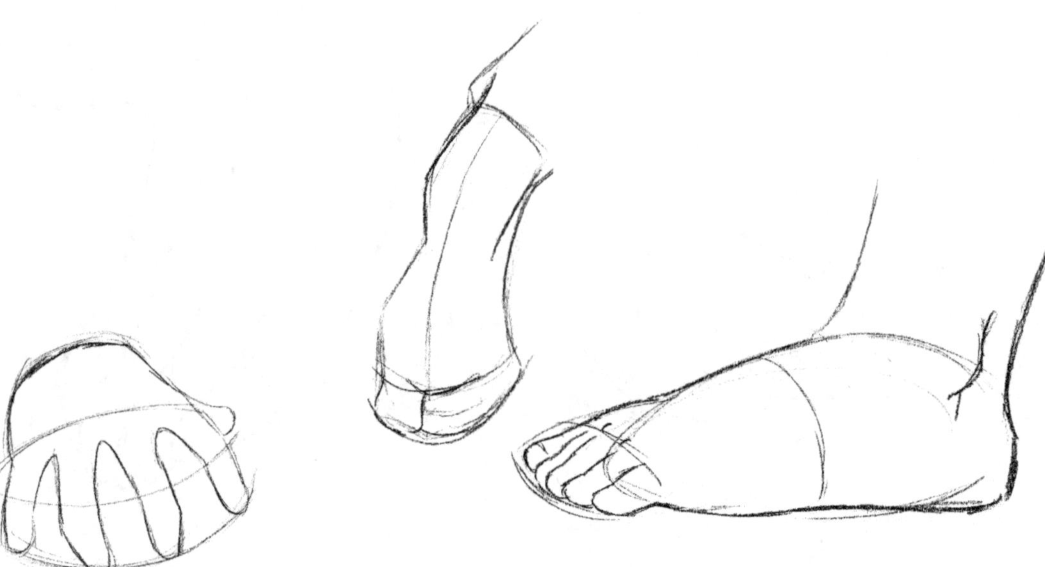

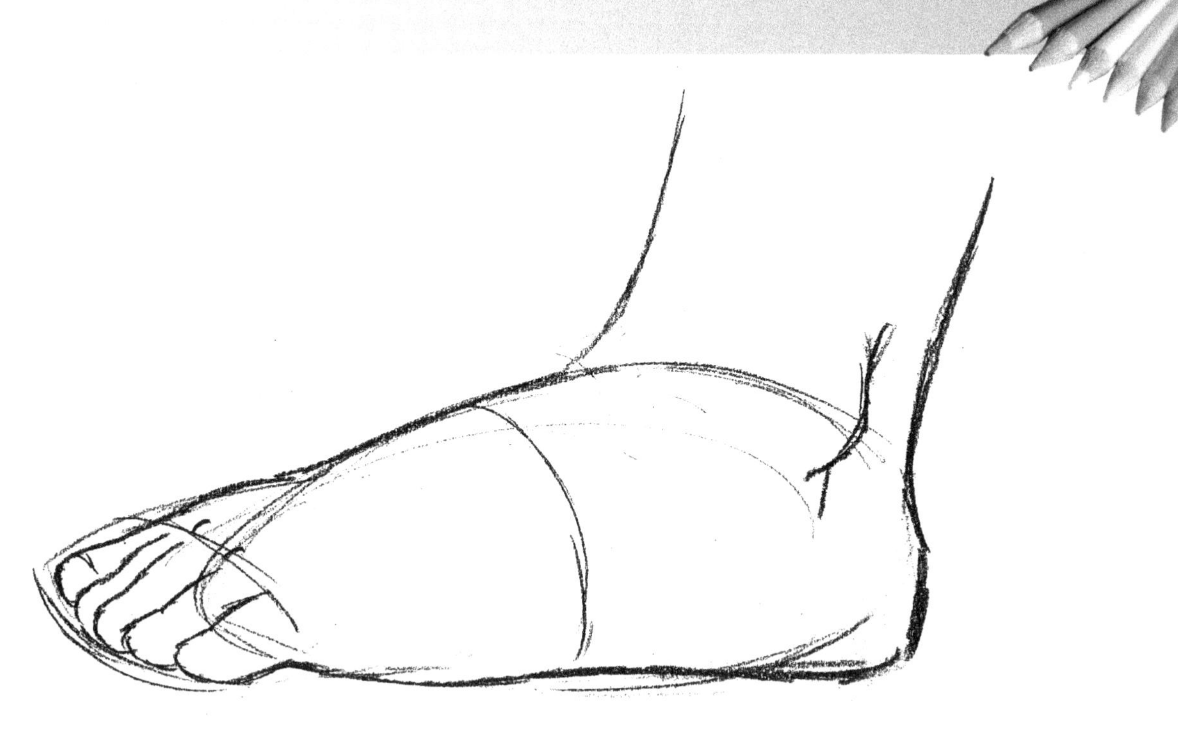

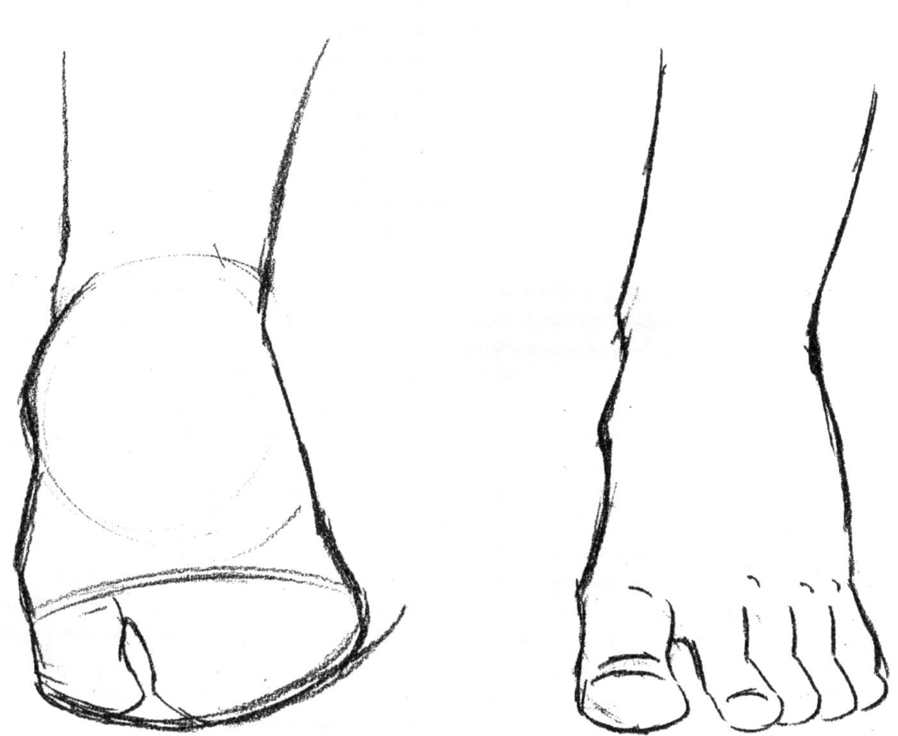

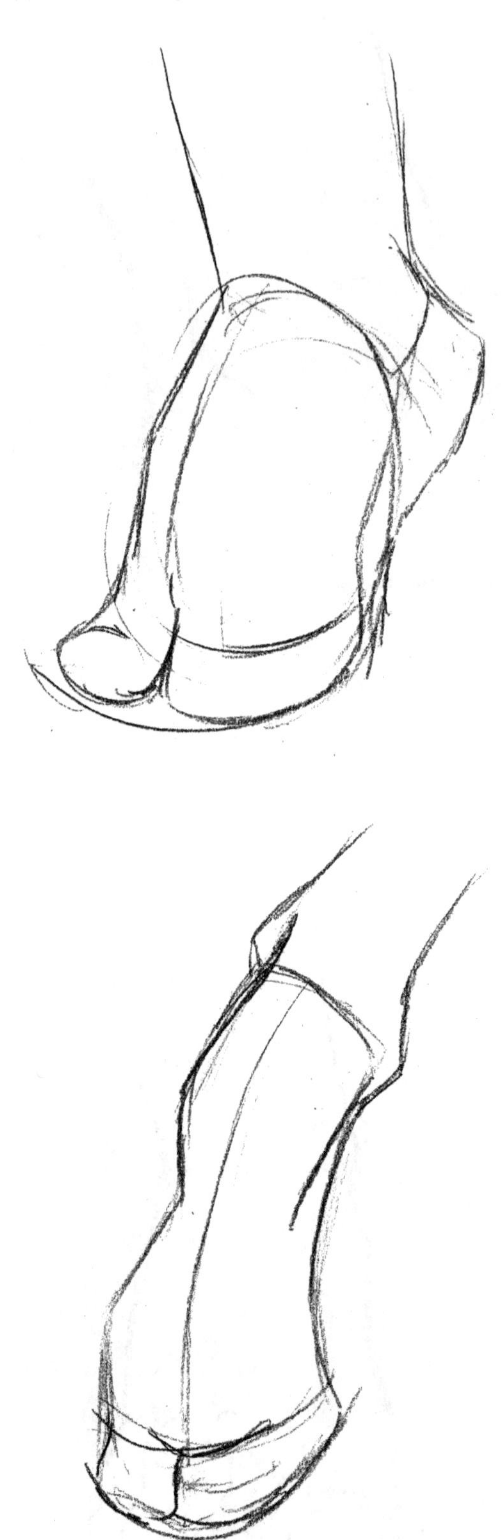

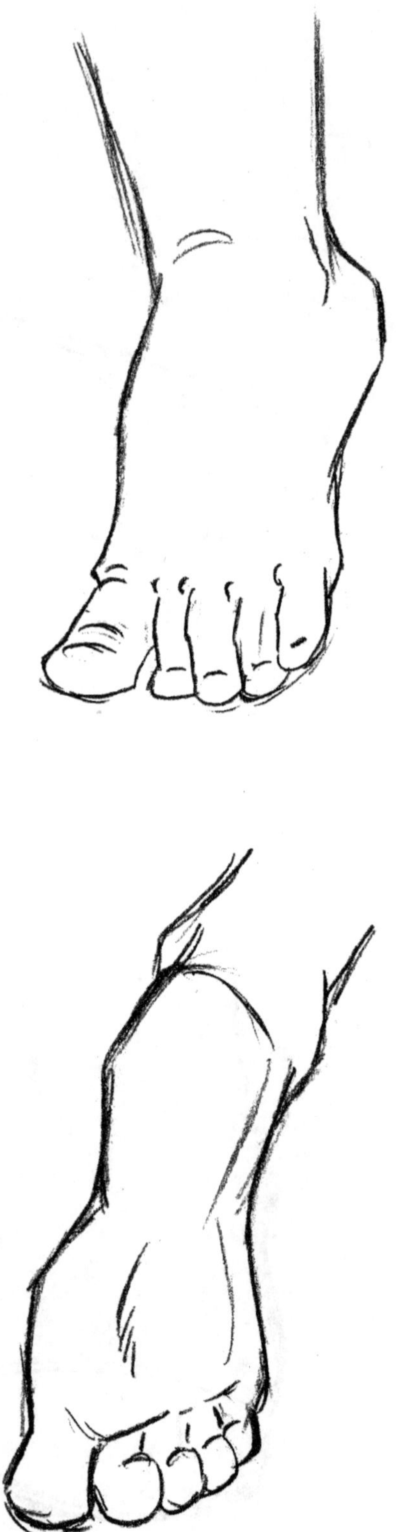

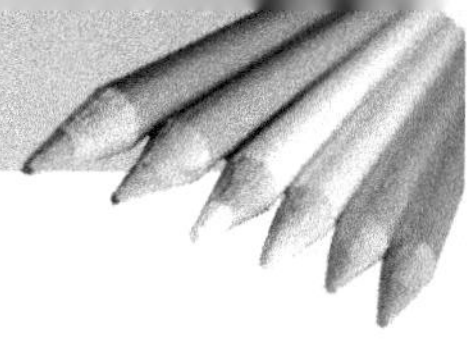

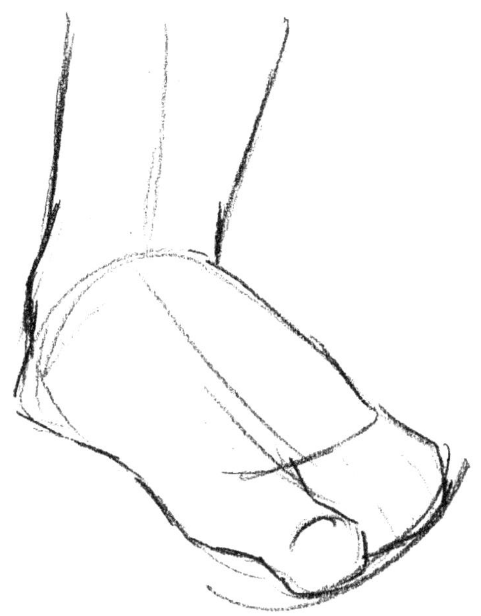

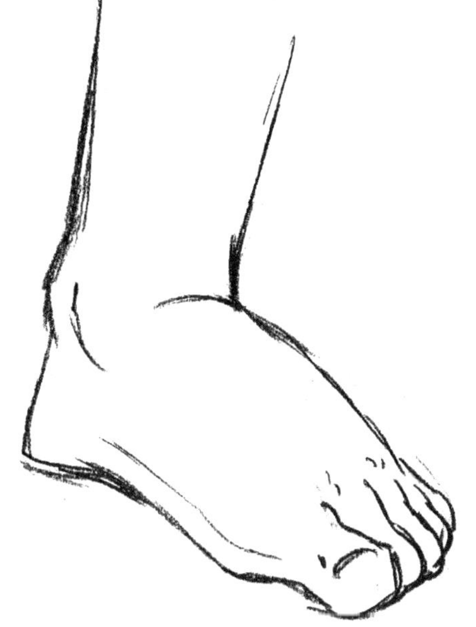

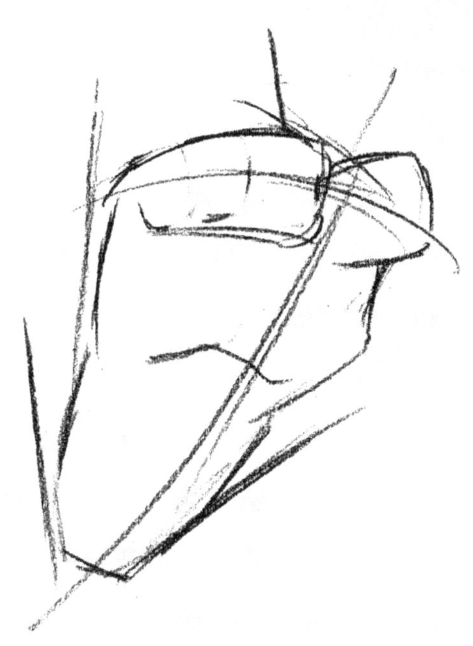

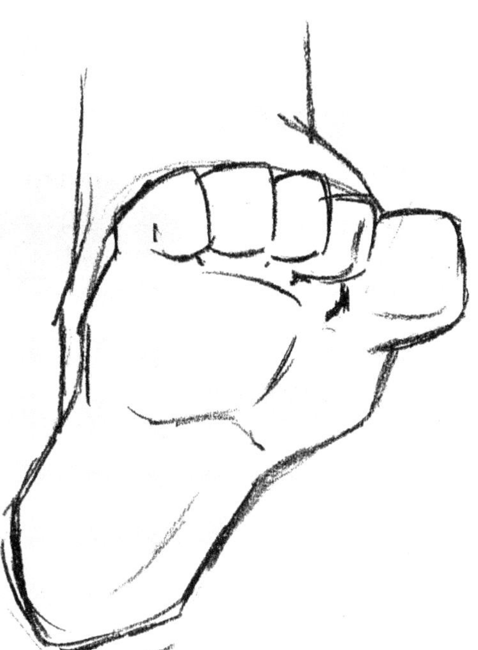

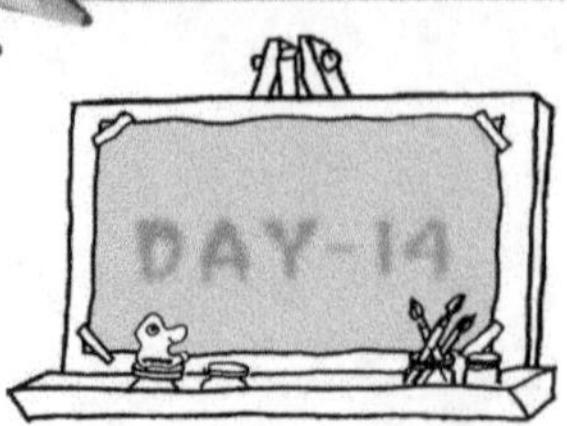

The drawings that you have made so far were of static things and of people showing no movement. That was simple. Now, let us come to a diffi cult topic, that is, to make pictures of things in motion and of people doing some work.

Illustrations

All the people that we see around us are doing something or the other. Whether they are sitting or standing or lying or are in any other state, they seem to be in movement. And, those people who are completely silent, and do not move, they are either ill, or are so much engrossed in meditation that they do not even care to move. Such people or objects are called lifeless.

The pictures of things in motion and people doing various works are called illustrations. The illustrations are very useful for an artist because through them any expression or emotion can be conveyed. The illustrations are prominently used in books, magazines, advertisements, calendars, etc. For making beautiful illustrations, not only should an artist be expert in making drawings, he should also be able to appreciate the beauty in things around him.

The illustration is a kind of decoration. The people decorate themselves with clothes, ornaments and cosmetics. Similarly, an artist decorates books, magazines, calendars and advertisements with illustrations. An illustration is the test of an artist's intelligence, expertise and tastes.

The foremost qualities of an illustration are its attractiveness and effectiveness in conveying the intended message. These two qualities decide the price of an illustration. So it is necessary that you understand the importance of illustrations. With pencil, pen and ink, you can produce good illustrations. But by using brushes, wash technique, pastels, crayons, etc. you can make illustrations more attractive.

For your convenience we have given here some illustrations. See them carefully. Keeping in mind their techniques, try to make some illustrations.

Different Methods of Making Illustration

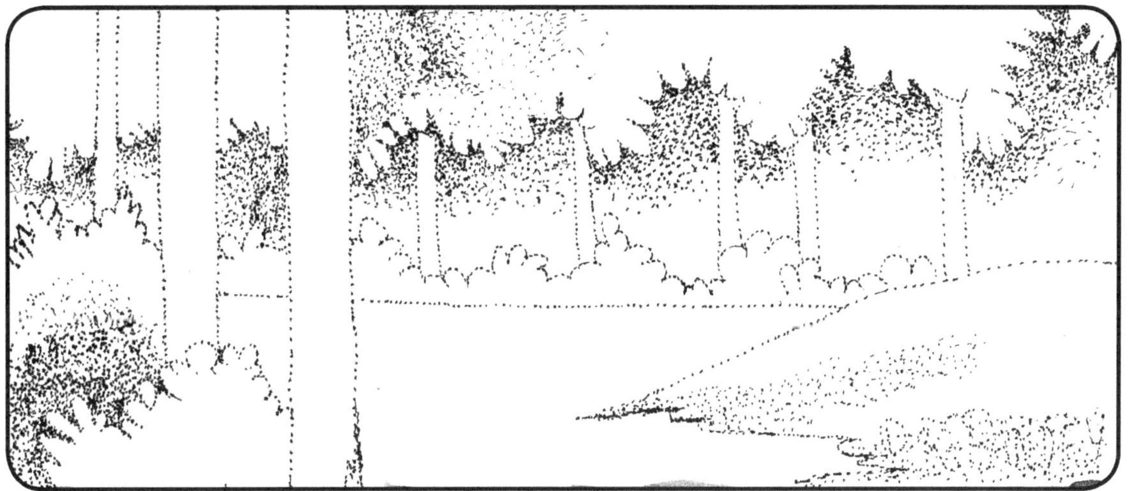

Drawing with pen

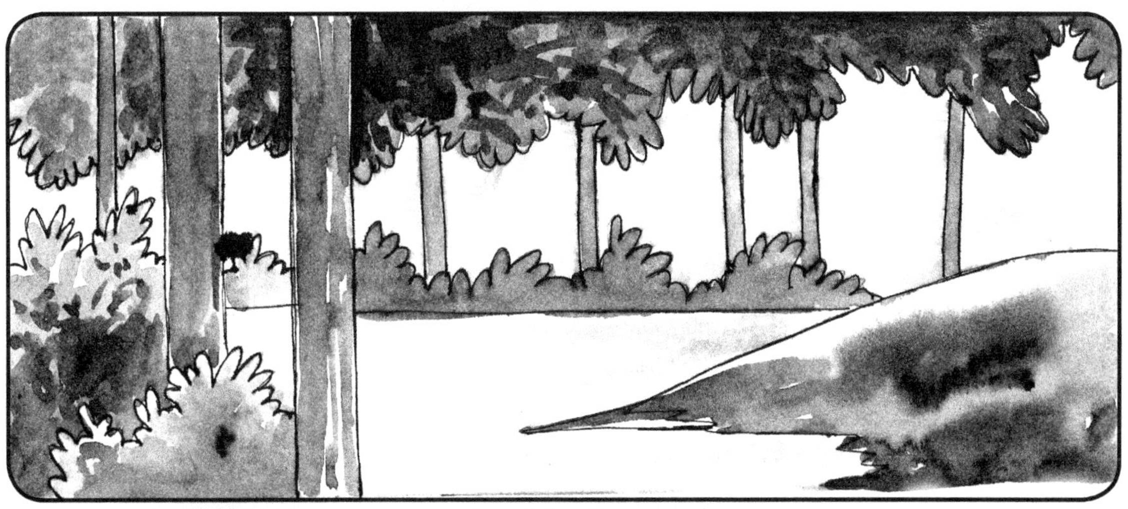

Line and half tone

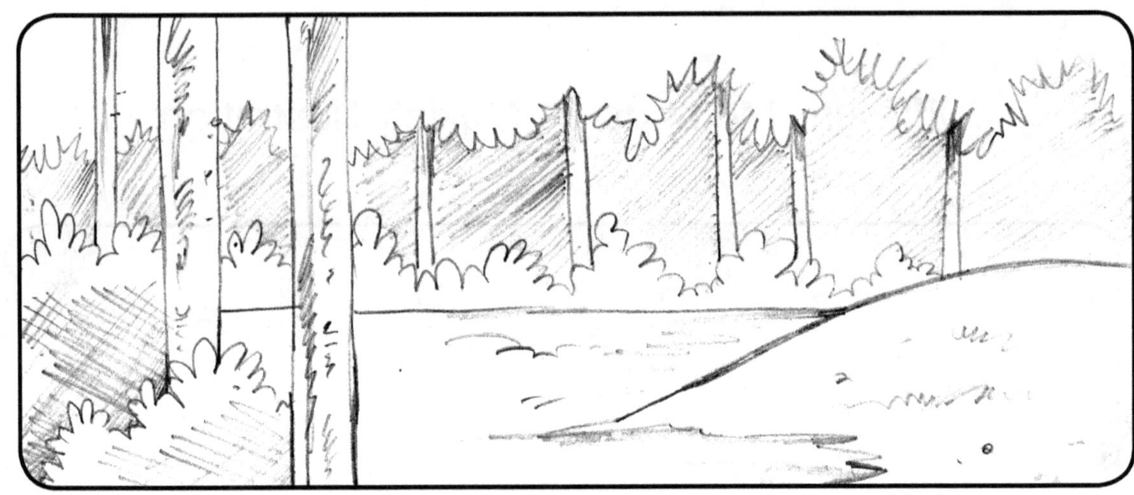

Drawing with pencil

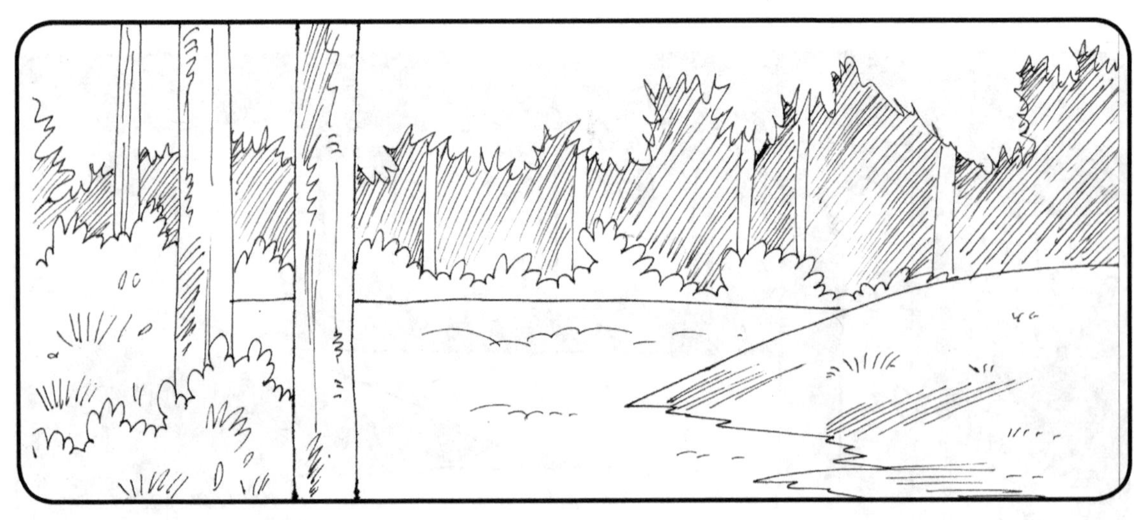

Drawing with pen

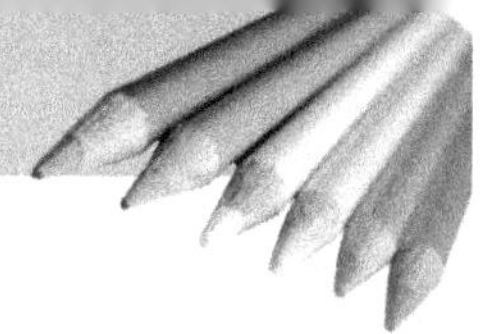

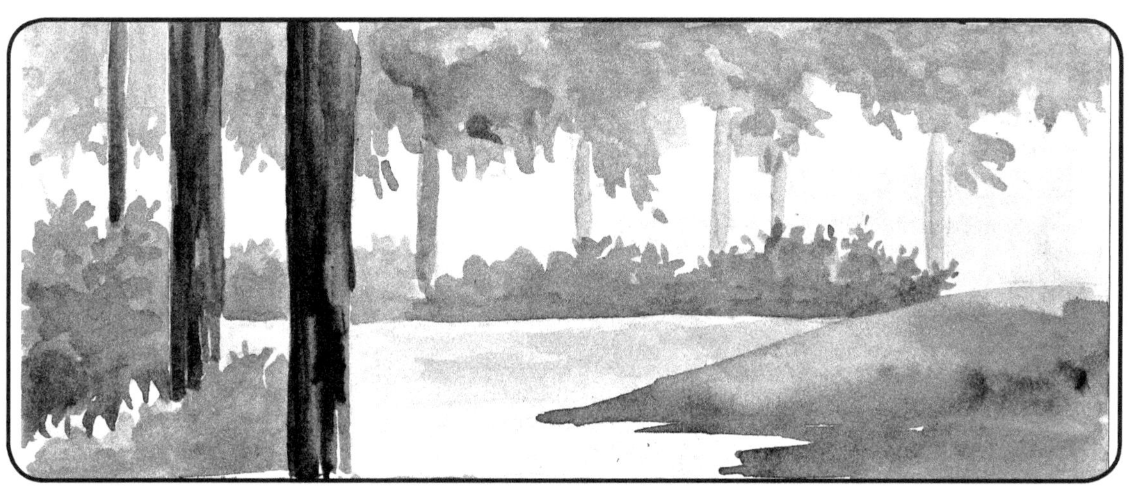

Half Tone

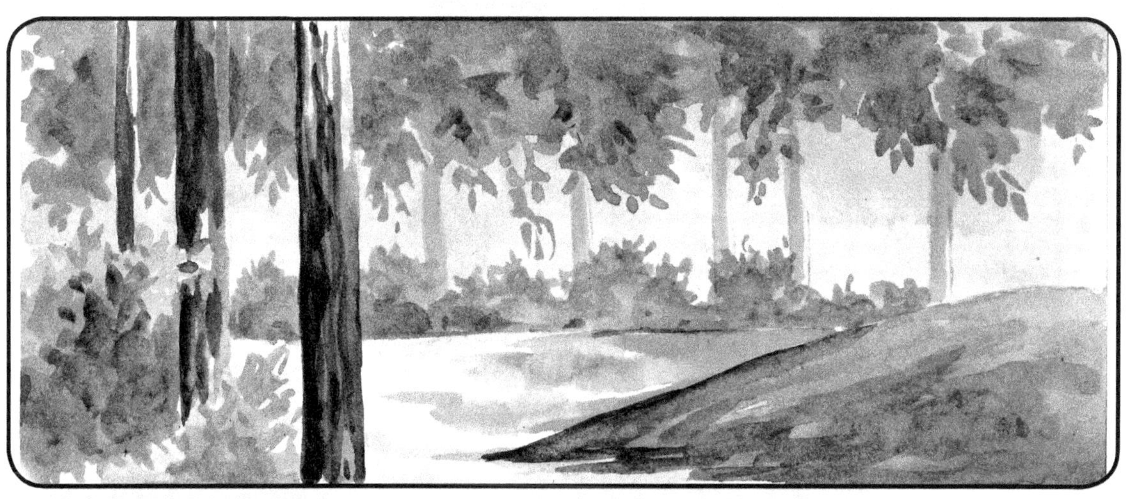

Wash (Painting with light water colours)

Animal caricatures

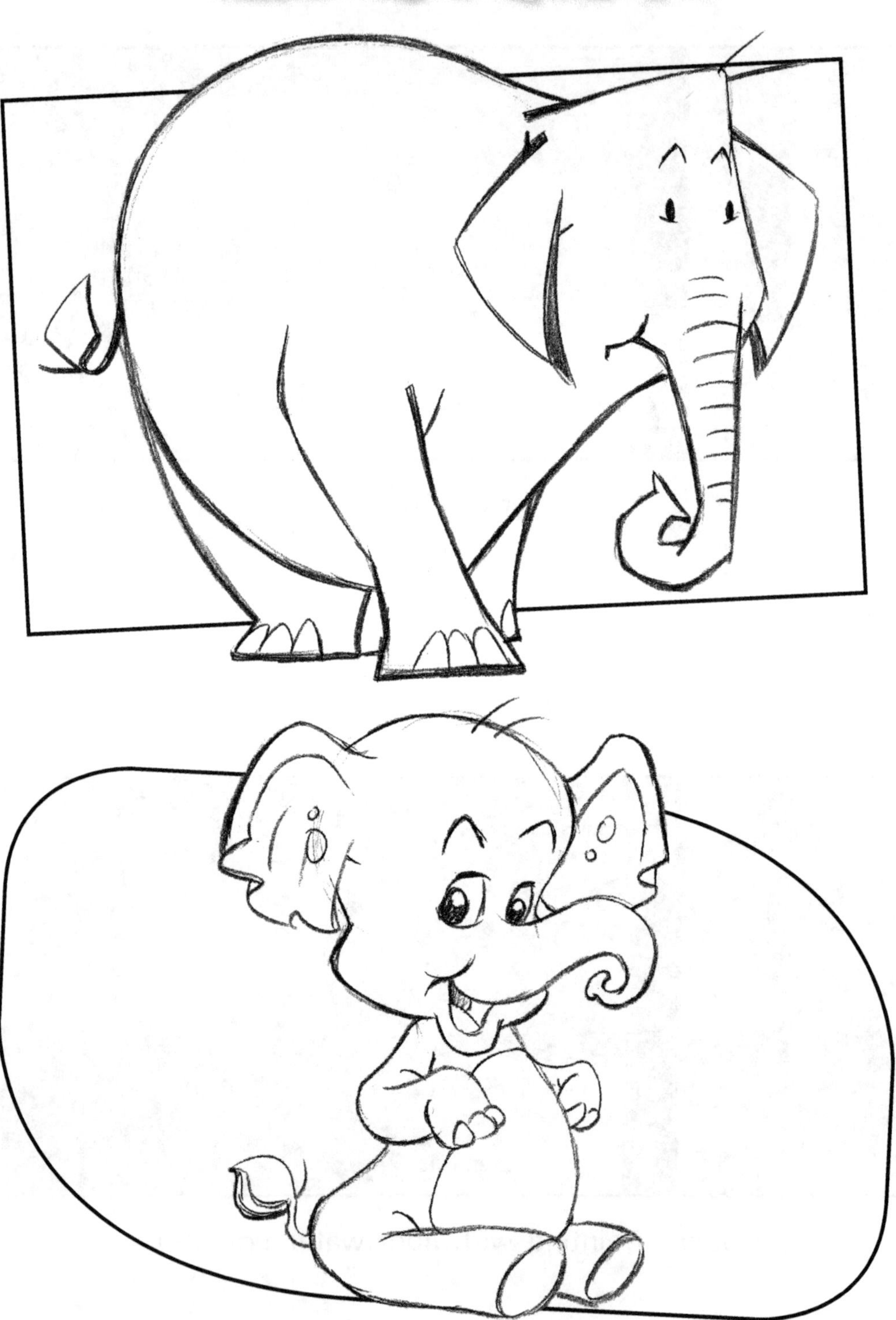

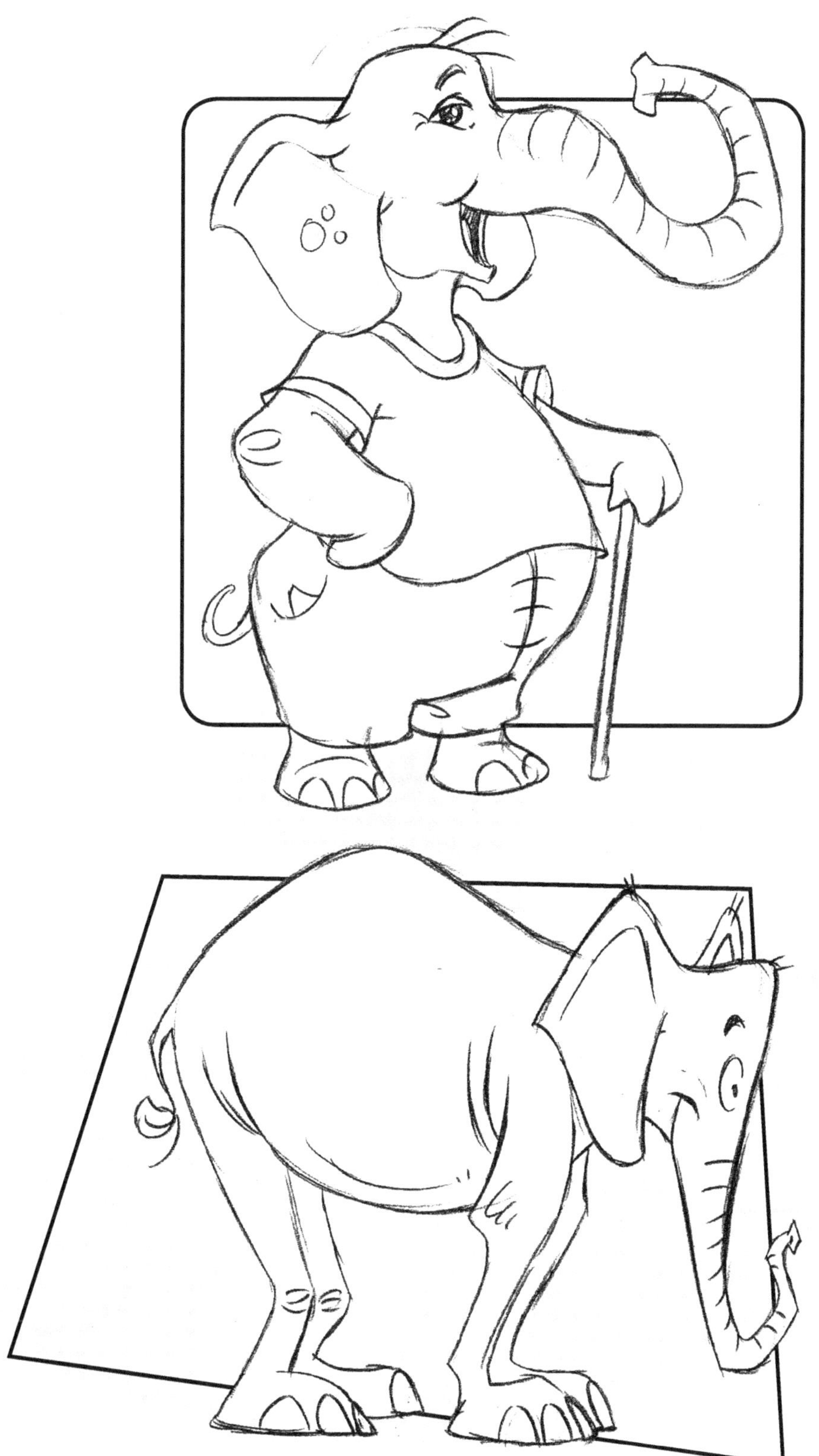

Girl's caricature

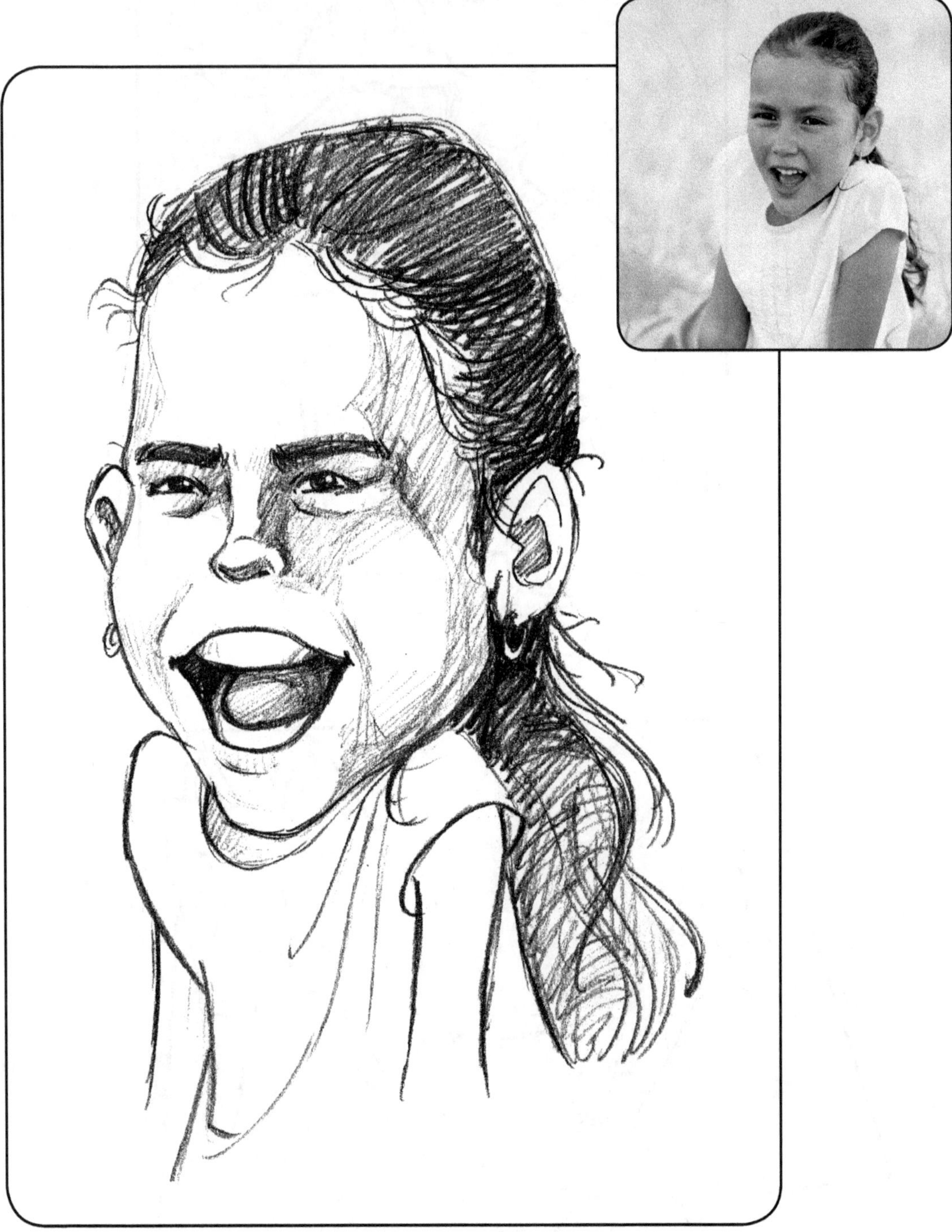

Boy's caricature

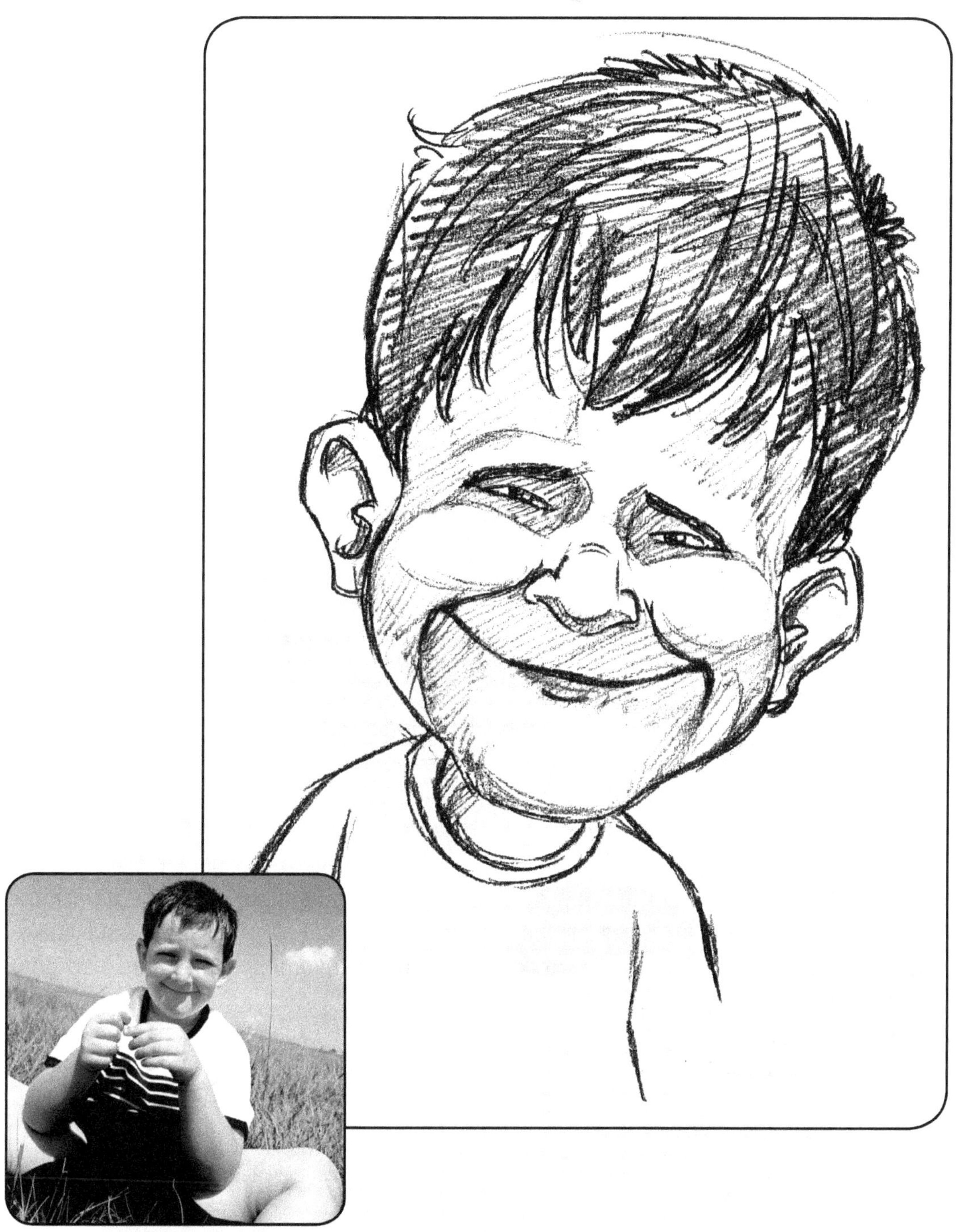

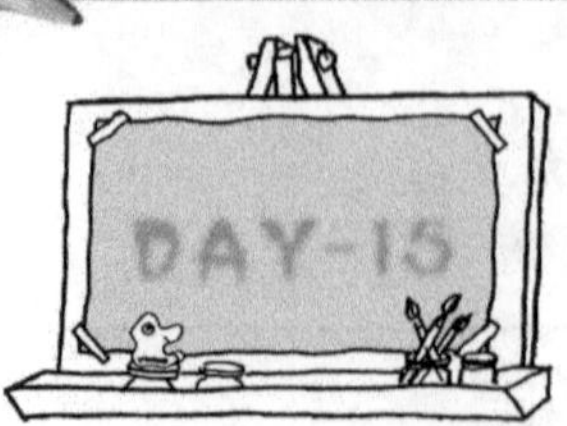

Usually water colour, oil colour and acrylic colour are used in painting. You can start painting in any medium. But it is better if you begin with water colour and do its regular practice.

Water Colour Painting

Water colours are available in cakes, tubes and bottles. Use good quality paint. For water colour painting, the surface of the paper should be rough. Drawing paper, handmade paper, cartridge paper, cant paper, mount board, etc. are useful for water colour painting. In this kind of painting the brushes are very important. The brush should be such that its hair are long and soft, and when soaked in water its tip becomes pointed and thin. Sable hair brushes are of this type. For painting you may need brushes from 1 to 6 numbers. For highlighting or special effects you should use some sharp pointed instrument or knife.

To start with, you can make paintings of fruits, fl owers and vegetables available at home. But for practice, it is better to copy the colour pictures printed in the magazines.

First of all, you must practice mixing of colours. You may remember the colour chart you had made on Day 2. When you mix yellow with red, red with blue and blue with yellow, you will get orange, violet and green, respectively. Similarly, you can obtain any colour by mixing these three colours. In the mixture of colours, the more a particular colour is added, the more effective will it become. When you have understood well the mixing of colours, then you should start the painting. You must use only the three primary colours—red, yellow and blue—and make different shades of them by intermixing. For your convenience, you may also buy the colours mentioned in the book.

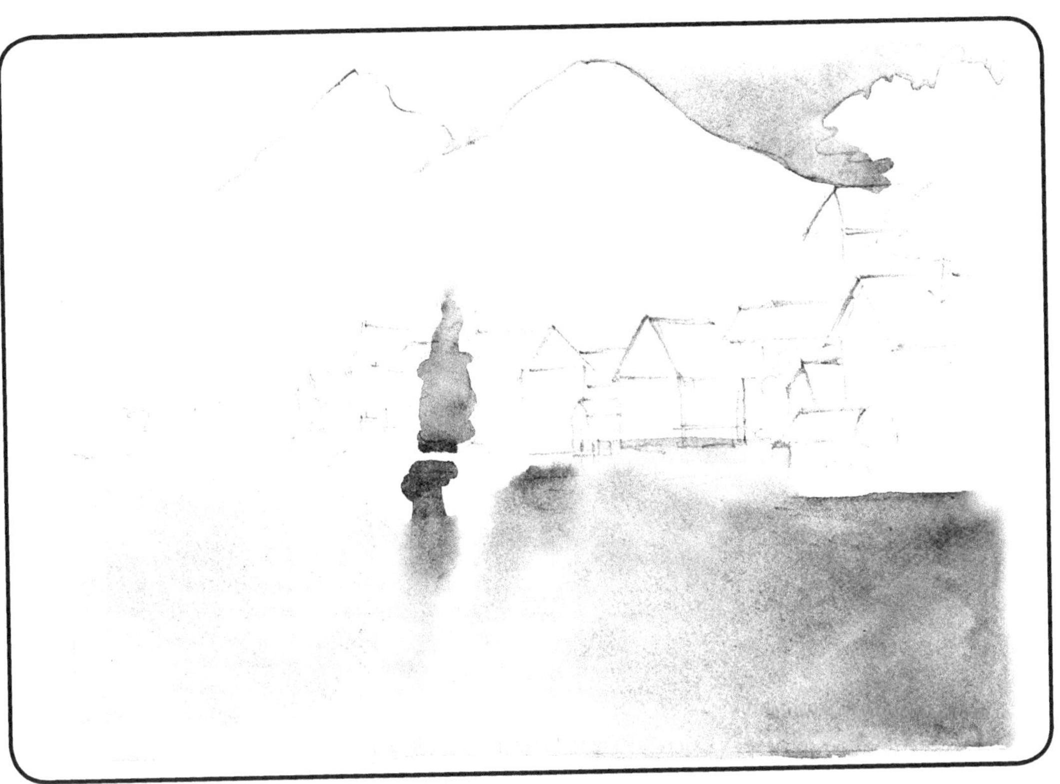

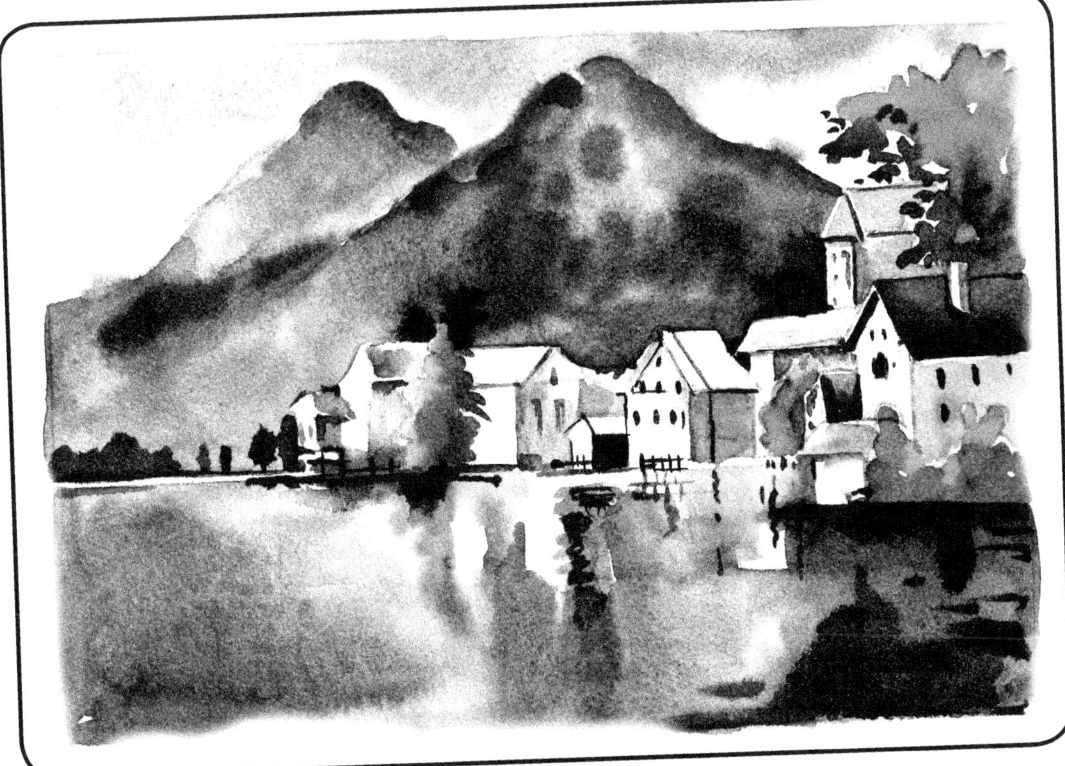

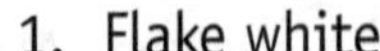

1. Flake white
2. Lemon or Cadmium yellow
3. Cadmium yellow medium
4. Cadmium yellow deep
5. Yellow ochre
6. Cadmium orange
7. Vermilion deep
8. Carmine red
9. Light red
10. Raw sienna
11. Burnt sienna
12. Crimson lake
13. Burnt umber
14. Emerald green
15. Permanent green
16. Sap green
17. Hooker's green
18. Violet
19. Ultramarine blue
20. Prussian blue
21. Ivory black

For your convenience, we have made pictures in water colour, oil colour and acrylic colour. See them carefully and practice them.

Method of Filling Colours

1. First of all, you must decide the size of the picture. You must not make a very small picture in the beginning. 11 x 15 inches size is good for practice. Divide the paper into three areas. This will make drawing easy. Keeping in mind a good composition, make a drawing with pencil.
2. Wet the area, where you have to fi ll a colour, with the brush.
3. If you are making a landscape, do the sky fi rst and then fi ll in the fore ground. After this you should take care of other areas.
4. First, fi ll in the light colours followed by dark colours. If the picture has a light background, then fi ll in the colours from light to dark areas. In case of the light front of a picture, you must go from dark to light.
5. If you don't want to show the effect of one colour upon another, then fi ll in the second colour only when the fi rst gets dry, otherwise they may intermix.
6. The fi nishing of picture should be done in the end. White colour can show the effect of highlight.

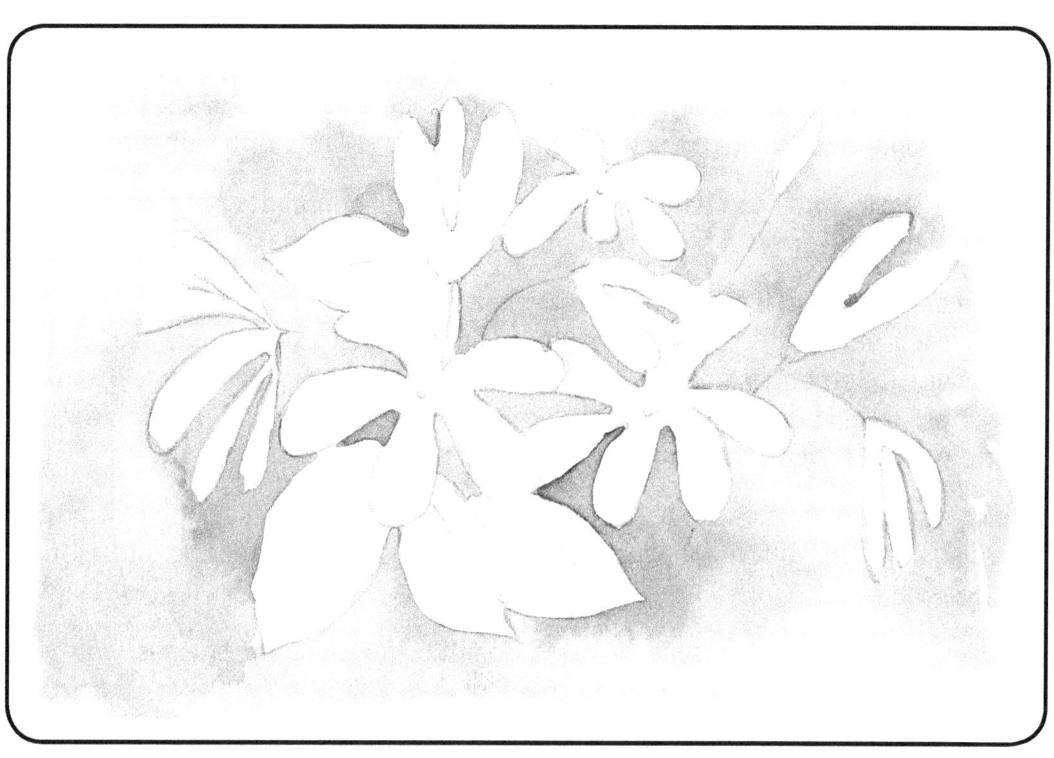

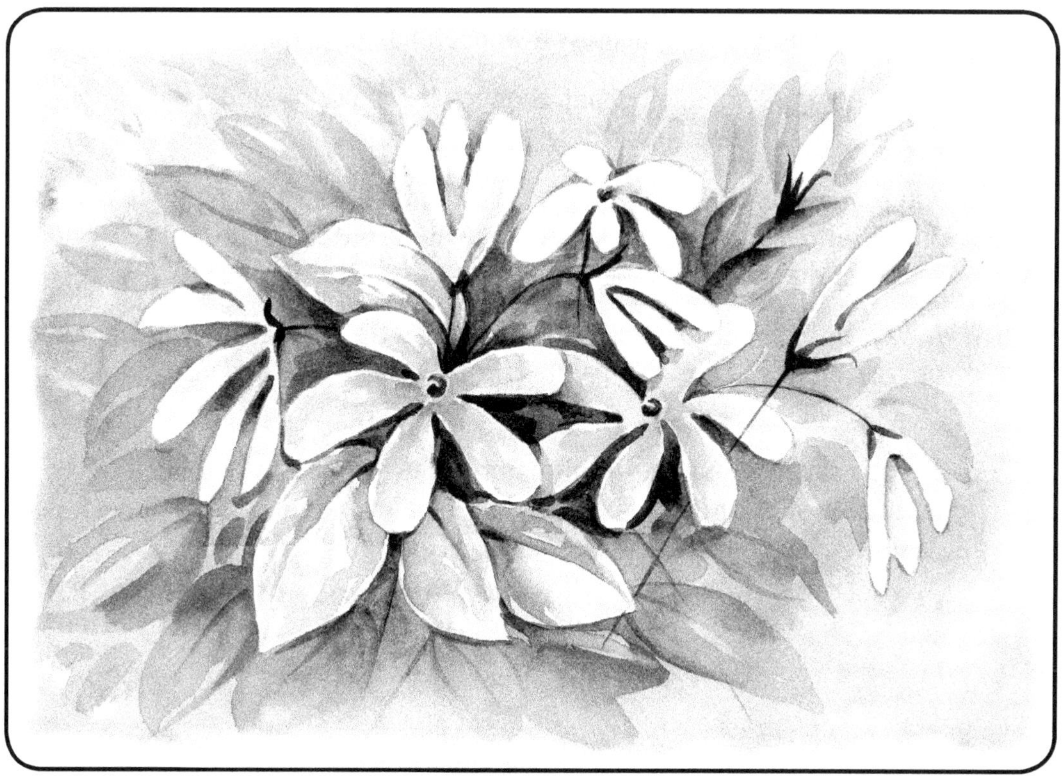

Oil Painting

There are many differences between oil colour and water colour. Oil painting is easy in comparison to water colour painting, but is slightly diffi cult too.

For oil painting, you can use canvas, hardboard, wooden panels, cardboard or oil paper. Prepared canvas may be costly. Oil paper may be cheap.

Oil colours are available in tubes. In comparison to water colours, you may not need many oil colours in the beginning. Cadmium yellow, Cadmium red, French ultramarine, Burnt sienna, Burnt umber, Viridian green, Alizarin crimson, Titanium white or Flake white and Ivory black are enough to begin with. In oil painting, white colour is used excessively, so you must buy a bigger tube of it.

Apart from colours, palette, palette knife, round, fi lbert and fl at hog hair brushes are also required. You will need Linseed oil (purifi ed) and Turpentine oil (purifi ed) to thin the paints.

You will also require kerosene or raw turpentine for cleaning brushes. You may need dippers to keep the two oils while working. Following are some important tips which you must follow while painting—

1. Use of easel is convenient in oil painting. If you cannot buy it, then you can keep your painting against a wooden box on a table.
2. If you are working on oil paper, then fi x the paper on cardboard or drawing board so that it does not move.
3. You can make the drawing with a pencil or charcoal. Burnt umber or French ultramarine thinned with turpentine oil can also be used with a brush for drawing.
4. Always mix the oil colours on a wooden palette and never try to mix them on the picture. Thin the paint with turpentine oil and use linseed oil as a medium.
5. If you commit a mistake in oil painting, it can be easily rubbed off by a cloth dipped in turpentine oil, while the paint is still wet. If required, you can also overpaint when the paint layer gets dry.

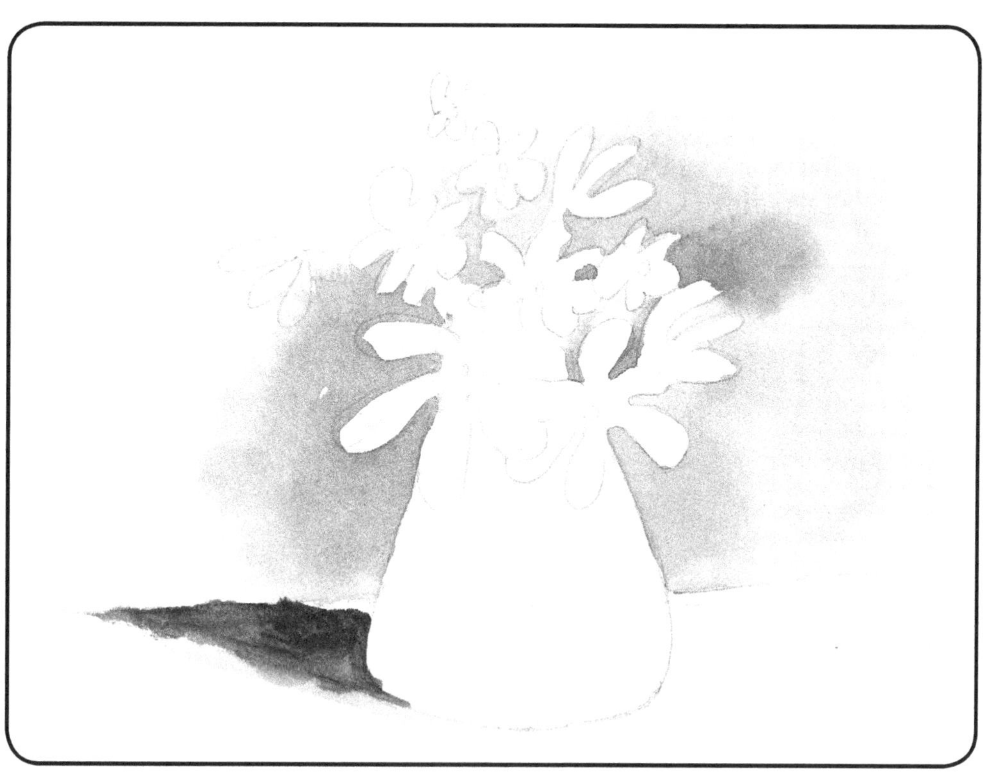

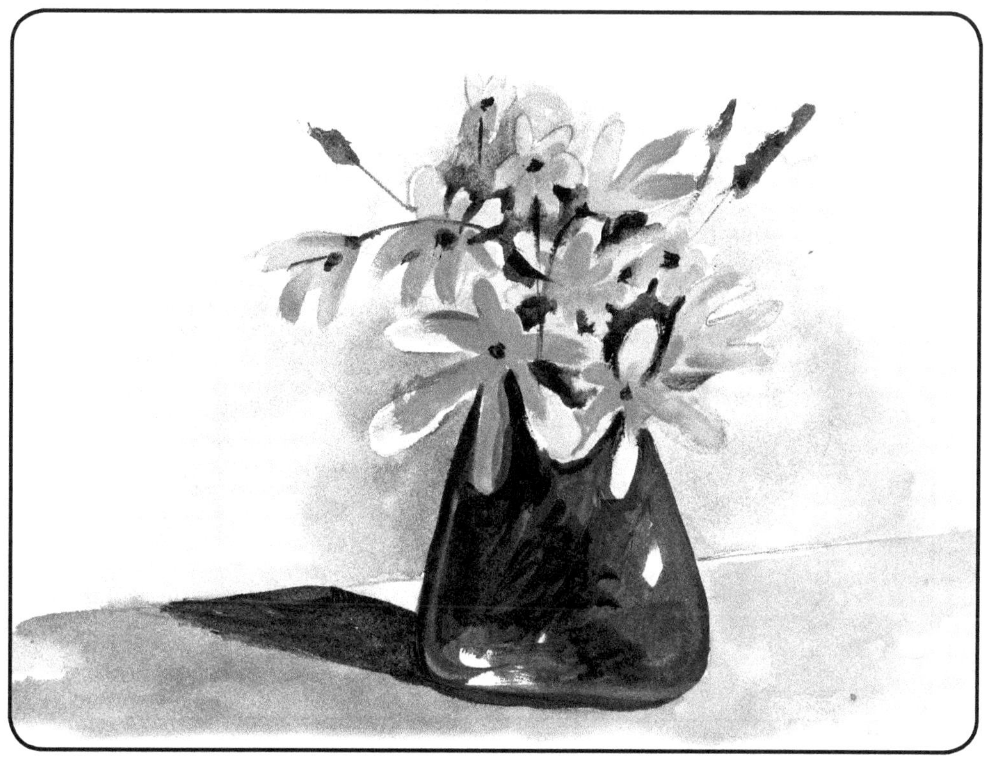

Acrylic Painting

Acrylic is a very flexible medium. This is used on canvas or illustration board. The colours can be thinned with water. These colours become water-proof after drying. Paintings made by this medium often look like an oil painting. The method is also like oil painting.

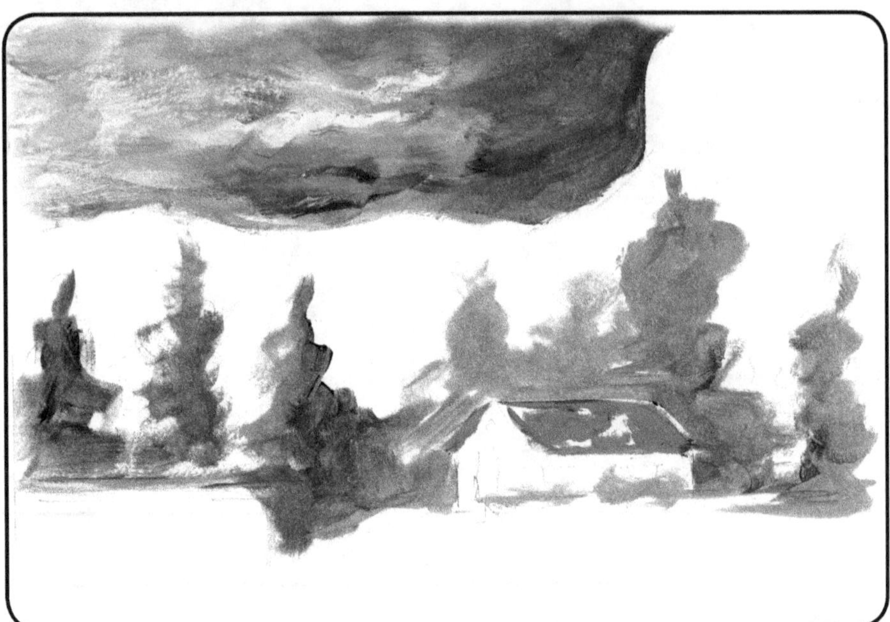

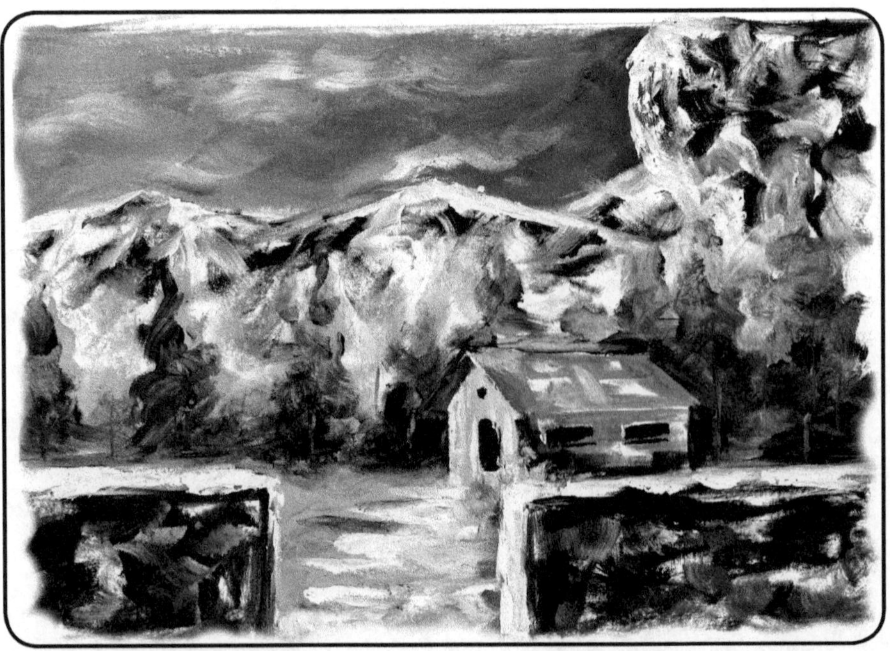

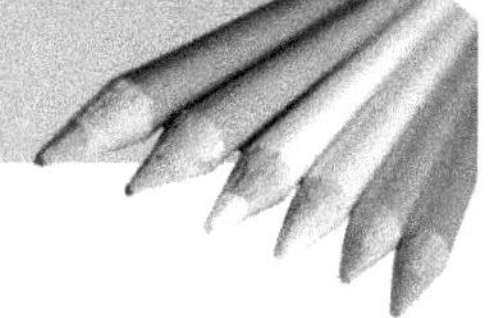

Batik

Batik is a very old form of art. For its invention credit cannot be given one person or place. It is believed that almost 2000 years ago, batik came into practice among the people of Egypt and Iran. They used to make designs on cloth with the help of this method. The art of batik was also developed in 7th century A.D. in China and in 1640 A.D. the Dutch brought it to Europe. Slowly this art became famous in India, Japan and Africa.

Few years ago, people had forgotten this art. But now again people of our country have developed an interest in batik. With the help of batik women can make new attractive designs on their clothes in their homes itself. Batik designs made on handloom cloth are in great demand in foreign countries. Women should specially learn this art.

It is very simple to make batik designs on clothes. A resisting agent is needed for this method. Usually wax is used as resisting agent.

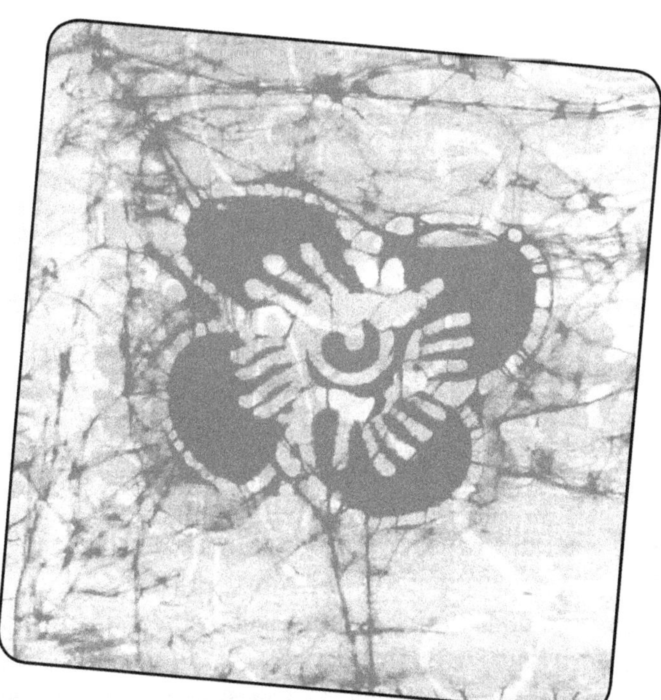

Things required

Very few things are needed for this method. One container is required to heat wax, along with a heater or stove. One plain table or plank of hardboard. A wooden frame on which the cloth is to be stretched for waxing. A pencil, charcoal or coloured chalk for drawing and a brush for blocking of drawing. Paraffi n wax for waxing and colours or dyes for colouring the clothes.

Method

For batik synthetic cloth should not be used. This work is done well on cotton or silk.

Before you begin the work, wash the cloth thoroughly in water, so that the starch comes out. Dry the cloth and press it, so that no fold is left on the cloth, otherwise there will be inconvenience in making the design. Now stretch the cloth on the frame and make the drawing with a pencil, charcoal or chalk. Make such a design that is not very minute. After making the design, heat the wax in a container and fi ll it in the drawing with a brush. When the wax gets dry, mix the colour in a container and soak the cloth in it. Do not rub the cloth, just dip it in the colour solution. When the cloth gets coloured well, take it out of the colour solution and wash it well with plain water, so that the extra colour gets washed away.

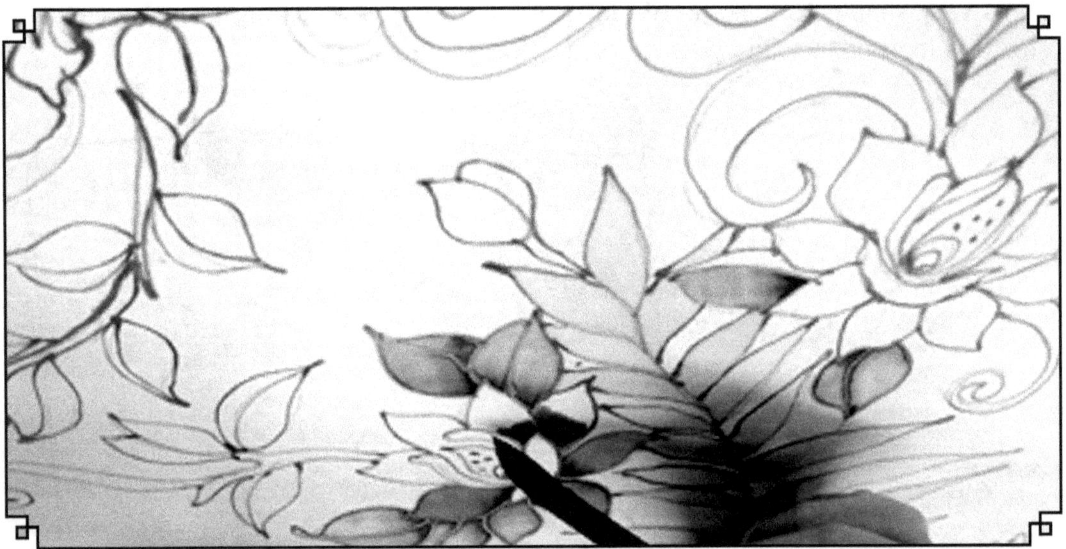

Now you have to remove the wax from the cloth. This process is called dewaxing. Take water in a container and mix a little soap in it. Soak the cloth into it and keep it to boil. During boiling, keep shaking the cloth so that the entire wax on the cloth gets mixed in the water. When the entire wax is removed, wash the cloth in plain water and dry it. In this way you can make a beautiful design on your clothes in a short time.

Dear readers, now that we have introduced you to the beautiful world of drawing and painting, we hope you will continue to practise and improve your skill.

SELF-IMPROVEMENT/PERSONALITY DEVELOPMENT

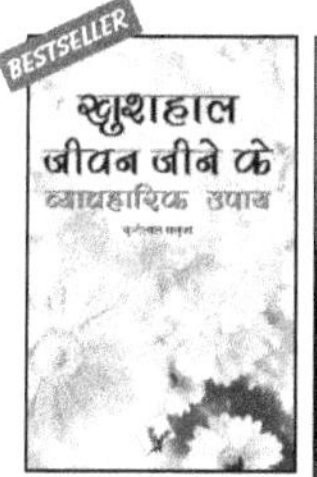

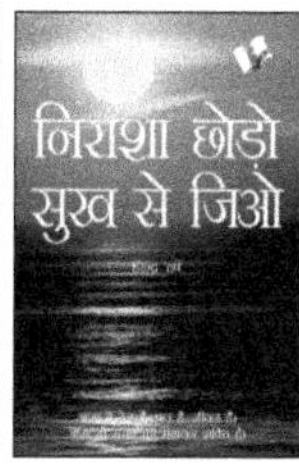

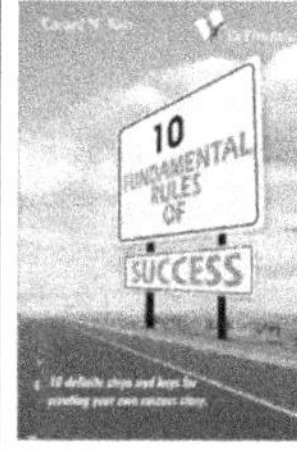

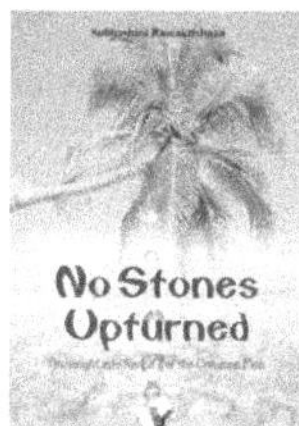

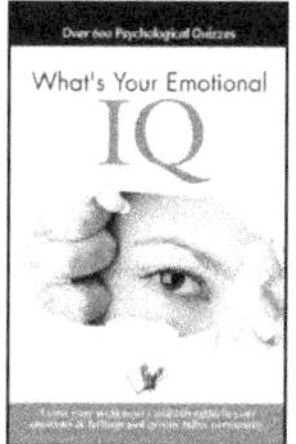

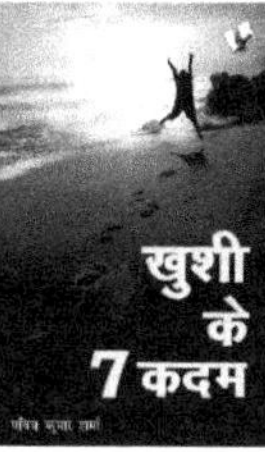

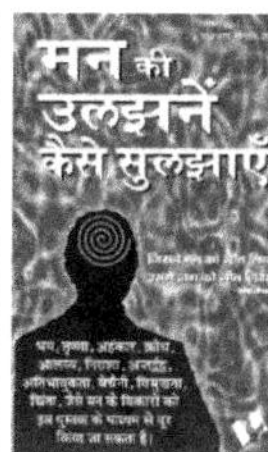

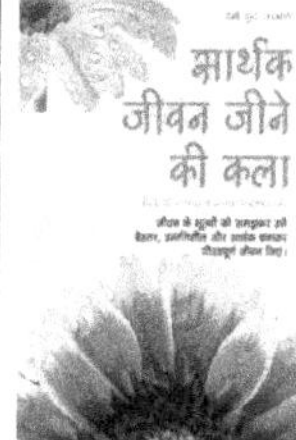

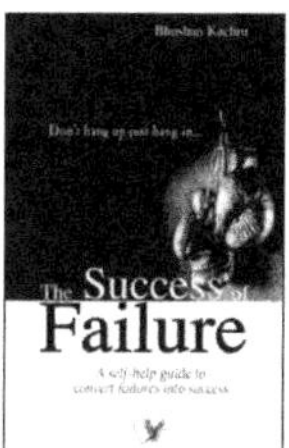

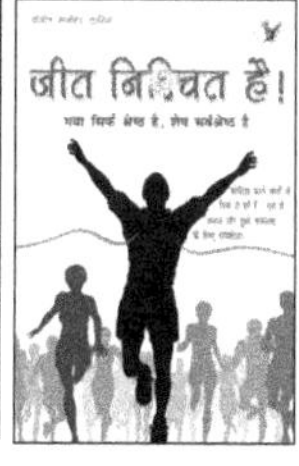

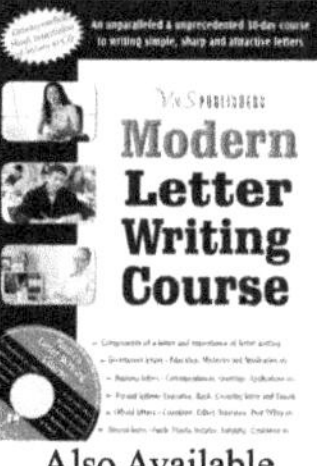

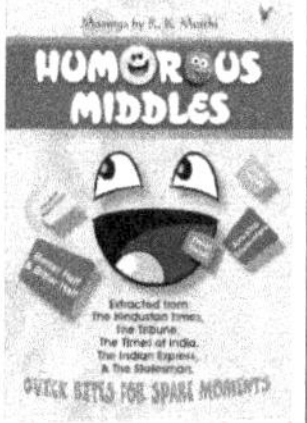

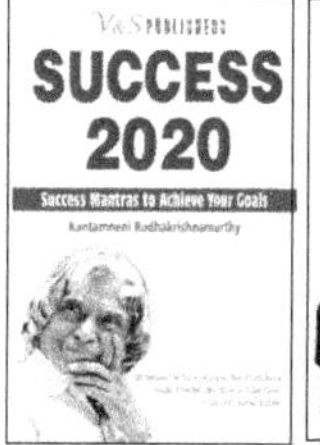

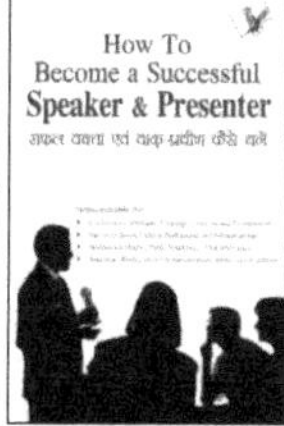

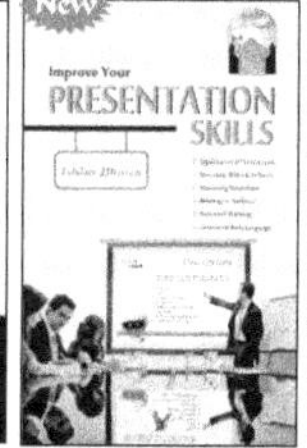

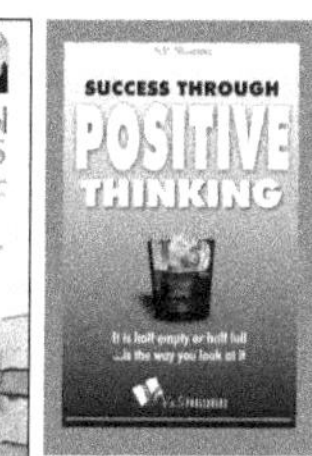

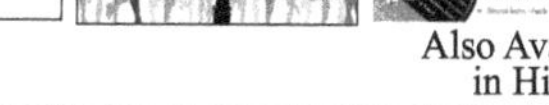
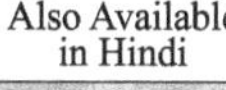

Also Available in Hindi

Also Available in Hindi

Also Available in Kannada, Tamil

स्वेट मार्डेन जीवन में सफल होने के उपाय

IMPROVE YOUR MEMORY POWER

MEMORY DEVELOPMENT COURSE

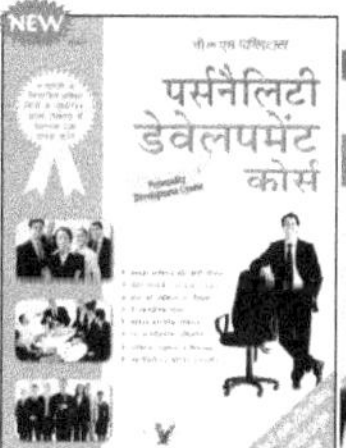

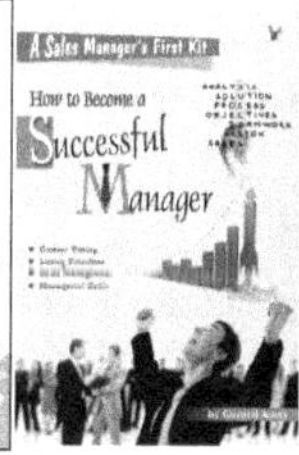

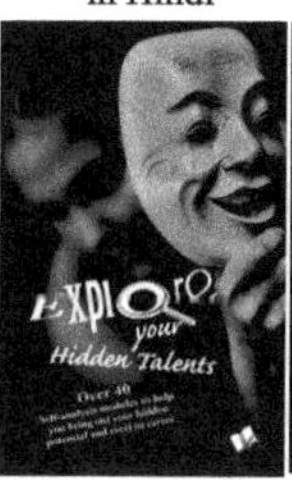

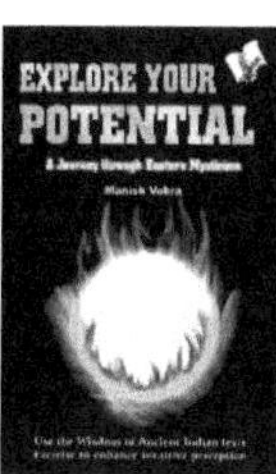

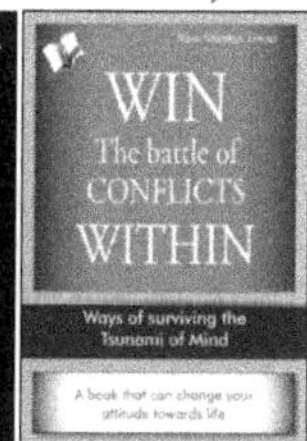

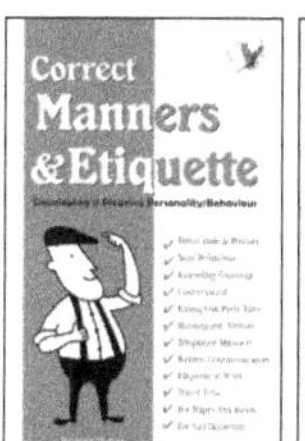

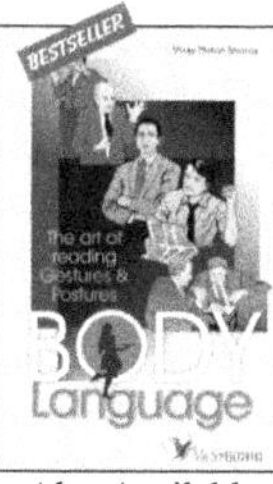

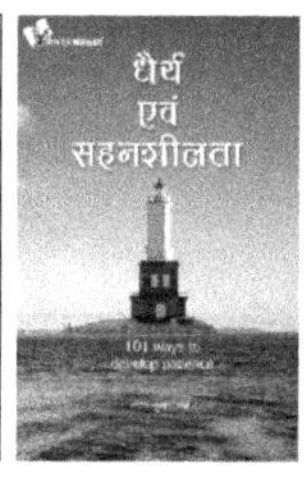

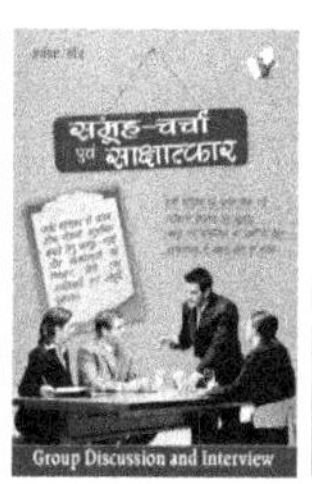

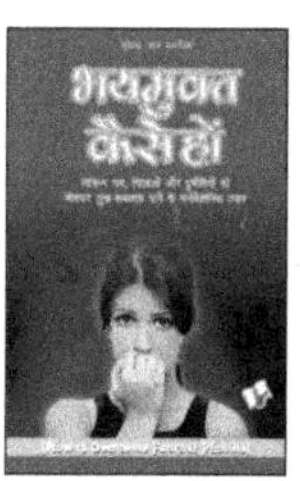

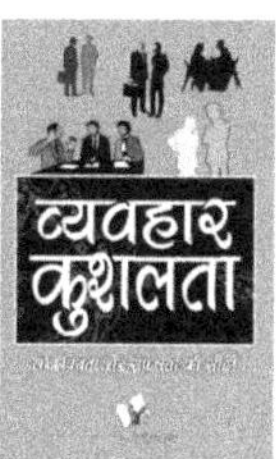

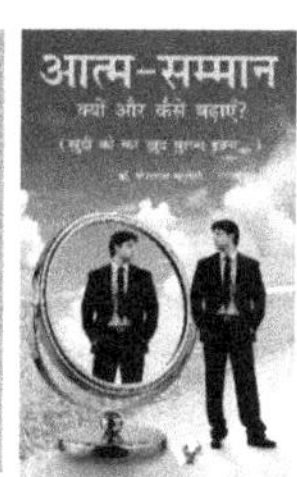

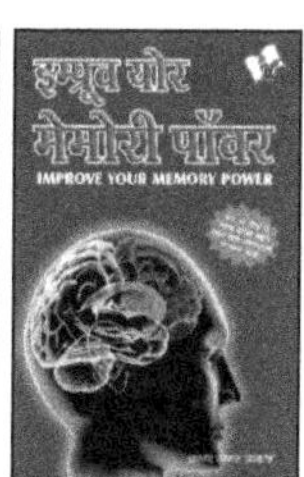

Also Available in Kannada

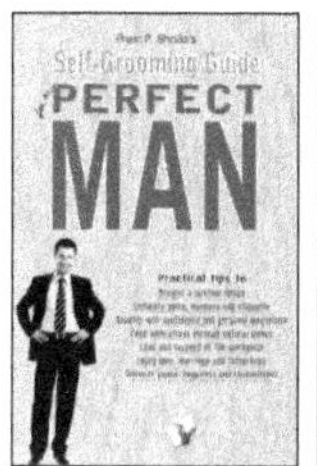

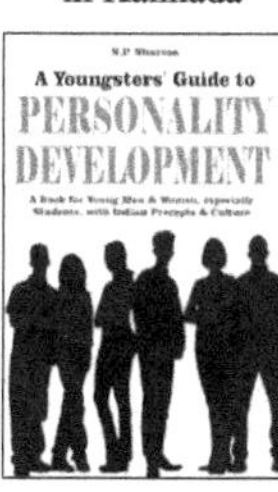

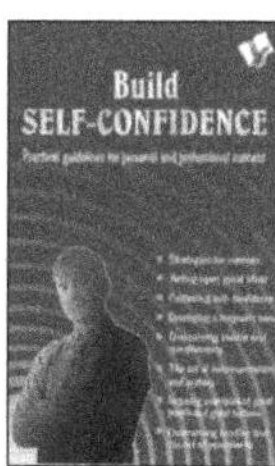

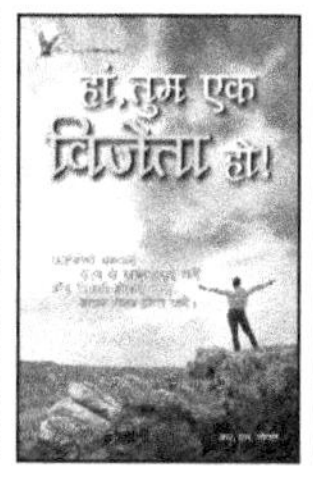

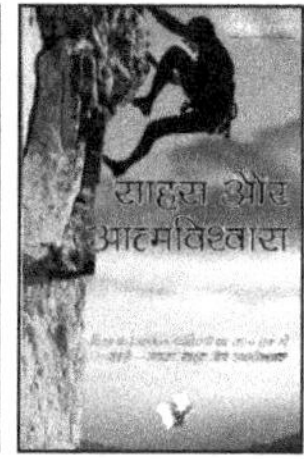

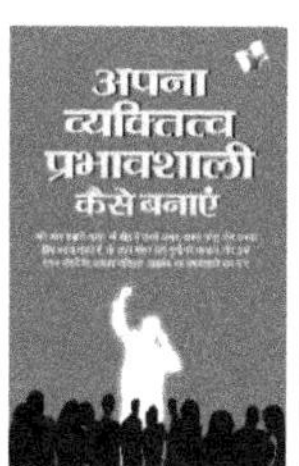

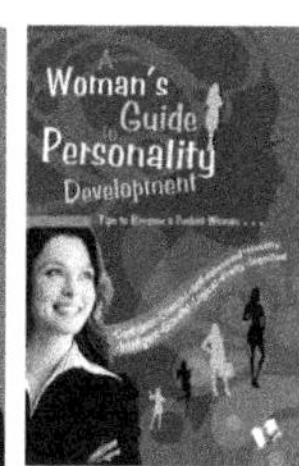

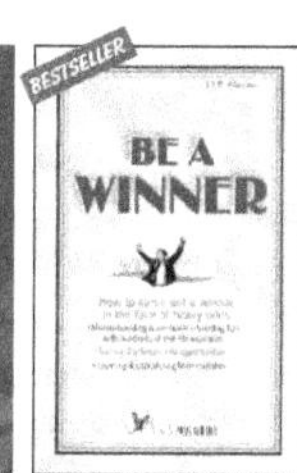

Also Available in Kannada

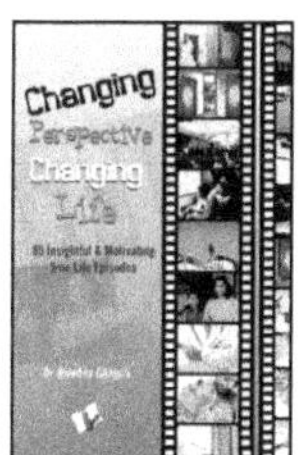

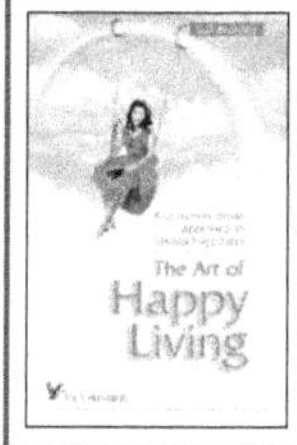

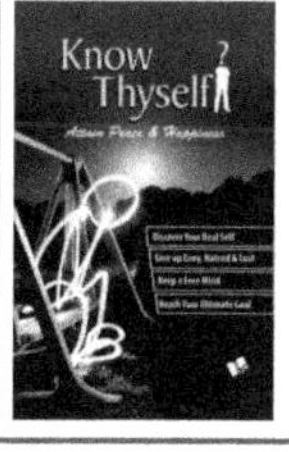

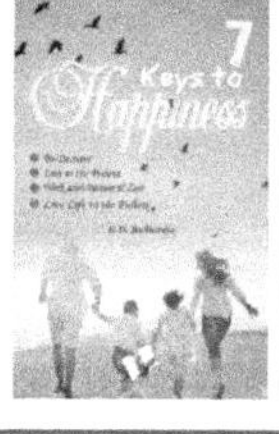

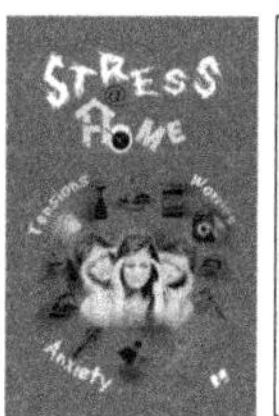

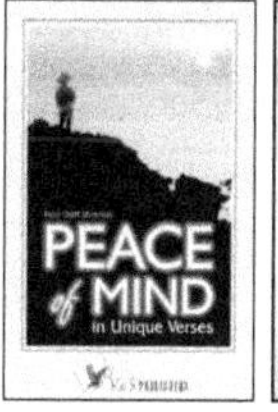

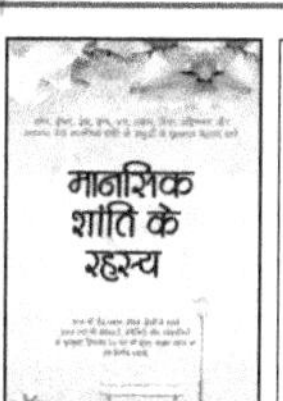

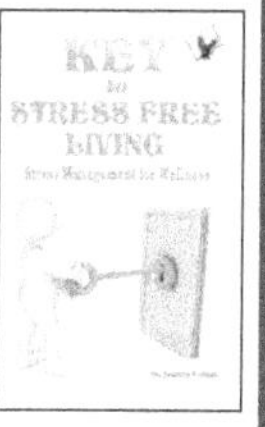

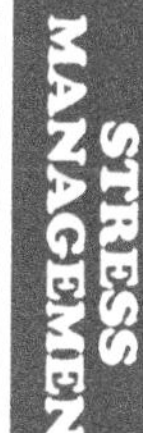

QUIZ BOOKS

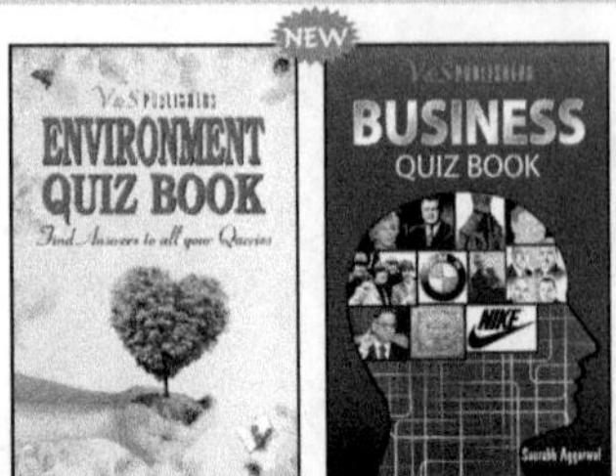

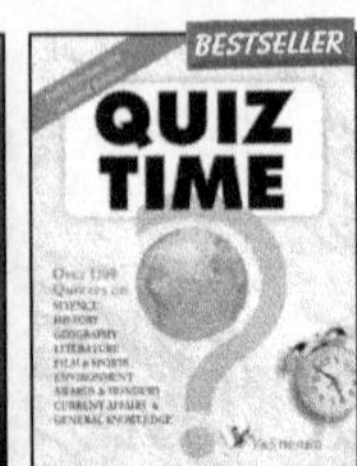

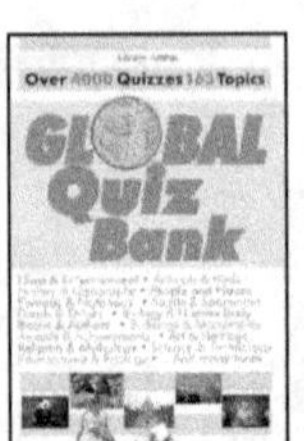

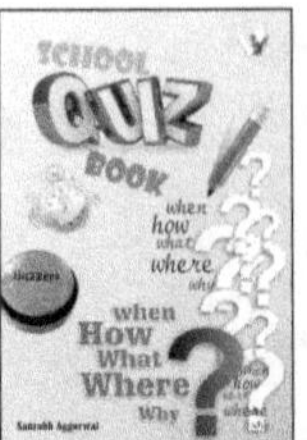

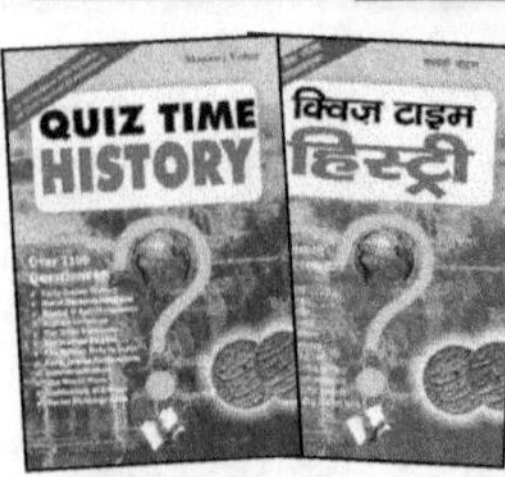

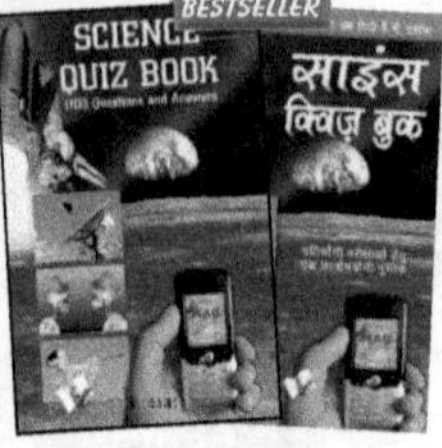

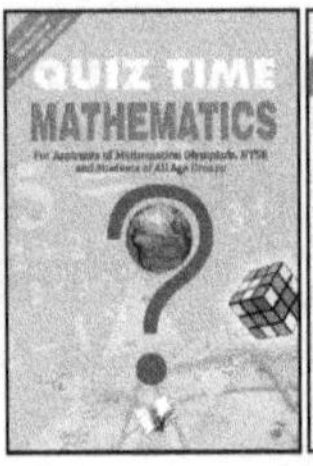

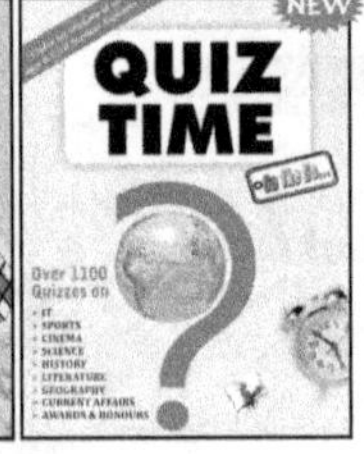

CTIVITIES BOOK

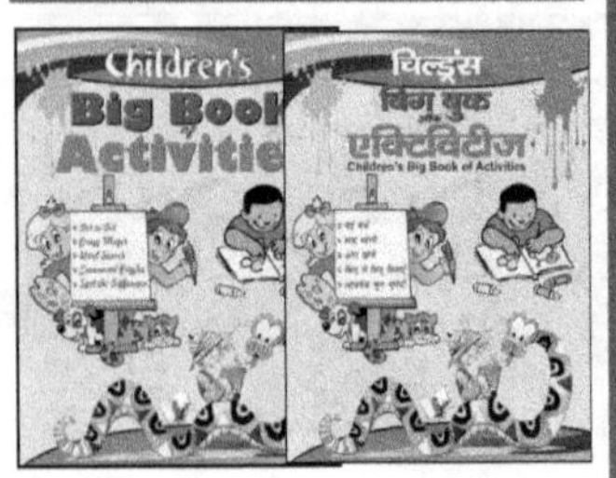

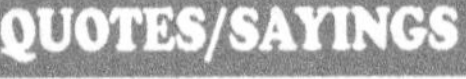

QUOTES/SAYINGS

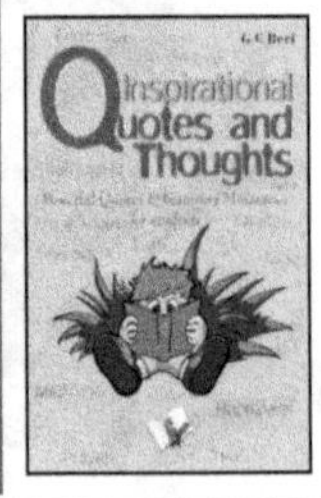

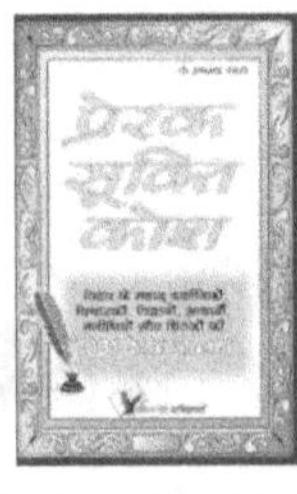

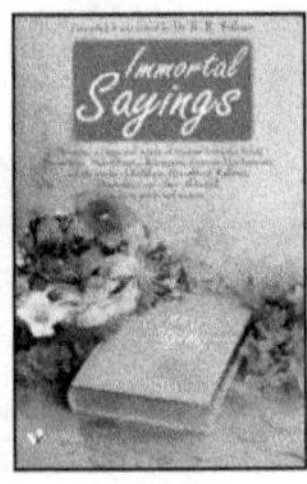

BIOGRAPHIES

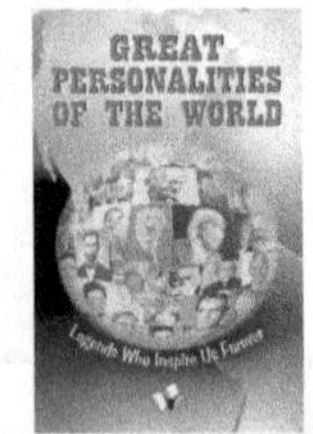

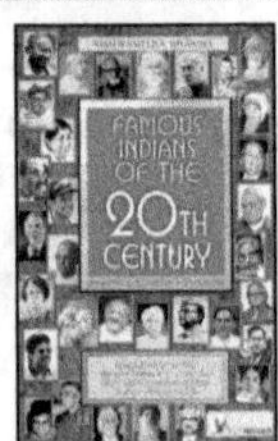

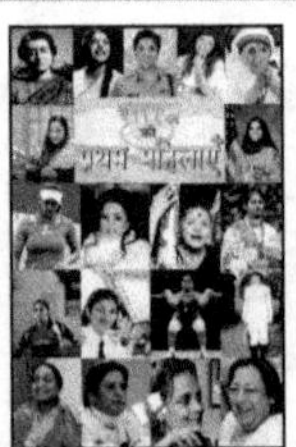

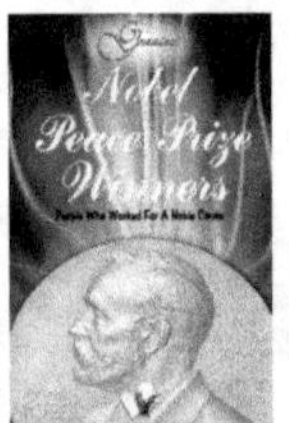

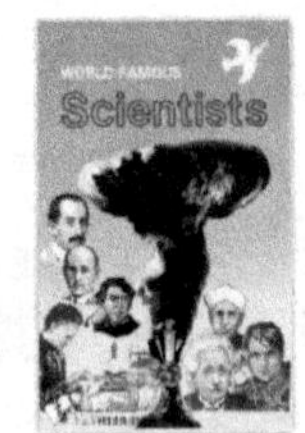

IELTS TECH

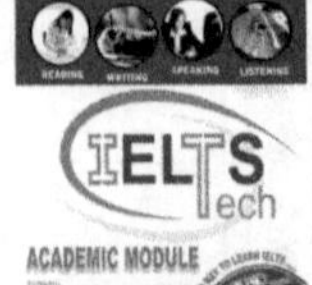

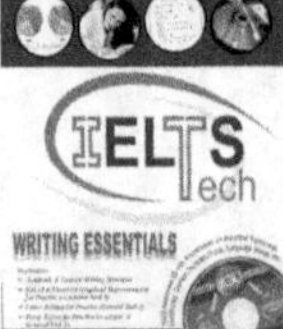

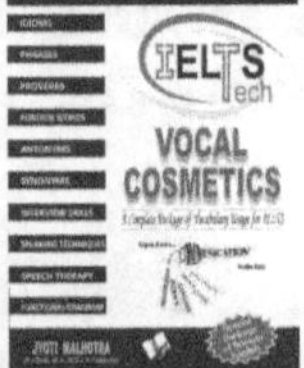

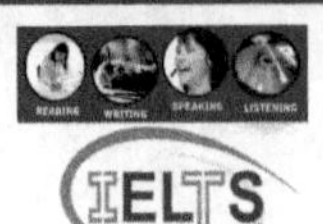

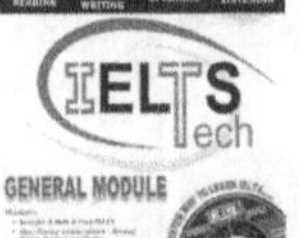

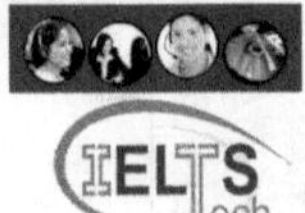

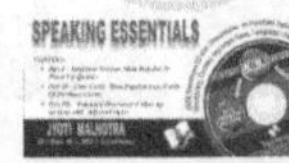

IELTS Tech — ACADEMIC MODULE · WRITING ESSENTIALS · VOCAL COSMETICS · GENERAL MODULE · SPEAKING ESSENTIALS

ENGLISH IMPROVEMENT

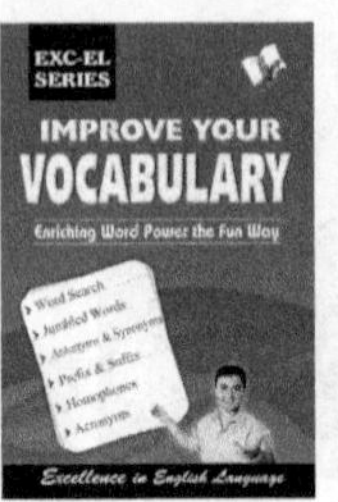

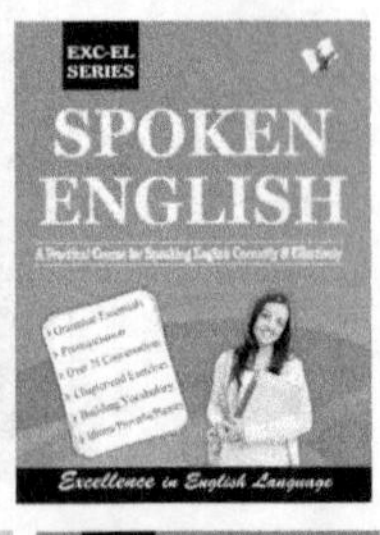

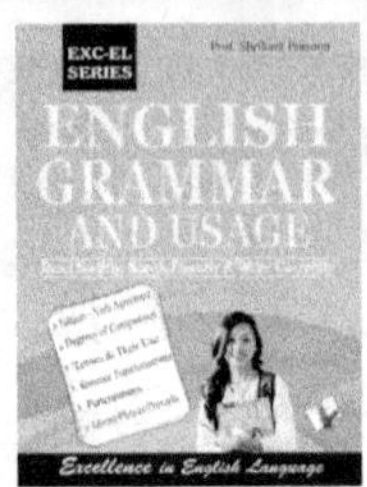

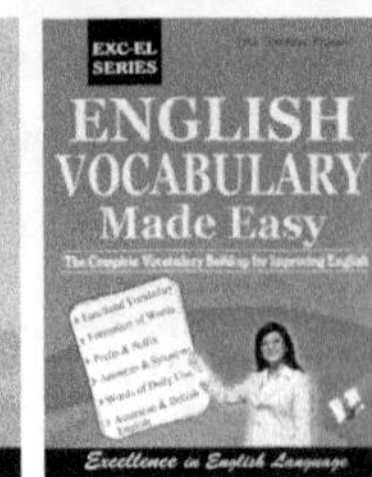

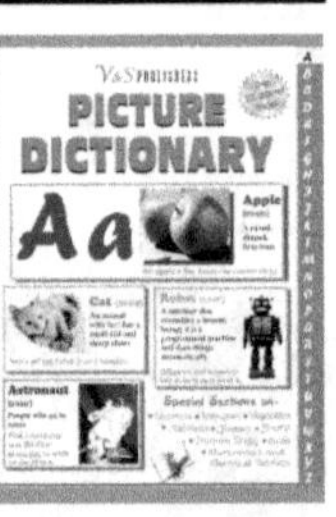

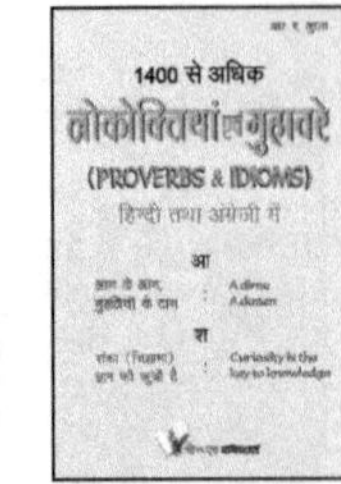

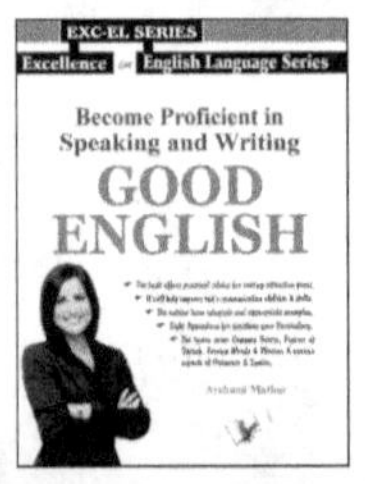

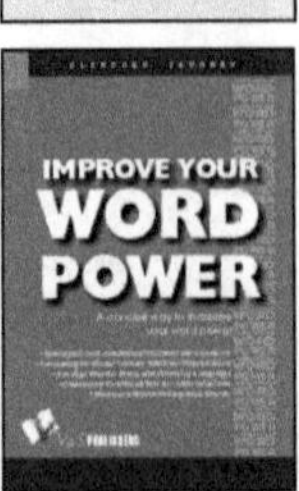

CHILDREN SCIENCE LIBRARY

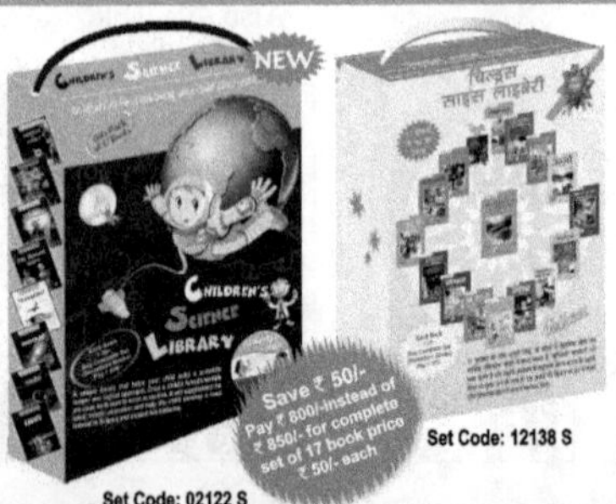

COMPUTER BOOKS

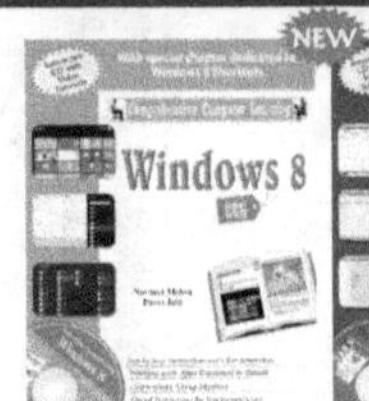

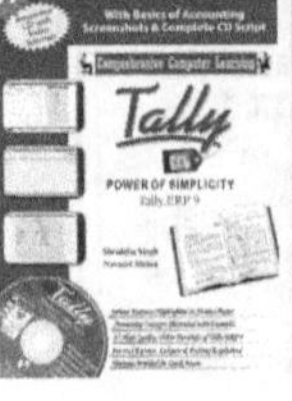

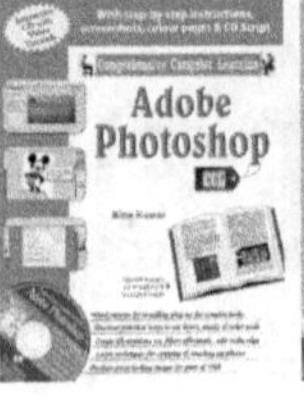

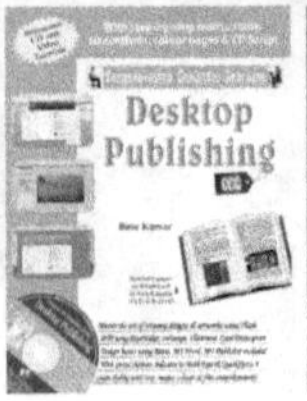

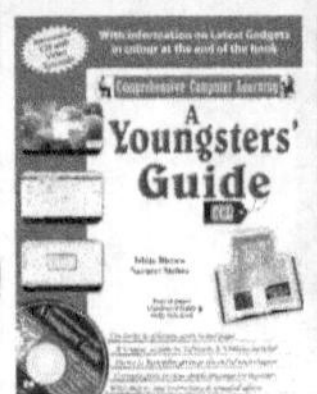

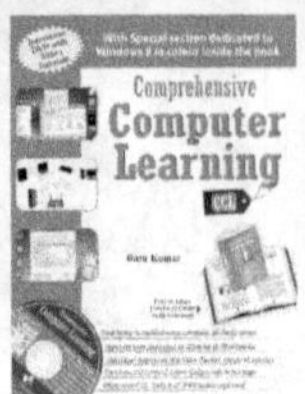

Also available in Hindi

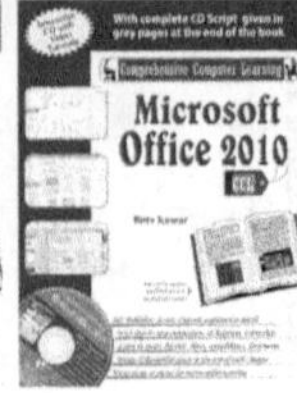

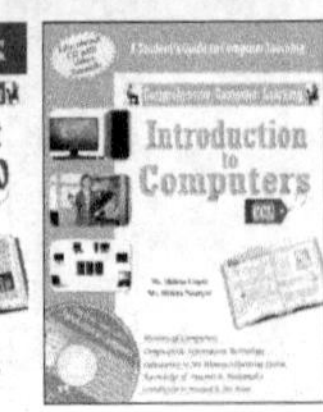

Also available in Hindi

All books available at www.vspublishers.com

STUDENT DEVELOPMENT/LEARNING

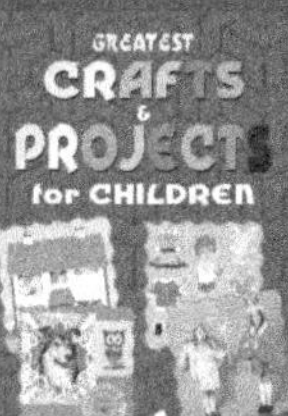

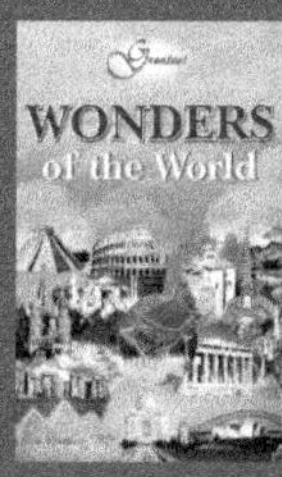

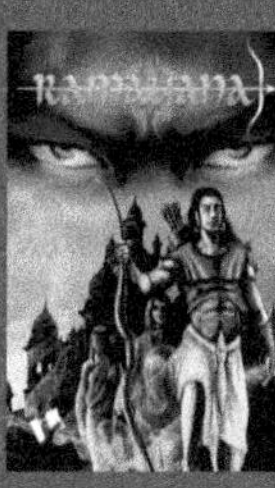

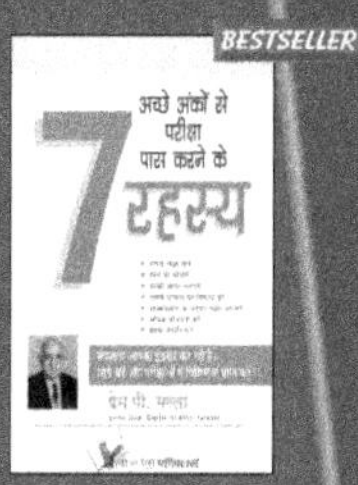
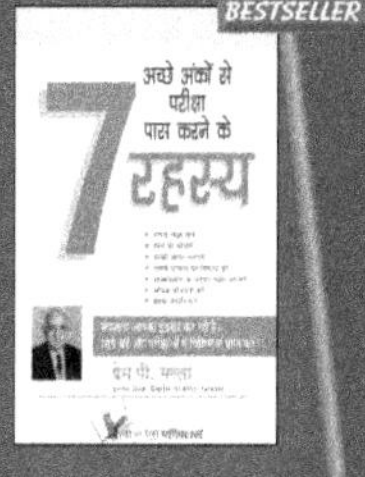

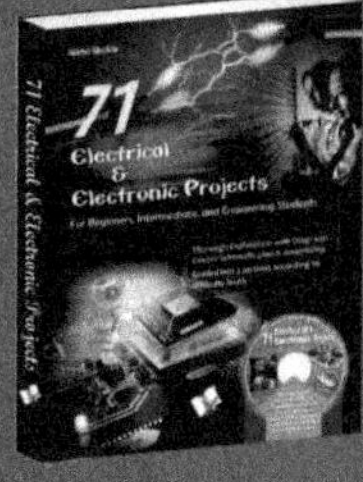

Also Available in Hindi

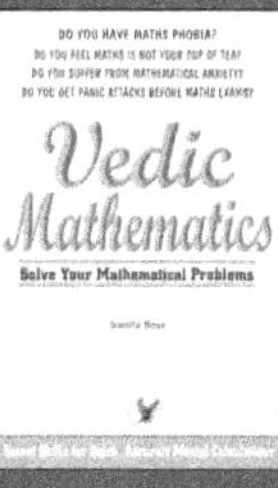

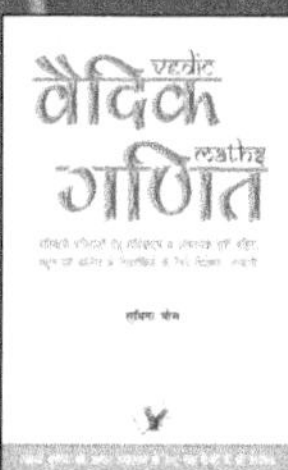

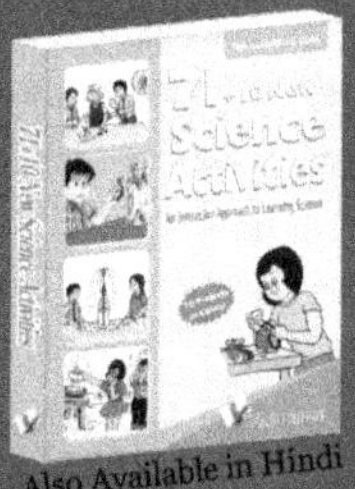

Also Available in Hindi

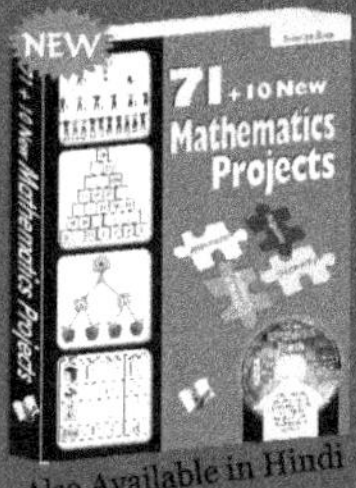

Also Available in Hindi

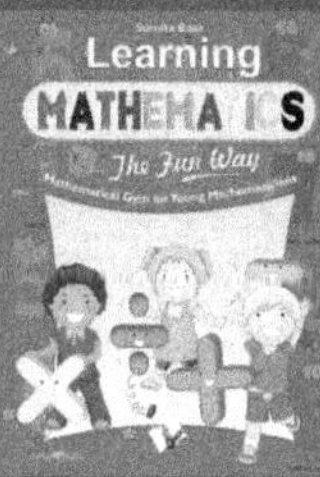

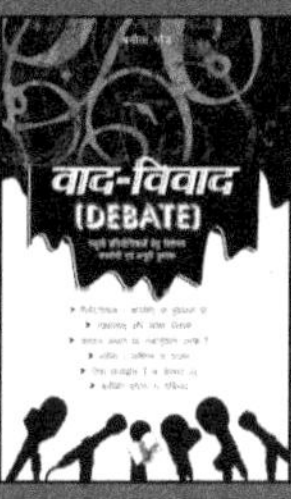

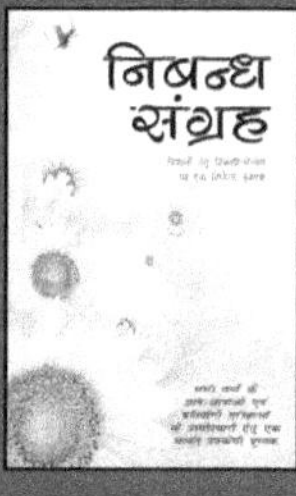

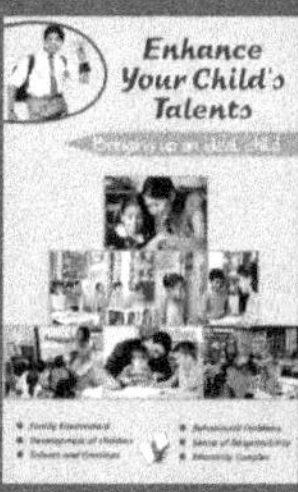

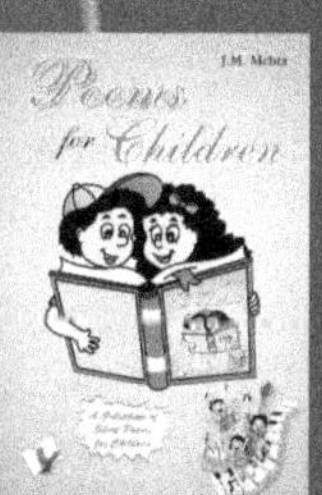

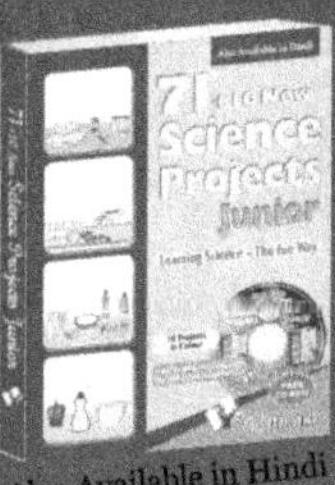

Also Available in Hindi

Also Available in Hindi

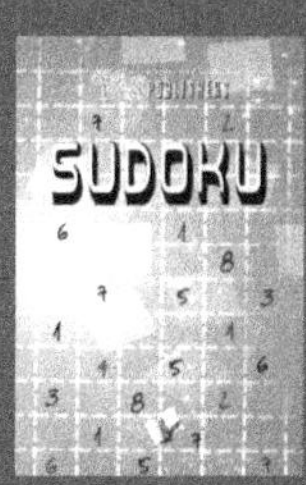

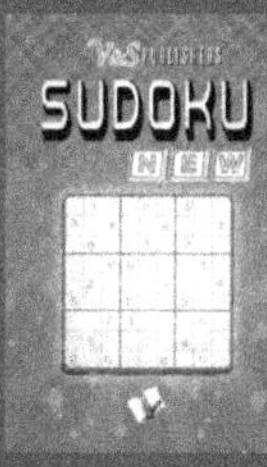

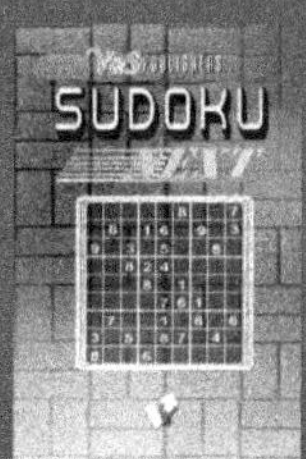

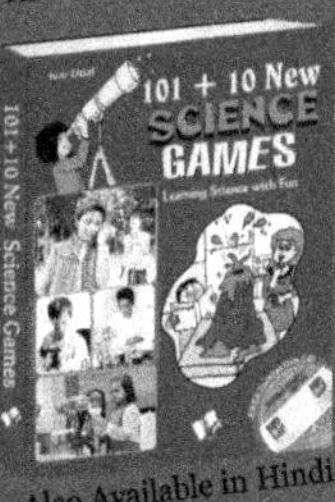

Also Available in Hindi

Also Available in Hindi, Tamil & Bangla

Spice in Science
The best of Science Funnies

71 ARTS & CRAFTS FOR SCHOOL CHILDREN

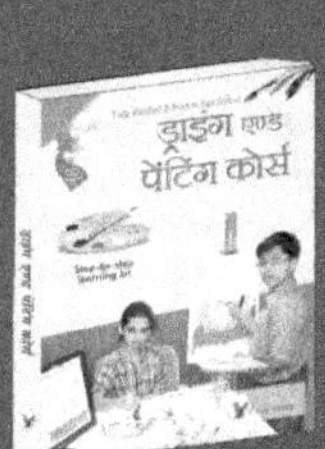

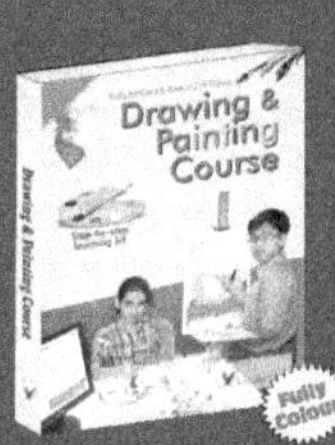
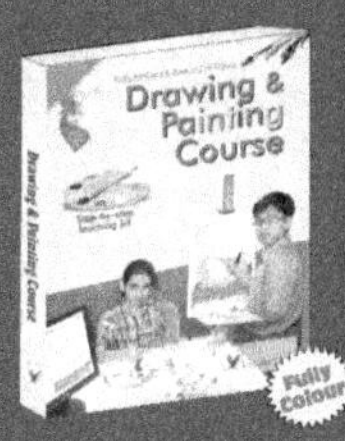
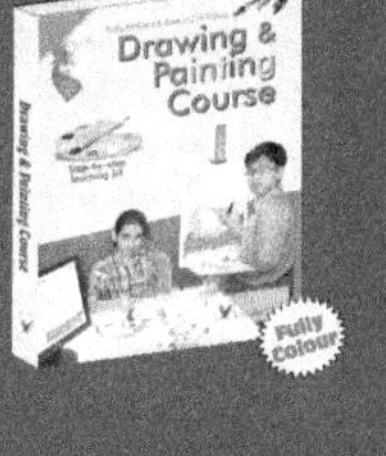

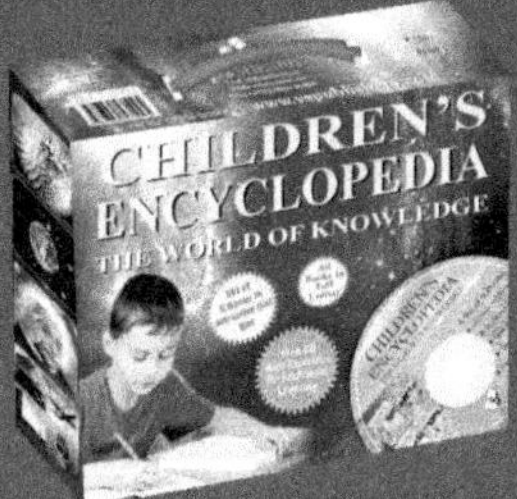

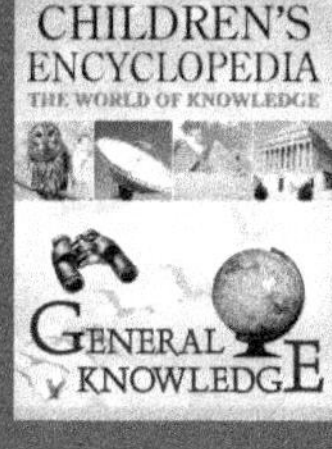

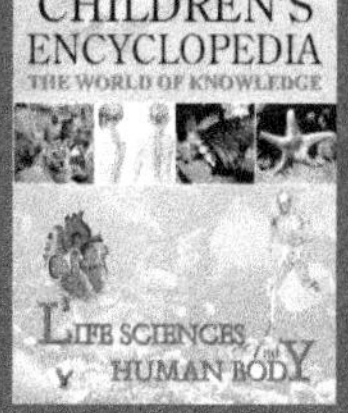

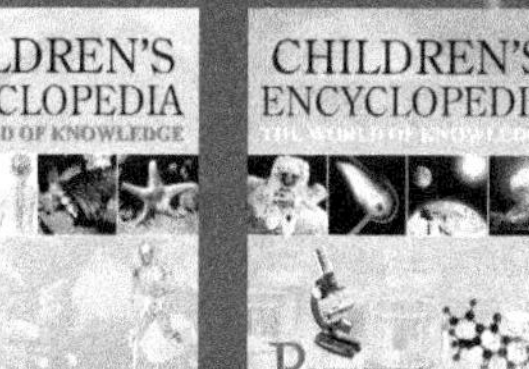

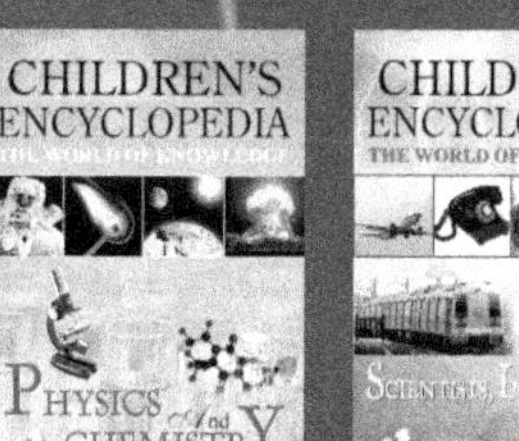

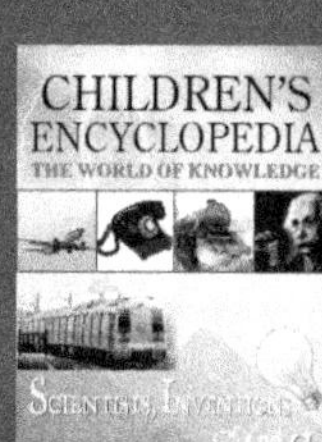

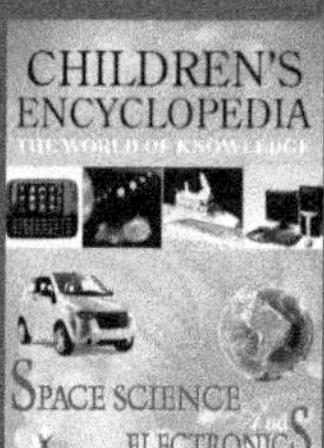

Contact us at sales@vspublishers.com

www.ingramcontent.com/pod-product-compliance
Lightning Source LLC
LaVergne TN
LVHW081319110826
845149LV00006B/1548

* 9 7 8 8 1 9 2 0 7 9 6 6 0 *